T0331648

Mathematical Tools in Signal Processing with
C++ & Java
Simulations

Mathematical Tools in
Signal Processing with
C++ & Java
Simulations

Willi-Hans Steeb
University of Johannesburg, South Africa

World Scientific

NEW JERSEY • LONDON • SINGAPORE • BEIJING • SHANGHAI • HONG KONG • TAIPEI • CHENNAI

Published by

World Scientific Publishing Co. Pte. Ltd.

5 Toh Tuck Link, Singapore 596224

USA office: 27 Warren Street, Suite 401-402, Hackensack, NJ 07601

UK office: 57 Shelton Street, Covent Garden, London WC2H 9HE

British Library Cataloguing-in-Publication Data
A catalogue record for this book is available from the British Library.

MATHEMATICAL TOOLS IN SIGNAL PROCESSING WITH C++ AND JAVA SIMULATIONS

ISBN-13 978-981-256-500-6
ISBN-10 981-256-500-0

Printed in Singapore

Preface

The word *signal* has several meanings. The one of interest for us is defined in Webster (1988) as 'a detectable physical quantity or impulse (as a voltage, current, or magnetic field strength) by which messages or information can be transmitted'. For example, the desired information can be a temperature, and the signal a voltage proportional to this temperature. The signal varies as a function of time. Many signals are continuous; some are discrete. The modelling of signals and systems is inherently mathematical and involves mathematical techniques not ordinarily studied by undergraduate science students, in particular newer techniques such as wavelets and the Radon transform. The book describes the mathematical tools used in signal processing together with C++ and Java implementations.

This book not only includes all the standard techniques used in signal processing such as the z-transform and digital linear filters, but also newer methods such as wavelets and neural networks. The book provides an excellent balance of theory and applications, beginning with a complete framework for understanding discrete-time signal processing. Speech signal processing is considered in detail.

The text consists of fourteen chapters. Sampling theory and transmission formats are introduced in chapter 1. Quantisation is discussed in chapter 2. The μ-law and A-law are also introduced. At the heart of signal processing is the design of digital linear filters. Chapter 3 gives a comprehensive introduction into this field. Digital filters of the FIR and IIR types are studied in some detail. Chapter 4 covers the circular and nonciruclar convolution. Chapter 5 is devoted to the discrete Fourier transform. A C++ program for the fast Fourier transform is also provided. In chapter 6 we introduce the discrete one-dimensional and two-dimensional cosine-transform together with a Java program. Chapter 7 gives an introduction into one- and two-dimensional wavelets together with a C++ and Java program. The z-transform as the discrete Laplace transform is introduced in chapter 8. It is also shown how linear difference equations can be solved using the z-transform. Discrete hidden Markov models can be used for pattern recognition. They are used particularly in speech recognition. Chapter 9 presents discrete hidden Markov models. Linear prediction analysis of speech is historically one of the most important speech analysis techniques. The basis is the source-filter model where the filter is constrained to be an all-pole linear filter. Chapter 10 covers this subject. Neural networks are also used in signal processing, in particular for pattern recognition. Chapter 11 introduces competitive learning and quantisation using neural networks and also the back-propagation algorithm. X-ray tomography which involves the Radon transform is described in chapter 12. The different data compression techniques are discussed in chapter 13 together with C++ and Java programs. The last chapter gives a survey on Digital Signal Processors and Microprocessors.

Without doubt, this book can be extended. If you have comments or suggestions, please send them to the author. The e-mail addresses of the author are:

`steeb_wh@yahoo.com`
`whs@na.rau.ac.za`

The websites of the author are:

`http://zeus.uj.ac.za`
`http://issc.uj.ac.za`

Contents

Chapter 1

Sampling Theory

1.1 Introduction

Samples are successive snapshots of a signal. In the case of audio, the signal is a sound wave. A microphone converts the acoustic signal into a corresponding analog electric signal, and an analog-to-digital converter transforms that analog signal into a sampled digital form. The accuracy of the digital approximation of the analog signal depends on its resolution in time (the *sampling rate*) and its *quantisation*, or resolution in amplitude (the number of bits used to represent each sample). For example, the audio recorded for storage on compact discs is sampled 44 100 times per second and represented with 16 bits per sample.

To convert an analog signal to a digital form it must first be band-limited and then sampled. Signals must be first filtered prior to sampling. Theoretically the maximum frequency that can be represented is half the sampling frequency. In practice a higher sample rate is used for non-ideal filters. The signal is now represented at multiples of the sampling period, T, as $s(nT)$ which is also written as s_n, where n is an integer.

A typical signal processing system includes an A/D converter, D/A converter and a CPU that performs the signal processing algorithm. The input analog signal $x(t)$ is first passed through an input filter (commonly called the anti-aliasing filter) whose function is to bandlimit the signal to below the *Nyquist rate* (one half the sampling frequency) to prevent aliasing. The signal is then digitised by the A/D converter at a rate determined by the sample clock to produce $x(n)$, the discrete-time input sequence. The system transfer function, $H(z)$, is typically implemented in the time-domain using a linear difference equation. The sample output, $y(n)$, is then converted back into a continuous-time signal, $y(t)$, by the D/A converter and out-

1

put low-pass filter. The calculation of the output signal using a difference equation requires a multiply and accumulate operation. This is typically a single-cycle instruction on DSP chips.

Telephone speech is sampled at 8 kHz. 16 kHz is generally regarded as sufficient for speech recognition and synthesis. The audio standard is a sample rate of 44.1 kHz (Compact Disc) or 48 kHz (Digital Audio Tape) to represent frequencies up to 20 kHz.

Sinusoidal sequences play an important role on frequency-domain analysis of digital filters. Given some *radian frequency* we can form the discrete-time sinusoidal sequences

$$\cos(\omega n), \qquad \sin(\omega n)$$

by evaluating these functions at the corresponding value of the argument. Strictly speaking, the units of ω are radians per sampling interval, i.e. we should write

$$\cos(\omega T n), \qquad \sin(\omega T n).$$

Since T is fixed we can absorb T into ω and thus ω is a dimensionless quantity.

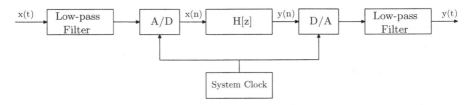

Figure 1.1. Typical Signal Processing System

We use the term sample to refer to a single output value from an A/D converter, i.e., a small integer number (usually 8 or 16 bits). Audio data is characterized by the following parameters, which correspond to settings of the A/D converter when the data was recorded. Naturally, the same settings must be used to play the data.

- `sampling rate (in samples per second)`, e.g. 8000 or 44100

- `number of bits per sample`, e.g. 8 or 16

- `number of channels (1 for mono, 2 for stereo, etc.)`

Approximate sampling rates are often quoted in Hz or kHz ([kilo-] Hertz), however, the correct term is samples per second (samples/sec). Sampling rates are always measured per channel, so for stereo data recorded at 8000 samples/sec, there are actually 16000 samples in a second.

Multi-channel samples are generally interleaved on a frame-by-frame basis: if there are N channels, the data is a sequence of frames, where each frame contains N samples, one from each channel. Thus, the sampling rate is really the number of frames per second. For stereo, the left channel usually comes first.

The specification of the number of bits for μ-LAW (pronounced mu-law – the mu stands for the Greek letter μ) samples is somewhat problematic. These samples are logarithmically encoded in 8 bits, like a tiny floating point number; however, their dynamic range is that of 12 bit linear data. Source for converting to/from μ-LAW is distributed as part of the SOX package. SOX stands for SoundeXchange. SOX is a universal sound processing utility. It is a popular cross-platform command line package to convert audio files between various formats and to apply effects on them. We can also use it to play and record audio files on some platforms. It can easily be ripped apart to serve in other applications.

There exists another encoding similar to μ-LAW, called A-LAW, which is used as a European telephony standard. There is less support for it in UNIX workstations.

Popular sampling rates

Some sampling rates are more popular than others, for various reasons. Some recording hardware is restricted to (approximations of) some of these rates, some playback hardware has direct support for some. The popularity of divisors of common rates can be explained by the simplicity of clock frequency dividing circuits.

```
Samples/sec  Description
===========  ===========
8000         Exactly 8000 samples/sec is a telephony standard
             that goes together with U-LAW (and also A-LAW)
             encoding. Some systems use an slightly different
             rate.

11 kHz       Either 11025, a quarter of the CD sampling rate,
             or half the Mac sampling rate.

16000        Used by, e.g. the G.722 compression standard.
```

18.9 kHz   CD-ROM/XA standard.

22 kHz   Either 22050, half the CD sampling rate, or the
             Mac rate; the latter is precisely
             22254.545454545454 but usually misquoted as 22000.

32000   Used in digital radio, NICAM (Nearly
             Instantaneous Compandable Audio Matrix
             [IBA/BREMA/BBC]) and other TV work,
             at least in the UK.

37.8 kHz   CD-ROM/XA standard for higher quality.

44056   This weird rate is used by professional audio
             equipment to fit an integral number of samples
             in a video frame.

44100   The CD sampling rate. DAT players recording
             digitally from CD also use this rate.

48000   The DAT (Digital Audio Tape) sampling rate for
             domestic use.

Files samples on SoundBlaster hardware have sampling rates that are divisors of 1000000.

While professional musicians disagree, most people do not have a problem if recorded sound is played at a slightly different rate, say, 1-2%. On the other hand, if recorded data is being fed into a playback device in real time (say, over a network), even the smallest difference in sampling rate can frustrate the buffering scheme used.

There may be an emerging tendency to standardise on only a few sampling rates and encoding styles, even if the file formats may differ. The suggested rates and styles are:

```
rate (samp/sec)   style mono/stereo

   8000           8-bit U-LAW mono
  22050           8-bit linear unsigned mono and stereo
  44100           16-bit linear signed mono and stereo
```

1.2 Nyquist Theorem

Given an analog signal $s_a(t)$. The sampled waveform (discrete signal) can be represented by

$$s(n) = s_a(nT), \qquad -\infty < n < \infty$$

where s_a is the analog waveform, n is an integer and T is the sampling time or the time difference between any two adjacent samples, which is determined by the bandwidth or the highest frequency in the input signal. For example, a sinusoidal tone of frequency $f = 20kHz$ sampled at $f_s = 44.1kHz$ is represented by only 2.205 samples per period. Calculation of many functions may lead in this case to some errors.

The *sampling theorem* (*Nyquist theorem*) states that if an analog signal $s_a(t)$ has a band limited *Fourier transform* $S_a(i\omega)$, given by

$$S_a(i\omega) := \int_{-\infty}^{\infty} s_a(t) \exp(-i\omega t) dt$$

such that

$$S_a(i\omega) = 0$$

for

$$\omega \geq 2\pi W$$

then the analog signal $s_a(t)$ can be reconstructed from its sampled version if

$$T \leq 1/2W .$$

The quantity W is called the *Nyquist frequency*. We can reconstruct the analog signal using (*Shannon's series* or *cardinal series*)

$$s_a(t) = \sum_{n=-\infty}^{\infty} s_a(nT) \frac{\sin(\pi(t-nT)/T)}{\pi(t-nT)/T}$$

$$= \sum_{n=-\infty}^{\infty} s_a(nT) \frac{\sin(\pi f_s(t-nT))}{\pi f_s(t-nT)}$$

where

$$f_s = 1/T$$

is the sampling frequency and t the continuous time. The series converges both uniformly and in the mean-square sense.

The Shannon series can be derived by expanding $S(i\omega)$ in a Fourier series, and then applying inversion. It can also derived from the classical *Poisson summation formula.* It is sometimes referred to as Whittaker's cardinal interpolation formula or the Whittaker-Shannon sampling series, having first been studied in detail by E. T. Whittaker in 1915 and later introduced into the literature of communications engineering by Shannon in 1949. By the Paley-Wiener theorem, since $s_a(t)$ is band-limited, it can be analytically extended from the real axis to the full complex plane, as an entire function of slow growth. The Shannon series converges for complex as well as real t.

Thus the function $s_a(t)$ will be represented digitally without any loss of information as long as sampling occurs in accordance with the Nyquist criteria. Often one introduces the short-cut notation

$$\text{sinc}(x) := \frac{\sin(x)}{x}$$

where $\text{sinc}(0) = 1$. Thus the sampling theorem states that a continuous signal must be discretely sampled at at least twice the frequency of the highest frequency in the signal. Normally the signal to be digitised would be appropriately filtered before sampling to remove higher frequency components. If the sampling frequency is not high enough the high frequency components in the signal will wrap around and appear in other locations in the discrete spectrum, thus corrupting it. The high frequency components are added into the low frequency range.

The information about the signal $s_a(t)$ at any given time $t \neq nT$ is distributed among all discrete samples $s(n)$ with appropriate weights. We are never presented with an infinite discrete time sequence and are therefore forced to perform the summation over a finite range. This is equivalent to a loss of information about the function $s_a(t)$ not only before and after our time window (which is understandable), but also at the time points between the sampling points. This can introduce errors into the process of reconstructing the function $s_a(t)$. For example, if

$$\frac{1}{T} = f_s < 2W$$

the analog signal image centred at $2\pi/T$ overlaps into the base band image. The distortion caused by high frequencies overlapping low frequencies is called *aliasing*. To avoid aliasing distortion, either the input analog signal has to be band limited to a maximum of half the sampling frequency, or the sampling frequency has to be increased to at least twice the highest frequency in the analog signal.

The sampling theorem can be extended to two and higher dimensions. For two dimensions we have

$$s_a(x_1, x_2) = \sum_{m_1=-\infty}^{\infty} \sum_{m_2=-\infty}^{\infty} s_a\left(\frac{m_1}{2W_1}, \frac{m_2}{2W_2}\right)$$

$$\times \text{sinc}\left(2\pi W_1\left(x_1 - \frac{m_1}{2W_1}\right)\right) \text{sinc}\left(2\pi W_2\left(x_2 - \frac{m_2}{2W_2}\right)\right).$$

The sampling theorem can also be extended to sampling lattices other than rectangular lattices, for example, hexagonal lattice.

1.3 Lagrange Sampling Theorem

It is possible to reconstruct functions with Fourier transform that have bounded support using samples that are irregularly spaced. The definition of the sampling theorem is ($z \in \mathbf{C}$)

$$f(z) = \sum_{n=-\infty}^{n=\infty} \frac{f(\lambda_n)G(z)}{G'(\lambda)(z - \lambda_n)}$$

where

$$G(z) := z \prod_{n=1}^{\infty} \left(1 - \frac{z^2}{\lambda_n^2}\right)$$

with $G'(z)$ denoting the derivative dG/dz and

$$|\lambda_n - n| \le L < \frac{1}{4}, \qquad n \in \mathbf{Z}.$$

λ_n is assumed to be a symmetric sequence of real numbers.

We can find the *Whittaker-Shannon sampling theorem* as a special case. We sample on a regular lattice, i.e.

$$\lambda_n = n.$$

Then the function G takes the form

$$G(z) = z \prod_{n=1}^{\infty} \left(1 - \frac{z^2}{n^2}\right) = \frac{\sin(\pi z)}{\pi}.$$

Since the derivative of G is given by

$$\frac{dG}{dz} = G'(z) = \cos(\pi z)$$

we find

$$\frac{dG(z = n)}{dz} = G'(n) = \cos(\pi n) = (-1)^n \, .$$

Given these expressions we find for f

$$f(z) = \sum_{n=-\infty}^{n=\infty} \frac{f(n)(-1)^n \sin(\pi z)}{\pi(z - n)} \, .$$

Owing to the identity

$$\sin(\pi(z - n)) \equiv (-1)^n \sin(\pi z)$$

we finally arrive at

$$f(z) = \sum_{n=-\infty}^{n=\infty} f(n) \frac{\sin(\pi(z - n))}{\pi(z - n)} \, .$$

1.4   Application

The following Java program `SineSound.java` shows how to save generated audio data to a file, in our case `sine.wav`. In the code we set the parameters: sampling frequency, signal frequency and amplitude. The operation `&` is the bitwise AND operation and `>>>` is the triple right shift to act as a logical right shift by inserting zeros at the top end. The `Math` class of Java is used for the number `Math.PI` and the function `Math.sin()`.

```
// SineSound.java

import java.io.ByteArrayInputStream;
import java.io.File;
import java.io.IOException;

import javax.sound.sampled.AudioFormat;
import javax.sound.sampled.AudioSystem;
import javax.sound.sampled.AudioInputStream;
import javax.sound.sampled.AudioFileFormat;

public class SineSound
{
  public static void main(String[] args)
  {
  byte[] data;
  AudioFormat format;
  int amplitude = 10000; // [0..32767]
```

```
int sampleF = 44100;
int signalF = 440;
float maximumBufferLengthInSeconds = 1.0F;
int maximumBufferLengthInFrames =
    (int) (maximumBufferLengthInSeconds*sampleF);
int periodLengthInFrames = sampleF/signalF;
if((periodLengthInFrames%2) != 0)
{
periodLengthInFrames++;
}
int numPeriodsInBuffer =
   maximumBufferLengthInFrames/periodLengthInFrames;
int numFramesInBuffer =
          numPeriodsInBuffer*periodLengthInFrames;

int bufferLength = numFramesInBuffer*4;
format = new AudioFormat(AudioFormat.Encoding.PCM_SIGNED,
                         sampleF,16,2,4,sampleF,false);
data = new byte[bufferLength];

for(int period=0;period<numPeriodsInBuffer;period++)
{
for(int frame=0;frame<periodLengthInFrames;frame++)
{
int value = 0;
value = (int)
 (Math.sin(((double)frame/(double)periodLengthInFrames)*
   2.0*Math.PI)*amplitude);

int baseAddr = (period*periodLengthInFrames+frame)*4;
data[baseAddr+0] = (byte) (value & 0xFF);
data[baseAddr+1] = (byte) ((value >>> 8) & 0xFF);
data[baseAddr+2] = (byte) (value & 0xFF);
data[baseAddr+3] = (byte) ((value >>> 8) & 0xFF);
} // end for frame
} // end for period

ByteArrayInputStream bais = new ByteArrayInputStream(data);
AudioInputStream ais =
  new AudioInputStream(bais,format,
                       data.length/format.getFrameSize());
try
{
AudioSystem.write(ais,AudioFileFormat.Type.WAVE,
```

```
                    new File("sine.wav"));
  }
  catch(IOException e)
  {
  e.printStackTrace();
  }
  } // end main()
}
```

1.5   Transmission Formats

Signals could be transmitted as continuous variations in intensity (or other parameters), or as digital pulses. Analog transmission was used for many years and remains common in cable television systems. It can pack more information into less bandwidth than digital signals, but it is much more vulnerable to noise and distortion and cannot be manipulated as easily as digital signals. Digital transmission requires simpler electronics and can encode any form of information. Digital signals are easy to process and manipulate. Digital and analog signals are transmitted by amplitude modulation. Digital modulation is not simply off-on-off-on. There are several digital modulation techniques. Each has its own distinct characteristics.

1) *Non Return To Zero Coding* (NRZ): Signal level is low for a 0 bit and high for a 1 bit and does not return to zero between successive 1 bits. In existing commercial optical fiber communications links, information is encoded with square-wave pulses in the non-return-to-zero format. These pulses propagate essentially linearly in existing systems. Dispersion, absorption and imperfections in the fiber cables deform them causing errors in the transmitted signal. To keep the signal error free, it is periodically corrected and amplified.

2) *Return To Zero Coding* (RZ): Signal level during the first half of a bit interval (data cell) is low for a 0 bit and high for a 1 bit. Then it returns to zero for either a 0 or 1 in the second half of the bit interval.

3) *Manchester Coding*: Signal level always changes in the middle of a bit interval (data cell). For a 0 bit, the signal starts out low and changes to high. For a 1 bit, the signal starts out high and changes to low. This means that the signal level changes at the end of a bit interval (data cell) only when two successive bits are identical (e.g., between two zeros). Thus Manchester coding represents binary values by a transition rather than a level. The transition occurs at mid-bit, with a low-to-high transition used to represent a logic "0", and a high-to-low transition represent a logic "1".

Depending on the data pattern, there may be a transition at the data cell boundary (beginning/end). A pattern of consecutive "1s" or "0s" results in a transition on the data cell boundary. When the data pattern alternates between "1" and "0", there is no transition on the cell data cell boundary.

4) *Miller Coding*: For a 1 bit the signal changes in the middle of a bit interval (data cell) but not at the beginning or end. For a 0 bit, the signal level remains constant through a bit interval, changing at the end of it if followed by another 0 but not if it is followed by a 1.

5) Biphase-M or Bifrequency Coding: For a 0 bit, the signal level changes at the start of an interval. For a 1 bit, the signal level changes at the start and at the middle of a bit interval.

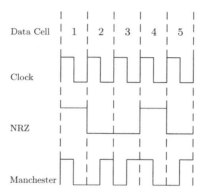

Figure 1.2. NRZ Encoding and Manchester Encoding for the bitstring 10010

In serial communication, clocks are used to define the size/boundary of a data cell (bit interval). With a non-self clocking code, since the clock and data are distinct, there can be skew between clock and data. In magnetic media applications, skew may be due to variations in the tape drive speed. In serial communication, skew results from differences in the transit delay between clock and data lines in long serial links.

In NRZ only one level/data cell is required, while in Manchester coding two levels are required. A DC component exist in NRZ when contiguous "1s" or contiguous "0s" are transmitted. When the data pattern alternates between "1s" and "0s", the frequency response is equal to 1/2 the clock rate. The frequency response for NRZ then ranges from DC to clock/2. The frequency response of Manchester code ranges from clock/2, occurring when the data pattern is alternating "1s" to "0s", to clock which occurs when the data pattern is consecutive "1s" or "0s". Two advantages of NRZ are that it does not require encoding/decoding, and it makes the most efficient use of a communication channels bandwidth. Manchester coding requires a modulation rate twice that of NRZ to transmit the same amount of information. This can be important in bandwidth limited communication channels. On the other hand, the receiver of NRZ requires a true DC response. Since Manchester code has no DC component, it can be transformer coupled.

Chapter 2

Quantisation

2.1 Introduction

Conversion of an analog signal (continuous-time, continuous-amplitude) into a digital signal (discrete-time, discrete-amplitude) consists of a sampling (described in chapter 1) and then a quantisation process. Sampling converts a continuous-time signal into a discrete-time signal by measuring the signal values at regular time intervals T_s, the so-called sampling time. Quantisation converts a continuous-amplitude signal into a discrete-amplitude signal that is different from the continuous-amplitude signal by the quantisation error or noise. When each of a set of discrete values is quantised separately, the process is known as *scalar quantisation*. Scalar quantisation processes samples of input signals one-by-one and independently.

Pulse code modulation (PCM) is a method of converting an analog signal into a digital signal. PCM does not mean any specific kind of compression, it only implies PAM (pulse amplitude modulation) - quantisation by amplitude and quantisation by time which means digitalisation of the analog signal. The range of values which the signal can achieve (quantisation range) is divided into segments, each segment has a segment representative of the quantisation level which lies in the middle of the segment. To every quantisation segment (and quantisation level) one unique code word (stream of bits) is assigned. The value that a signal has at a certain time is called a sample.

Can we already exploit dependencies during quantisation?

In *vector quantisation* we use dependency between k consecutive samples to break-up an k-dimensional space into cells in a more efficient way than with scalar quantisation. The signal to be quantised is considered as a series of vectors $\mathbf{x}_m$ containing N-samples

$$\mathbf{x}_m = (x_0, x_1, \ldots, x_{N-1})_m \,.$$

Thus we first have to set up a *codebook*. The codebook consists of L vectors $\mathbf{y}_i$ ($i = 0, 1, \ldots, L-1$). The bit rate is determined by the size L of the code book. Each codevector is also of length N. A distortion measure (distance measure) $d(\mathbf{x}_m, \mathbf{y}_i)$ is needed to weight the quantisation errors and generate a metric in the N-dimensional space. This is needed to avoid explicitly describing the boundaries of the cells.

Differential pulse code modulation (DPCM) is a procedure of converting an analog to a digital signal in which the analog signal is sampled and then the difference between the actual sample value and its predicted value (predicted value is based on previous sample or samples) is quantised and then encoded forming a digital value. DPCM code words represent differences between samples unlike PCM where code words represented a sample value. Basic concept of DPCM - coding a difference, is based on the fact that most source signals show significant correlation between successive samples so encoding uses redundancy in sample values which implies lower bit rates. Realisation of the basic concept is based on a technique in which we have to predict a current sample value based upon previous samples (or sample) and we have to encode the difference between the actual value of the sample and the predicted value (difference between samples can be interpreted as prediction error). Since it is necessary to predict the sample value, DPCM is part of predictive coding. DPCM compression depends on the chosen prediction technique. Well-conducted prediction techniques lead to good compression rates, in other cases DPCM could mean expansion compared to regular PCM encoding. Thus differential pulse-code modulation is a pulse-code modulation in which an analog signal is sampled and the difference between the actual value of each sample and its predicted value, derived from the previous sample or samples, is quantised and converted, by encoding, to a digital signal. Note there are several variations of differential pulse-code modulation.

Adaptive differential pulse-code modulation (ADPCM) is a differential pulse-code modulation in which the prediction algorithm is adjusted in accordance with specific characteristics of the input signal. Embedded adaptive differential pulse code modulation (embedded ADPCM): Modulation is achieved using algorithms that quantise the difference between the input and the estimated signal into core bits and enhancement bits.

2.2 Scalar Quantisation

A sampling process converts a continuous-time signal $x(t)$ into a discrete-time sequence $x(n)$. In practice, this sampling is performed with an analog-to-digital converter (ADC) that represents the sampled value with a finite number of bits, usually in fixed-point notation. Hence, the ADC also simultaneously converts the continuous-valued sample $x(n)$ into one that has been quantised. In the following we denoted it by $x_q(n)$. The value of $x_q(n)$ is assigned to one of the numbers represented by the finite number of bits in the ADC. The process of converting the $x(n)$ into $x_q(n)$ can be modeled by the quantiser characteristic. The quantiser range is expressed in terms of 2's complement numbers that span the amplitude range from $-M$ to $M-1$ in K steps, each of size

$$\Delta = 2M/K.$$

If the quantiser contains b bits,

$$K = 2^b$$

then

$$\Delta = \frac{2M}{2^b}.$$

For a given quantiser range, increasing the number of bits reduces the step size, making the staircase pattern approach a straight line.

Thus in scalar quantisation each sampled value of the input analog signal, which can have an infinite range, is compared against a finite set of amplitude values, and the closest value from the finite set is chosen to represent the analog amplitude. The distance between the finite set of amplitude levels is called the quantiser step size, which is usually denoted by Δ. Each discrete amplitude level Δ_n is represented by a code-word $c(n)$ for transmission purposes. At the de-quantiser, which is usually at the digital receiver, the code-word $c(n)$ indicates which discrete amplitude is to be used.

Example. Assume we have the range $[-1, 1]$ and 4 bits for quantisation. Owing to 4 bits we have the range

$$-8, -7, -6, -5, -4, -3, -2, -1, 0, 1, 2, 3, 4, 5, 6, 7$$

with the bit representation

```
-8 -> 1000    -7 -> 1001
-6 -> 1010    -5 -> 1011
-4 -> 1100    -3 -> 1101
-2 -> 1110    -1 -> 1111
```

```
0  -> 0000    1 -> 0001
2  -> 0010    3 -> 0011
4  -> 0100    5 -> 0101
6  -> 0110    7 -> 0111
```

where we used *two's complement* for negative numbers. If the most significant bit is 1 the integer number is negative. Thus we have to find a linear map

$$f(x) = ax + b$$

where

$$f : \{ -8, -7, \ldots, 6, 7\} \to [-1, 1].$$

The boundary conditions are $f(-8) = -1$ and $f(7) = 1$. We obtain two equations with two unknowns

$$-1 = -8a + b, \qquad 1 = 7a + b.$$

The solutions is

$$a = \frac{2}{15}, \qquad b = \frac{1}{15}.$$

Thus

$$f(x) = \frac{2}{15}x + \frac{1}{15}.$$

For example, if $x = 6$, then we have $f(6) = 13/15$. We can solve the equation with respect to x under the constraint that x takes only the values $-8, -7, \ldots, 7$. We find

$$x = \frac{15}{2}f(x) - \frac{1}{2}.$$

If $f(x) = 0.3$ we have $x = 1.75$ and owing to the constraint we have $x = 2$ since 1.75 is closer to 2 than 1.

The general case is as follows. We have $(M > 0)$

$$f : \{ -2^n, -2^n + 1, \ldots, 2^n - 1\} \to [-M, M].$$

From

$$f(x) = ax + b$$

we have

$$f(-2^n) = -M$$

and

$$f(2^n - 1) = +M.$$

Therefore

$$-M = -2^n a + b, \qquad M = (2^n - 1)a + b \equiv 2^n a - a + b.$$

The solution is

$$a = \frac{2M}{2^{n+1} - 1}, \qquad b = \frac{M}{2^{n+1} - 1}.$$

Thus

$$f(x) = \frac{2M}{2^{n+1} - 1}x + \frac{M}{2^{n+1} - 1}.$$

The following picture shows the quantisation

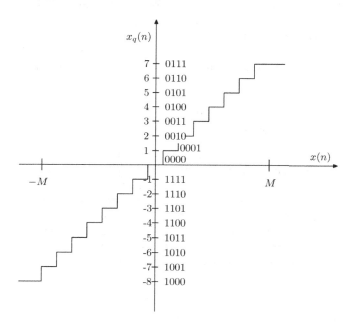

Figure 2.1. Quantiser characteristics for a 4-bit quantiser

There are two types of errors that can be introduced by such a quantiser. The first is *granular error*, which occurs when $|x(n)| < M$, and is denoted by $\epsilon_g(n)$, where

$$\epsilon_g(n) := x(n) - x_q(n).$$

Note that the magnitude of this error is always less than the step size Δ. The second error occurs when $|x(n)| > M$, when the amplitude exceeds the quantiser limits, and is called the *clipping error*, denoted by $\epsilon_c(n)$, where

$$\epsilon_c(n) := \begin{cases} x(n) - M - 1 \text{ for } x(n) > M - 1 \\ x(n) + M \quad \text{ for } \ x(n) < -M \end{cases}.$$

2.3   Mu-Law and A-Law

Pulse Code Modulation is a sampling technique for digitising analog signals, especially audio signals. PCM samples the signal 8000 times a second. Each sample is represented by 8 bits for a total of 64 Kbps. There are two standards for coding the sample level. Both of these algorithms are used as telecommunication standards. The μ-Law standard is used in North America and Japan while the A-Law standard is used in most other countries. The A-Law and μ-Law compression are standard forms of audio compression for 16 bit sounds. Like most audio compression techniques, they are lossy, which means that when we expand them back from their compressed state, they will not be exactly the same as when we compressed them. The compression is always 2:1, meaning that audio compressed with either of these algorithms will always be exactly half of their original size.

μ-Law and A-Law compression are both logarithmic forms of data compression, and are very similar. One definition of μ-Law is

```
...a form of logarithmic data compression for audio data.
Due to the fact that we hear logarithmically,
sound recorded at higher levels does not require the same
resolution as low-level sound. This allows us to disregard
the least significant bits in high-level data.
This turns out to resemble a logarithmic transformation.
The resulting compression forces a 16-bit number to be
represented as an 8-bit number.
```

Another definition is:

```
Mu-law encoding is a form of logarithmic quantisation.
It is based on the observation that many signals are
statistically more likely to be near a low signal level
than a high signal level. Therefore, it makes more sense
to have more quantisation points near a low level than
a high level. In a typical mu-law system, linear samples
of 14 to 16 bits are companded to 8 bits. Most telephone
quality codecs use mu-law encoded samples.
```

The formula for the μ-Law is

$$y(x) = \mathrm{sgn}(x)\frac{V_0 \log_{10}\left(1 + \frac{\mu|x|}{V_0}\right)}{\log_{10}(1 + \mu)}$$

where $|x| \leq 1$ and $V_0 = L\sigma_x$, in which L is the loading factor and σ_x is the rms value of the input speech signal. A typical value of the compression factor μ is 255.

The formula for the A-law is

$$y(x) = \frac{Ax}{1 + \log_{10}(A)}, \qquad \text{for} \quad 0 \leq x \leq \frac{1}{A}$$

$$y(x) = \frac{1 + \log_{10}(Ax)}{1 + \log_{10}(A)}, \qquad \text{for} \quad \frac{1}{A} \leq x \leq 1$$

where A is the compression parameter with typical values of 86 for 7 bit (North American PCM) and 87.56 for 8 bits (European PCM) speech quantisers.

The above expressions show that the A-Law is a combination of a logarithmic curve used for large amplitudes, while for small amplitudes the curve becomes linear. The μ-Law, on the other hand, is not exactly linear or logarithmic in any range, but is approximately linear for small and logarithmic for large amplitudes.

In simpler terms, this means that sound is represented as a wave, and humans can only hear audio in the middle of the wave. We can remove data from the upper and lower frequencies of a sound, and humans will not be able to hear a significant difference. Both μ-Law and A-Law take advantage of this, and are able to compress 16-bit audio in an manner acceptable to human ears. A-Law and μ-Law compression have been developed at around the same time, and basically only differ by the particular logarithmic function used to determine the translation. When we get to the work of implementing the algorithms, we see that the differences are nominal. The main difference is that μ-Law attempts to keep the top five bits of precision, and uses a logarithmic function to determine the bottom three bits, while A-Law compression keeps the top four bits and uses the logarithmic function to figure out the bottom four.

The purpose of the algorithms is to compress a 16-bit source sample down to an 8-bit sample. The crux of μ-Law functionality is deciding which of the samples need to keep most of their precision. Even the most-important sample will still lose precision. It simply becomes a matter of determining how much each sample loses, and minimising the loss on samples deemed more important.

To generate a compressed μ-Law sample from an uncompressed sample, the following algorithm is applied to the 16-bit source sample.

First, the algorithm stores the sign. It then adds in a bias value which (due to wrapping) will cause high valued samples to lose precision. The top five most significant bits are pulled out of the sample (which has been previously biased). Then, the bottom three bits of the compressed byte are generated using a small look-up table, based on the biased value of the source sample. The 8-bit compressed sample is then finally created by logically OR'ing together the 5 most important bits, the 3 lower bits, and the sign when applicable. The bits are then logically NOT'ed, which is for transmission reasons.

C μ-Law Compression Code:

```
const int cBias = 0x84;
const int cClip = 32635;

static char MuLawCompressTable[256] =
{
0,0,1,1,2,2,2,2,3,3,3,3,3,3,3,3,
4,4,4,4,4,4,4,4,4,4,4,4,4,4,4,4,
5,5,5,5,5,5,5,5,5,5,5,5,5,5,5,5,
5,5,5,5,5,5,5,5,5,5,5,5,5,5,5,5,
6,6,6,6,6,6,6,6,6,6,6,6,6,6,6,6,
6,6,6,6,6,6,6,6,6,6,6,6,6,6,6,6,
6,6,6,6,6,6,6,6,6,6,6,6,6,6,6,6,
6,6,6,6,6,6,6,6,6,6,6,6,6,6,6,6,
7,7,7,7,7,7,7,7,7,7,7,7,7,7,7,7,
7,7,7,7,7,7,7,7,7,7,7,7,7,7,7,7,
7,7,7,7,7,7,7,7,7,7,7,7,7,7,7,7,
7,7,7,7,7,7,7,7,7,7,7,7,7,7,7,7,
7,7,7,7,7,7,7,7,7,7,7,7,7,7,7,7,
7,7,7,7,7,7,7,7,7,7,7,7,7,7,7,7,
7,7,7,7,7,7,7,7,7,7,7,7,7,7,7,7,
7,7,7,7,7,7,7,7,7,7,7,7,7,7,7,7
};

unsigned char LinearToMuLawSample(short sample)
{
int sign = (sample >> 8) & 0x80;

if(sign) sample = (short) -sample;
if(sample > cClip) sample = cClip;
sample = (short) (sample + cBias);

int exponent = (int) MuLawCompressTable[(sample >> 7) & 0xFF];
int mantissa = (sample >> (exponent+3)) & 0x0F;
int compressedByte = ~(sign | (exponent << 4) | mantissa);
```

```
return (unsigned char) compressedByte;
}
```

A-Law Compression:

A-Law compression is very similar to μ-Law compression. They differ primarily in the way that they keep precision. We give a short description of the encoding algorithm, and then the code example. First, the sign is stored off. Then the code branches. If the absolute value of the source sample is less than 256, the 16-bit sample is simply shifted down 4 bits and converted to an 8-bit value, thus losing the top 4 bits in the process. However, if it is more than 256, a logarithmic algorithm is applied to the sample to determine the precision to keep. In that case, the sample is shifted down to access the seven most significant bits of the sample. Those seven bits are then used to determine the precision of the bottom 4 bits. Finally, the top seven bits are shifted back up four bits to make room for the bottom 4 bits. The two are then logically OR'd together to create the eight bit compressed sample. The sign is then applied, and the entire compressed sample is logically XOR'd for transmission reasons.

C A-Law Compression Code:

```
char ALawCompressTable[128] =
{
1,1,2,2,3,3,3,3,4,4,4,4,4,4,4,4,
5,5,5,5,5,5,5,5,5,5,5,5,5,5,5,5,
6,6,6,6,6,6,6,6,6,6,6,6,6,6,6,6,
6,6,6,6,6,6,6,6,6,6,6,6,6,6,6,6,
7,7,7,7,7,7,7,7,7,7,7,7,7,7,7,7,
7,7,7,7,7,7,7,7,7,7,7,7,7,7,7,7,
7,7,7,7,7,7,7,7,7,7,7,7,7,7,7,7,
7,7,7,7,7,7,7,7,7,7,7,7,7,7,7,7
};

unsigned char LinearToALawSample(short sample)
{
int sign;
int exponent;
int mantissa;
unsigned char compressedByte;

sign = ((~sample) >> 8) & 0x80;
```

```
if(!sign) sample = (short) -sample;
if(sample > cClip) sample = cClip;
if(sample >= 256)
{
  exponent = (int) ALawCompressTable[(sample >> 8) & 0x7F];
  mantissa = (sample >> (exponent + 3)) & 0x0F;
  compressedByte = (unsigned char)((exponent << 4) | mantissa);
}
else
{ compressedByte = (unsigned char)(sample >> 4); }

compressedByte ^= (sign ^ 0x55);
return compressedByte;
}
```

Decompression:

The most obvious way to decompress a compressed μ-Law or A-Law sample would be to reverse the algorithm. However a more efficient method exists. Consider for a moment the fact that A-Law and μ-Law both take a 16-bit value and crunch it down to an 8-bit value. The reverse of that is to take an 8-bit value and turn it into a 16-bit value. In the graphics world, it is common to convert 32 and 24 bit values with an eight bit index into a palette table. Thus can we use palettes for the μ-Law and A-Law compression look up? In fact, these palettes will be smaller than their 24 and 32-bit cousins because we only need to represent 16-bit values, not 24 and 32. We create static lookup tables to do the reverse conversion from A-Law and μ-Law. The two differing tables are presented below. To convert from our compressed sample back to the raw 16-bit sample, just use the compressed sample as the index into the table, and the corresponding value in the table is our decompressed 16-bit sample. Obviously, this method requires the memory overhead for the tables, but each table is only 512 bytes.

Decompression Code:

```
static short MuLawDecompressTable[256] =
{
-32124,-31100,-30076,-29052,-28028,-27004,-25980,-24956,
-23932,-22908,-21884,-20860,-19836,-18812,-17788,-16764,
-15996,-15484,-14972,-14460,-13948,-13436,-12924,-12412,
-11900,-11388,-10876,-10364, -9852, -9340, -8828, -8316,
-7932, -7676, -7420, -7164, -6908, -6652, -6396, -6140,
-5884, -5628, -5372, -5116, -4860, -4604, -4348, -4092,
-3900, -3772, -3644, -3516, -3388, -3260, -3132, -3004,
```

```
-2876, -2748, -2620, -2492, -2364, -2236, -2108, -1980,
-1884, -1820, -1756, -1692, -1628, -1564, -1500, -1436,
-1372, -1308, -1244, -1180, -1116, -1052,  -988,  -924,
 -876,  -844,  -812,  -780,  -748,  -716,  -684,  -652,
 -620,  -588,  -556,  -524,  -492,  -460,  -428,  -396,
 -372,  -356,  -340,  -324,  -308,  -292,  -276,  -260,
 -244,  -228,  -212,  -196,  -180,  -164,  -148,  -132,
 -120,  -112,  -104,   -96,   -88,   -80,   -72,   -64,
  -56,   -48,   -40,   -32,   -24,   -16,    -8,     0,
32124, 31100, 30076, 29052, 28028, 27004, 25980, 24956,
23932, 22908, 21884, 20860, 19836, 18812, 17788, 16764,
15996, 15484, 14972, 14460, 13948, 13436, 12924, 12412,
11900, 11388, 10876, 10364,  9852,  9340,  8828,  8316,
 7932,  7676,  7420,  7164,  6908,  6652,  6396,  6140,
 5884,  5628,  5372,  5116,  4860,  4604,  4348,  4092,
 3900,  3772,  3644,  3516,  3388,  3260,  3132,  3004,
 2876,  2748,  2620,  2492,  2364,  2236,  2108,  1980,
 1884,  1820,  1756,  1692,  1628,  1564,  1500,  1436,
 1372,  1308,  1244,  1180,  1116,  1052,   988,   924,
  876,   844,   812,   780,   748,   716,   684,   652,
  620,   588,   556,   524,   492,   460,   428,   396,
  372,   356,   340,   324,   308,   292,   276,   260,
  244,   228,   212,   196,   180,   164,   148,   132,
  120,   112,   104,    96,    88,    80,    72,    64,
   56,    48,    40,    32,    24,    16,     8,     0
};

static short ALawDecompressTable[256] =
{
 -5504,  -5248,  -6016,  -5760,  -4480,  -4224,  -4992,  -4736,
 -7552,  -7296,  -8064,  -7808,  -6528,  -6272,  -7040,  -6784,
 -2752,  -2624,  -3008,  -2880,  -2240,  -2112,  -2496,  -2368,
 -3776,  -3648,  -4032,  -3904,  -3264,  -3136,  -3520,  -3392,
-22016,-20992,-24064,-23040,-17920,-16896,-19968,-18944,
-30208,-29184,-32256,-31232,-26112,-25088,-28160,-27136,
-11008,-10496,-12032,-11520, -8960, -8448, -9984, -9472,
-15104,-14592,-16128,-15616,-13056,-12544,-14080,-13568,
  -344,   -328,   -376,   -360,   -280,   -264,   -312,   -296,
  -472,   -456,   -504,   -488,   -408,   -392,   -440,   -424,
   -88,    -72,   -120,   -104,    -24,     -8,    -56,    -40,
  -216,   -200,   -248,   -232,   -152,   -136,   -184,   -168,
 -1376,  -1312,  -1504,  -1440,  -1120,  -1056,  -1248,  -1184,
 -1888,  -1824,  -2016,  -1952,  -1632,  -1568,  -1760,  -1696,
  -688,   -656,   -752,   -720,   -560,   -528,   -624,   -592,
```

```
-944,   -912, -1008,  -976,  -816,  -784,  -880,  -848,
5504,   5248,  6016,  5760,  4480,  4224,  4992,  4736,
7552,   7296,  8064,  7808,  6528,  6272,  7040,  6784,
2752,   2624,  3008,  2880,  2240,  2112,  2496,  2368,
3776,   3648,  4032,  3904,  3264,  3136,  3520,  3392,
22016, 20992, 24064, 23040, 17920, 16896, 19968, 18944,
30208, 29184, 32256, 31232, 26112, 25088, 28160, 27136,
11008, 10496, 12032, 11520,  8960,  8448,  9984,  9472,
15104, 14592, 16128, 15616, 13056, 12544, 14080, 13568,
344, 328, 376, 360, 280, 264, 312, 296,
472, 456, 504, 488, 408, 392, 440, 424,
88, 72, 120, 104, 24, 8, 56, 40,
216, 200, 248, 232, 152, 136, 184, 168,
1376, 1312, 1504, 1440, 1120, 1056, 1248, 1184,
1888, 1824, 2016, 1952, 1632, 1568, 1760, 1696,
688, 656, 752, 720, 560, 528, 624, 592,
944, 912, 1008, 976, 816, 784, 880, 848
};
```

2.4   Application

The following C++ program au.cpp shows an application of the μ-law. We generate a file for the sound format au for a sine wave. The au-format is as follows:

OFFSET	BYTES	Remarks
00h	4	signature .snd
04h	4	data location
08h	4	data size
0Ch	4	data format
10h	4	sampling rate (Hz)
14h	4	channel count
18h	n	char info (optional text information)

where $n = 4, 8, 12, \ldots$. Thus 28 (base 10 and 1C in hex) is the minimum value for data location. After the char info (ASCII) the audio data follow. ASCII stands for American Standard Code for Information Interchange. It is a coding scheme whereby every character the computer can represent is assigned an integer code between 0 and 127. ASCII can be defined as the first 127 codes in the Unicode set.

We use $n = 4$ in the following. The first four bytes contain the signature
.snd with the hex values (ASCII table) 0x2E, 0x73, 0x6E, 0x64. We have

```
hex-values        BYTES   Remarks
================  =====   ==================================
2E, 73, 6E, 64    4       signature .snd
00, 00, 00, 1C    4       data location, 28
00, 00, 1F, A0    4       data size, 8000
00, 00, 00, 01    4       data format, 1 for mu-law 8bits
00, 00, 1F, 40    4       sampling rate (Hz), 8000Hz
00, 00, 00, 01    4       channel count, 1 channel mono
00, 00, 00, 00    4       char info
==================================================================
```

The data size is 8000 bytes, since

```
1F 40 => 1*16^3 + 15*16^2 + 4*16^1 = 8000
```

The sampling rate is 8000 Hz since

```
1F 40 => 1*16^3 + 15*16^2 + 4*16^1 = 8000
```

The C++ program is given by

```cpp
// au.cpp

#include <cstdio>
#include <cmath>
using namespace std;

int sgn(double yg)
{
  if(yg > 0) return 1;
  if(yg < 0) return -1;
  if(yg == 0) return 0;
}

double f(double xf)
{
  int mu = 255;
  return (sgn(xf)*(log(1.0 + (mu*fabs(xf))))/(log(1.0+mu)));
}

int main(void)
{
```

```
unsigned char hex[28];
hex[0] = 0x2E; hex[1] = 0x73; hex[2] = 0x6E; hex[3] = 0x64;
hex[4] = 0x00; hex[5] = 0x00; hex[6] = 0x00; hex[7] = 0x1C;
hex[8] = 0x00; hex[9] = 0x00; hex[10] = 0x1F; hex[11] = 0x40;
hex[12] = 0x00; hex[13] = 0x00; hex[14] = 0x00; hex[15] = 0x01;
hex[16] = 0x00; hex[17] = 0x00; hex[18] = 0x1F; hex[19] = 0x40;
hex[20] = 0x00; hex[21] = 0x00; hex[22] = 0x00; hex[23] = 0x01;
hex[24] = 0x00; hex[25] = 0x00; hex[26] = 0x00; hex[27] = 0x00;
const int N = 8000;
char data[N];
int freq = 440;
double pi = 3.14159;
for(int i=0;i<N;i++)
{
double xf = sin(freq*2.0*pi*i/N);
double fs = f(xf);
char t;
if(i==0) t = 127;
if(sgn(fs) == -1) t = (unsigned char) (127.0-fabs((127.0*fs)));
if(sgn(fs) == 1) t = (unsigned char) (255.0-(127.0*fs));
data[i] = t;
}
FILE* in;
in = fopen("sin440.au","wb");
for(int k=0;k<28;k++) fputc(hex[k],in);
for(int l=0;l<8000;l++) fputc(data[l],in);
fclose(in);
return 0;
}
```

2.5   Vector Quantisation

2.5.1   Introduction

Vector quantisation (VQ) is a lossy data compression method based on the principle of block coding. It is a fixed-to-fixed length algorithm. Before 1980, the design of a vector quantiser was considered to be a challenging problem due to the need for multi-dimensional integration. In 1980, Linde, Buzo and Gray [37] proposed a vector quantisation design algorithm based on a training sequence. The use of a training sequence bypasses the need for multi-dimensional integration. A vector quantisation that is designed using this algorithm are referred to in the literature as an *LBG-vector quantisation*.

Example. Consider the codebook with vectors in $\mathbf{R}^2$

```
codenumber    vector
==========    =========
0             (0.0,0.0)
1             (2.0,1.0)
2             (1.0,3.0)
3             (1.0,4.0)
==========    =========
```

Each vector has a code number. Assume that the signal is the sequence of vectors

(0.0,1.0),   (2.0,3.0),   (2.0,0.5)

As a distance measure we use the *Euclidean distance*

$$d(\mathbf{x}, \mathbf{y}) := \sqrt{(x_1 - y_1)^2 + (x_2 - y_2)^2}, \qquad \mathbf{x}, \mathbf{y} \in \mathbf{R}^2.$$

Thus the vector $(0.0, 1.0)$ is closest to $(0.0, 0.0)$. Thus 0.0 is transmitted. The vector $(2.0, 3.0)$ is closest to $(1.0, 3.0)$. Thus 2.0 is transmitted. The vector $(2.0, 0.5)$ is closest to $(2.0, 1.0)$. Thus 1.0 is transmitted. The transmitted sequence is therefore

$$0.0, \quad 2.0, \quad 1.0.$$

The decoded signal is therefore

$$(0.0, 0.0), \quad (1.0, 3.0), \quad (2.0, 1.0)$$

2.5.2   Design Problem

The vector quantisation problem can be stated as follows. Given a vector source with its statistical properties known, given a distortion measure, and given the number of codevectors, find a codebook and a partition of the space which result in the smallest average distortion.

Assume that there is training sequence T consisting of M source vectors

$$T := \{ \mathbf{x}_0, \mathbf{x}_1, \ldots, \mathbf{x}_{M-1} \}.$$

This training sequence can be obtained from some large database. For example if the source is a speech signal, then the training sequence can be obtained by recording several long telephone conversations. Here M is assumed to be sufficiently large so that all the statistical properties of the source are captured by the training sequence T. We assume that the source vectors are k-dimensional, e. g.,

$$\mathbf{x}_m = (x_{m,1}, x_{m,2}, \ldots, x_{m,k})^T, \qquad m = 0, 1, \ldots, M - 1$$

where ^{T} denotes transpose. Let N be the number of codevectors and let

$$C := \{\, \mathbf{c}_0, \mathbf{c}_1, \ldots, \mathbf{c}_{N-1} \,\}$$

represent the codebook. Obviously each codevector is also k-dimensional, i.e.,

$$\mathbf{c}_n = (c_{n,1}, c_{n,2}, \ldots, c_{n,k})^T, \qquad n = 0, 1, \ldots, N - 1 \,.$$

Let S_n be the encoding region associated with codevector $\mathbf{c}_n$ and let

$$P := \{\, S_0, S_1, \ldots, S_{N-1} \,\}$$

denote the partition of the space. If the source vector $\mathbf{x}_m$ is in the encoding region S_n, then its approximation (denoted by $Q(\mathbf{x}_m)$) is $\mathbf{c}_n$:

$$Q(\mathbf{x}_m) = \mathbf{c}_n \qquad \text{if} \quad \mathbf{x}_m \in S_n \,.$$

Assuming a squared-error distortion measure, the average distortion is given by

$$D_{ave} := \frac{1}{Mk} \sum_{m=0}^{M-1} \|\mathbf{x}_m - Q(\mathbf{x}_m)\|^2$$

where $\|...\|$ denotes the norm, for example the Euclidean norm.

The design problem for the code book can now be formulated as follows. Given

$$T \qquad \text{(the training set)}$$

and

$$N \qquad \text{(number of codevectors)}$$

find C and P such that D_{ave} is minimised.

If C and P are a solution to the above minimisation problem, then it must satisfy the following two criteria.

Nearest Neighbour Condition:

$$S_n = \{\, \mathbf{x} : \|\mathbf{x} - \mathbf{c}_n\|^2 \leq \|\mathbf{x} - \mathbf{c}_{n'}\|^2 \quad \text{for all} \quad n' = 0, 1, \ldots, N - 1 \,\}\,.$$

This condition tells us that the encoding region S_n consists of all vectors that are closer to $\mathbf{c}_n$ than any of the other codevectors. For those vectors lying on the boundary, any tie-breaking procedure will do.

Centroid Condition:

$$\mathbf{c}_n = \frac{\sum_{\mathbf{x}_m \in S_n} \mathbf{x}_m}{\sum_{\mathbf{x}_m \in S_n} 1}, \qquad n = 0, 1, \ldots, N-1.$$

This condition says that the codevector $\mathbf{c}_n$ should be average of all those training vectors that are in encoding region S_n. In implementation, one must make sure that at least one training vector belongs to each encoding region so that the denominator in the above equation is nonzero.

2.5.3 LBG Design Algorithm

The LBG design algorithm is an iterative algorithm which alternatively solves the above two optimality criteria. This algorithm requires an initial codebook $C^{(0)}$. This initial codebook is obtained by the *splitting method*. In this method, an initial codevector is the average of the entire training set. This codevector is split into two. The iteration runs with these two vectors as the initial codebook. After the iteration the final two codevectors are split into four and the iteration process is repeated until the desired number of codevectors is obtained. The LBG design algorithm is as follows.

1) Given T the training set. Set $\epsilon > 0$ to a small number.

2) Let $N = 1$ (number of codevectors) and

$$\mathbf{c}_1^* := \frac{1}{M} \sum_{m=0}^{M-1} \mathbf{x}_m$$

Calculate

$$D_{ave}^* = \frac{1}{Mk} \sum_{m=0}^{M-1} \|\mathbf{x}_m - \mathbf{c}_1^*\|^2$$

3) **Splitting.** For $i = 0, 1, \ldots, N-1$, set

$$\mathbf{c}_i^{(0)} := (1 + \epsilon)\mathbf{c}_i^*$$

$$\mathbf{c}_{N+i}^{(0)} := (1 - \epsilon)\mathbf{c}_i^*$$

Thus at the beginning we start of with two vectors. Set $N = 2N$.

4) **Iteration.** Set the iteration index $j = 0$ and let

$$D_{ave}^{(0)} = D_{ave}^*$$

a) For $m = 0, 1, \ldots, M - 1$ find the minimum value of

$$\|\mathbf{x}_m - \mathbf{c}_n^{(j)}\|^2$$

over all $n = 0, 1, \ldots, N - 1$. Let n^* be the index which provides the minimum for a given m. Thus each m has a certain n^*. Set

$$Q(\mathbf{x}_m) = \mathbf{c}_{n^*}^{(j)} .$$

b) For $n = 0, 1, \ldots, N - 1$ update the codevector

$$\mathbf{c}_n^{(j+1)} = \frac{\sum_{Q(\mathbf{x}_m)=\mathbf{c}_n^{(j)}} \mathbf{x}_m}{\sum_{Q(\mathbf{x}_m)=\mathbf{c}_n^{(j)}} 1}$$

c) Set $j = j + 1$

d) Calculate

$$D_{ave}^{(j)} = \frac{1}{Mk} \sum_{m=0}^{M-1} \|\mathbf{x}_m - Q(\mathbf{x}_m)\|^2$$

e) If

$$\frac{D_{ave}^{(j-1)} - D_{ave}^{(j)}}{D_{ave}^{(j-1)}} > \epsilon$$

go back to step (a).

f) Set

$$D_{ave}^* = D_{ave}^{(j)}$$

For $n = 0, 1, \ldots, N - 1$, set

$$\mathbf{c}_n^* = \mathbf{c}_n^{(j)}$$

as the final codevectors for this iteration step.

5) Repeat steps 3) and 4) until the desired number of codevectors is obtained.

The algorithm guarantees a locally optimal solution. The size of the training sequence for practical application should be sufficiently large. It is recommended that $M \geq 1000N$. A typical value for ϵ is 0.001.

2.5.4 Example

Consider in the Euclidean space $\mathbf{R}^2$ the training set T of nine vectors

$$\mathbf{x}_0 = (-1.5, -1.5), \quad \mathbf{x}_1 = (-1.5, 2.0), \quad \mathbf{x}_2 = (-2.0, -2.0)$$

$$\mathbf{x}_3 = (1.0, 1.0), \quad \mathbf{x}_4 = (1.5, 1.5), \quad \mathbf{x}_5 = (1.0, 2.0)$$

$$\mathbf{x}_6 = (1.0, -2.0), \quad \mathbf{x}_7 = (1.0, -3.0), \quad \mathbf{x}_8 = (1.0, -2.5).$$

Thus the number of training vectors is $M = 9$. Let $\epsilon = 0.005$. The following Java program gives an implementation of the algorithm.

```java
// LGB.java

import java.util.*;

class Vect
{
  private double x;
  private double y;

  Vect() { init(0.0,0.0); }

  Vect(double x,double y) { init(x,y); }

  private void init(double x,double y)
  { this.x = x; this.y = y; }

  void addSelf(Vect addend)
  { x += addend.x; y += addend.y; }

  void divSelf(double divisor)
  { x /= divisor; y /= divisor; }

  Vect mul(double factor)
  { return new Vect(x*factor,y*factor); }

  double euclidDist2(Vect vect)
  { return Math.pow(x-vect.x,2) + Math.pow(y-vect.y,2); }

  public String toString()
  { return "(" + x + ", " + y + ")"; }
} // end class Vect

class LGB
```

```
{
  private static final double EPSILON = 0.005;
  private static final int K = 2;   // K-dimensional

  private int N, M, NUMOF_N;
  private Vect samples[];
  private Vect codebook[];
  private int Qxm[];

  private double dave_j;

  LGB(Vector samples,int numofCodebookVects)
  {
  NUMOF_N = numofCodebookVects;
  M = samples.size();
  Qxm = new int[M];

  this.samples = new Vect[M];

  for(int i=0;i<M;i++)
  { this.samples[i] = (Vect) samples.get(i); }

  start();
  iteration();
  }

  private void start()
  {
  N = 1;
  Vect c1 = new Vect();

  for(int m=0;m<M;m++)
  { c1.addSelf(samples[m]); }
  c1.divSelf(M);

  for(int m=0;m<M;m++)
  { dave_j += samples[m].euclidDist2(c1); }
  dave_j /= (M*K);
  codebook = new Vect[N];
  codebook[0] = c1;
  }

  private void iteration()
  {
```

```
while(N < NUMOF_N)
{
split();
double dave_j_1 = 0.0;
int j = 0;

do
{
dave_j_1 = dave_j;

// a) find the min val of ||samples - codebook||^2
for(int m=0;m<M;m++)
{
double euclidDistMinVal = Double.MAX_VALUE;

for(int n=0;n<N;n++)
{
double euclidDist = samples[m].euclidDist2(codebook[n]);
if(euclidDist < euclidDistMinVal)
{
euclidDistMinVal = euclidDist;
Qxm[m] = n;
}
}
}
// b) update codebook
for(int n=0;n<N;n++)
{
Vect cn = new Vect();
int numof = 0;

for(int m=0;m<M;m++)
{
if(Qxm[m] == n)
{
cn.addSelf(samples[m]);
numof++;
}
}
cn.divSelf(numof);
codebook[n]   = cn;
}
// step c)
j++;
```

```
// step d)
dave_j = 0.0;

for(int m=0;m<M;m++)
{
dave_j += samples[m].euclidDist2(codebook[Qxm[m]]);
}
dave_j /= (M*K);
}
while((dave_j_1 - dave_j)/dave_j_1 > EPSILON);

// step f)
}
}

private void split()
{
Vect codebookOld[] = codebook;
codebook = new Vect[2+N];

for(int i=0;i<N;i++)
{
codebook[i] = codebookOld[i].mul(1+EPSILON);
codebook[i+N] = codebookOld[i].mul(1-EPSILON);
}
N *= 2;
} // end method split()

public String toString()
{
String str = "\nCodebook\n" +
     "--------\n\n";

for(int i=0;i<codebook.length;i++)
{
str += codebook[i] + "\n";
}
return str;
}

public static void main(String args[])
{
Vector samples = new Vector();
samples.add(new Vect(-1.5,-1.5));
```

```
    samples.add(new Vect(-1.5,2.0));
    samples.add(new Vect(-2.0,-2.0));
    samples.add(new Vect(1.0,1.0));
    samples.add(new Vect(1.5,1.5));
    samples.add(new Vect(1.0,2.0));
    samples.add(new Vect(1.0,-2.0));
    samples.add(new Vect(1.0,-3.0));
    samples.add(new Vect(1.0,-2.5));
    int numof = 4;

    LGB lgb = new LGB(samples,numof);
    System.out.println (lgb);
    }
}
```

The output is

```
Codebook
-------------
(1.0,-2.5)
(1.1667,1.5)
(-1.75,-1.75)
(-1.5,2.0)
=============
```

Chapter 3

Digital Linear Filters

3.1 Introduction

One of the most common problems encountered in digital signal processing is that of constructing a filter with given magnitude characteristics at different frequencies ([2], [44], [57]). Thus the function of a filter is to remove unwanted parts of the signal, such as random noise, or to extract useful parts of the signal, such as the components lying within a certain frequency range. There are two main kinds of filter, analog and digital. They are quite different in their physical makeup and in how they work. An analog filter uses analog electronic circuits made up from components such as resistors, capacitors and op amps to produce the required filtering effect. Such filter are widely used in such applications as noise reduction, video signal enhancement, graphics equalisers in hi-fi systems and many other areas. There are well-established standard techniques for designing an analog filter circuit for a given requirement. At all stages, the signal being filtered is an electrical voltage or current which is the direct analogue of the physical quantity (e.g. sound or video signal or transducer output) involved. A digital filter uses a digital processor to perform numerical calculations on sampled values of the signal. The processor may be a general-purpose computer such as a PC, or a specialised Digital Signal Processor (DSP) chip.

As described in chapter 1, the analog input signal must first be sampled and digitised (quantisation) using an analog to digital converter (ADC). The resulting binary numbers, representing successive sampled values of the input signal, are transferred to the processor, which carries out numerical calculation on them. These calculations typically involve multiplying the input values by constants and adding the products together. If necessary, the results of these calculations, which now represent sampled values of the filtered signal, are output through a digital to analog converter (DAC) to convert the signal back to analog form. Thus in a digital filter the signal is represented by a sequence of numbers, rather than a voltage or current.

Thus a digital filter consists of the interconnection of three simple elements:

$$\text{adder,} \quad \text{multiplier,} \quad \text{delays}.$$

The adder and multiplier are conceptually simple components that are readily implemented in the arithmetic logic unit of the computer. Delays are components that allow access to future and past values of the input sequence. Open-headed arrows indicate direction of information flow, while the larger closed arrows indicate multipliers. This convention will be useful for drawing complicated digital filters. There are two types of delays: positive and negative. A positive delay, or simply delay, is implemented by a memory register that stores the current value of a sequence for one sample interval, thus making it available for future calculations. A positive delay is conventionally indicated by a box labelled z^{-1}. A negative delay, or advance, is used to look ahead to the next value in the input sequence, and is indicated by a box denoted by z. Let $x(n)$ be the digital signal. Then

$$zx(k) := x(k+1)$$

and

$$z^{-1}x(k) := x(k-1).$$

Advances are typically used for applications, such as image processing, in which the entire data sequence to be processed is available at the start of processing, so that the advance serves to access the next data sample in the sequence. The availability of the advance will simplify the analysis of digital filters. However, the advance cannot be implemented in all applications. For example, when the data sequence is obtained by sampling a function of time, each new sample is usually processed as it is acquired. In this case, advances are not allowed, since we cannot gain access to future data values. A digital filter design involves selecting and interconnecting a finite number of these elements and determining the multiplier coefficient values.

A digital filter has a number of advantages over an analog filter. A digital filter is programmable, i.e. its operation is determined by a program stored in the processor's memory. This means the digital filter can be changed without affecting the circuitry (hardware). An analog filter can only be changed by redesigning the filter circuit. Digital filters are easily designed, tested and implemented on a general-purpose computer or workstation. The characteristics of analog filter circuits (particularly those containing active components) are subject to drift and are dependent on temperature. Digital filter do not suffer from these problems. Unlike their analog counterparts, digital filters can handle low frequency signals accurately. As the rate of DSP technological development continues to increase, digital filters are being applied to high frequency signal in the RF (radio frequency) domain, which in the past was the exclusive domain of analog technology. Digital filters also can adapt to changes in the characteristics of the signal. Furthermore they do not drift. The frequency response characteristic can be made to approximate closely to the ideal. They can be made to have no insertion loss and linear phase characteristics are possible. Adaptive filtering is relatively simple to achieve. Digital word-length may be controlled by the filter designer, and therefore the accuracy of the filter may be precisely controlled.

Given the sampled sequence

$$x(0), \quad x(1), \quad x(2), \quad \ldots , x(N-1) \,.$$

The digital output from the processor to the digital analog converter is

$$y(0), \quad y(1), \quad y(2), \ldots , y(N-1) \,.$$

The way in which the $y(n)$'s are calculated from the sequence $x(0)$, $x(1)$, ... determines the filtering action of the digital filter.

Examples of simple digital filters are: unity gain filter $y(n) = x(n)$, simple gain filter

$$y(n) = Kx(n)$$

(K is a constant), pure delay filter

$$y(n) = x(n-1),$$

two-term difference filter

$$y(n) = x(n) - x(n-1),$$

two-term average filter

$$y(n) = \frac{1}{2}(x(n) + x(n-1))$$

three-term average filter

$$y(n) = \frac{1}{3}(x(n) + x(n-1) + x(n-2))$$

central difference filter

$$y(n) = \frac{1}{2}(x(n) - x(n-2)) \,.$$

The order of a digital filter is defined as the number of previous inputs. All of the examples given above can be written in the following form

$$y(n) = a_0 x(n)$$

$$y(n) = a_0 x(n) + a_1 x(n-1)$$

$$y(n) = a_0 x(n) + a_1 x(n-1) + a_2 x(n-2).$$

A *low-pass filter* is one which does not affect low frequencies and rejects high frequencies. The simplest (and by no means ideal) low-pass filter is given by the following difference equation

$$y(n) = x(n) + x(n-1), \qquad n = 0, 1, 2, \ldots$$

where $x(n)$ is the filter input amplitude at time (or sample) n, and $y(n)$ is the output amplitude at time n. A more physical way of writing the filter equation is

$$y(nT) = x(nT) + x((n-1)T)$$

where T is the sampling interval in seconds. It is customary in digital signal processing to omit T. The simplest possible low-pass filter is also somehow the worst possible low-pass filter. To see this we have to look at the frequency response of the filter.

The time-domain performance of digital filters is described in terms of the filter's unit-sample response sequence, denoted by $\{h(n)\}$. This sequence is analogous to the impulse response of analog filters. A convolutional equation allows us to determine the output sequence $\{y(n)\}$ from the input sequence $\{x(n)\}$ and the unit sample response $\{h(n)\}$. The unit-sample response sequence also permits us to determine whether a filter is stable. Linear difference equations provide a time-domain description that is useful for implementing digital filter structures.

Filter specifications are also expressed in the frequency domain. Thus we can investigate the frequency domain properties of signals and filters. The Fourier transform of the unit-sample response $\{h(n)\}$ is the transfer function $H(e^{i\omega})$ of the filter and it describes the gain of the filter at different frequencies. The Fourier transform of a data input sequence $\{x(n)\}$ is called the spectrum $X(e^{i\omega})$ and it defines the frequency contents of the signal. Another analytic technique used to study the signal is the z-transform (see chapter 8). The system function $H(z)$ is defined as the z-transform of the unit-sample response $\{h(n)\}$ and is used for the analysis and synthesis of digital filters. The complex z-plane is the domain for the z-transform. The representation of a digital filter as a collection of poles and zeros in the z plane will provide a useful interpretation of the filter frequency.

If the input is the impulse sequence $\delta(n)$, the resulting output is called the *impulse response* of the filter and is denoted by $h(n)$. The input and output of a linear time-invariant filter may be related via the impulse response of the filter as follows

$$y(n) = x(n) * h(n)$$

where $*$ denotes the convolution. Thus the output of the filter corresponds to the convolution of the input with the impulse response of the filter.

A *rational filter H* of order N, applied to a given sequence x of sampled data, produces a new sequence y, related to x by the linear difference equation

$$a_0 y(n) + a_1 y(n-1) + \cdots + a_N y(n-N) = b_0 x(n) + b_1 x(n-1) + \cdots + b_N x(n-N) \,.$$

The filter coefficients

$$B = [b_0, b_1, ..., b_N], \qquad A = [a_0, a_1, ..., a_N]$$

are uniquely defined up to a multiplicative nonzero coefficient. Thus we can assume without loss of generality that they are normalized by a_0. Moreover, at least one of the coefficients a_N or b_N should be different from 0, otherwise the filter could be defined by shorter vectors A and B, and it would be of order strictly lower than N. Using the time shift operator z defined above, the filter H can be represented (see also chapter 7 on z-transform) by the rational function

$$H(z) = \frac{B(z)}{A(z)} = \frac{b_0 + b_1 z^{-1} + \cdots + b_{N-1} z^{-(N-1)}}{a_0 + a_1 z^{-1} + \cdots + a_{N-1} z^{-(N-1)}}$$

with $a_0 = 1$ and at least one of the coefficients a_{N-1} or b_{N-1} different from zero. For example a digital filter of order 4 should be defined by the vectors

$$B = [b_0, b_1, b_2, b_3, b_4], \qquad A = [a_0, a_1, a_2, a_3, a_4] \,.$$

The frequency response of a digital filter depends on the sampling rate. Half the sampling frequency is called the *Nyquist frequency*. Thus we can introduce a nondimensional frequency, that is, by definition, the frequency in Hz divided by the Nyquist frequency. Thus, for example, if the sampling rate is 1000 Hz, the frequency of 50 Hz will correspond to the nondimensional frequency of $50/(1000/2) = 0.1$ and 150 Hz will correspond to $150/(1000/2) = 0.3$.

Filters are frequently used to separate or reject sinusoidal components from a composite signal. For example we have signal from two sinusoidal waves

$$x(t) = \sin(2\pi 100 t) + \sin(2\pi 400 t)$$

one with the frequency of 100 Hz and the other with the frequency of 400 Hz, over an interval of 0.1 seconds. The sampling frequency could be 2000 Hz. The filter should now separate the low frequency from the high frequency.

3.2 Finite Impulse Response Filters

As described above a rational filter H of order N, applied to a given sequence x of sampled data, produces a new sequence y, related to x by the linear difference equation

$$a_0 y(n) + a_1 y(n-1) + \cdots + a_N y(n-N) = b_0 x(n) + b_1 x(n-1) + \cdots + b_N x(n-N) .$$

If the coefficients $a_1, a_2, \ldots, a_{N-1}$ are all equal to zero, the filter is called finite impulse response filter (FIR), otherwise an infinite impulse response filter (IIR). Thus for a finite impulse response filter we obtain

$$y(n) = \frac{b_0}{a_0} x(n) + \frac{b_1}{a_0} x(n-1) + \cdots + \frac{b_N}{a_0} x(n-N) .$$

Thus a finite impulse response filter produces an output $y(n)$ that is the weighted sum of the current and past inputs $x(n)$.

In the literature there is an alternative terminology in which a Finite Impulse Response filter is known as a non-recursive filter. The impulse response of a digital filter is the output from the filter when a unit impulse is applied at its input. A unit impulse is the input sequence consisting of a single value of 1 at time $t = 0$, followed by zeros at all subsequent instants. An FIR filter is one whose impulse response is of finite duration. An IIR filter is one whose impulse response continues forever, since the recursive previous output terms feed back energy into the filter input and keep it going.

Example. Consider supplying an FIR filter with a sine-wave

$$x(n) = \sin(\omega n T) .$$

Thus

$$y(n) = \sum_{j=0}^{q} b_j \sin(\omega(n-j)T) .$$

Using the identity

$$\sin(\alpha + \beta) \equiv \sin(\alpha)\cos(\beta) + \cos(\alpha)\sin(\beta)$$

we find

$$y(n) = \left(\sum_{j=0}^{q} b_j \cos(-\omega jT) \right) \sin(\omega nT) + \left(\sum_{j=0}^{q} b_j \sin(-\omega jT) \right) \cos(\omega nT).$$

The terms in the parentheses are independent of n and hence the expression for $y(n)$ is a sinusoid with amplitude

$$\sqrt{ \left(\sum_{j=0}^{q} b_j \cos(\omega jT) \right)^2 + \left(\sum_{j=0}^{q} b_j \sin(-\omega jT) \right)^2 }$$

and phase

$$\tan^{-1} \left(\frac{\sum_{j=0}^{q} b_j \sin(-\omega jT)}{\sum_{j=0}^{q} b_j \cos(-\omega jT)} \right).$$

3.3   Infinite Impulse Response Filters

If the coefficients $a_1, a_2, \ldots, a_{N-1}$ are not all 0 the filter is called infinite impulse response filter. In the literature there is an alternative terminology in which a Infinite Impulse Response filter is known as recursive filter.

Infinite impulse response digital filters are usually designed by extending classical analog filter design procedures. An IIR filter design is typically accomplished in three steps. First, an analog lowpass filter is designed to meet the desired passband specification. The most commonly employed are the Butterworth, Chebyshev and elliptic analog lowpass filter design procedures. Second, an analog-to-digital filter transformation is employed to obtain a digital lowpass filter. The impulse-invariance method and the bilinear z-transform are used for transferring these analog designs into their digital counterparts. In the final step, a frequency transformation is employed to obtain a highpass, bandpass or bandreject filter.

For example the implementation of a second-order IIR filter is done by using a second-order difference equation. A second order infinite impulse response filter has a transfer function of the form

$$H(z) = \frac{b_0 + b_1 z^{-1} + b_2 z^{-2}}{1 + a_1 z^{-1} + a_2 z^{-2}}$$

where a_1, a_2, b_0, b_1, and b_2 are the coefficients of the polynomials of the system transfer function that, when factored, yield the system poles and zeros (see chapter 7 on z-transform). The difference equation found by taking the inverse z-transform and applying the shift theorem is

$$y(n) = b_0 x(n) + b_1 x(n-1) + b_2 x(n-2) - a_1 y(n-1) - a_2 y(n-2).$$

This second order filter can be used to implement low-pass, high-pass, bandpass, and bandstop filters.

A bandpass filter is a filter that passes one frequency band and attenuates frequencies above and below that band. A band reject filter rejects (attenuates) one frequency band and passes both a lower and a higher frequency band.

Example 1. Consider the given signal

$$x(0) = 5.0, \quad x(1) = 16.0, \quad x(2) = 8.0,$$

$$x(3) = -3.0, \quad x(4) = 0.0, \quad x(5) = 2.0.$$

Thus $N = 6$. A first order digital filter is given by

$$y(n) = 2x(n) - x(n-1) + 0.8y(n-1)$$

with $x(-1) = 0$ and $y(-1) = 0$. Thus we find

$$y(0) = 10.0, \quad, y(1) = 35.0, \quad, y(2) = 28.0,$$

$$y(3) = 8.4, \quad y(4) = 9.72, \quad y(5) = 11.776.$$

A C++ implementation is given by

```
// filter.cpp

#include <iostream>
using namespace std;

int main(void)
{
  int N = 6;
  double* x = new double[N];
  double* y = new double[N];
  x[0] = 5.0; x[1] = 16.0; x[2] = 8.0;
  x[3] = -3.0; x[4] = 0.0; x[5] = 2.0;
  y[0] = 2.0*x[0];

  for(int i=1;i<N;i++)
  {
```

```
    y[i] = 2.0*x[i] - x[i-1] + 0.8*y[i-1];
    }
    for(int k=0;k<N;k++)
    {
    cout << "y[" << k << "] = " << y[k] << endl;
    }
    delete[] x;
    delete[] y;
    return 0;
}
```

Example 2. Consider the given signal

$$x(n) = \sin(2\pi n/100) + f(n), \qquad n = 0, 1, ..., 99$$

where $f(n)$ is a small noise signal and

$$y(0) = x(0).$$

Then

$$y(n+1) = 0.9y(n) + 0.1x(n+1), \qquad n = 0, 1, ..., 98$$

defines a recursive filter. The following Java program simulates this difference equation. The method **random()** in the **Math** class of Java provides a random number in the range $[0, 1]$ of data type **double**. We multiply this random numbers by 0.05 to add a small noise signal to the sine-signal.

```
// Noise.java

public class Noise
{
  public static void main(String[] args)
  {
  int N = 100;
  double[] x = new double[N];
  double[] y = new double[N];
  double[] f = new double[N];

  for(int n=0;n<N;n++)
  {
  f[n] = Math.random();
  x[n] = Math.sin(2.0*Math.PI*n/N) + 0.05*f[n];
  }

  y[0] = x[0];
```

```
for(int n=0;n<(N-1);n++)
y[n+1] = 0.9*y[n] + 0.1*x[n+1];

for(int n=0;n<N;n++)
System.out.println("y[" + n + "]= " + y[n]);
}
}
```

Example 3. Another example is the two pole resonator with center frequency ω and bandwidth related to r

$$y(n) = 2r\cos(\omega T)y(n-1) - r^2 y(n-2) + x(n) - \cos(\omega T)x(n-1)\,.$$

Common types of IIR filter:

```
Type          Characteristics
===========   ====================================
Butterworth   maximally flat amplitude
Bessel        maximally flat group delay
Chebyshev     equiripple in passband or stopband
Elliptic      equiripple in passband and stopband
====================================================
```

The Bessel function is used to produce the most linear phase response of all IIR filters with no consideration of the frequency magnitude response. Specifically, filter designs based on Bessel functions have maximally constant group delay.

The Butterworth function is used to produce maximally flat filter magnitude responses with no consideration of phase linearity or group delay variations. Filter designs based on a Butterworth function have no amplitude ripple in either the passband or the stopband. The *passband* is the frequency range over which a filter passes signal energy. Usually defined as the frequency range where the filter's frequency response is equal to or greater than -3 DB. The stopband is the band of frequencies attenuated by a digital filter. The term *ripple* refers to fluctuations (measured in dB) in the passband, or stopband, of a filter's frequency magnitude response curve. Unfortunately, for a given filter order, Butterworth designs have the widest transition region of the most popular filter design functions.

The Chebyshev function is used to produce passband, or stopband ripples constrained within fixed bounds. There are families of Chebyshev functions based on the amount of ripple such as 1 dB, 2 dB, and 3 dB of ripple. Chebyshev filters can be designed to have a frequency response with ripples

in the passband and flat stopbands (Chebyshev type I), or flat passbands
and ripples in the stopband (Chebyshev type II). Chebyshev filters cannot
have ripples in both the passband and the stopband. Digital filters based
upon Chebyshev functions have steeper transition region roll-off but more
nonlinear phase response characteristics than, say, Butterworth filters.

The elliptic functions are used to produce the sharpest roll-off for a given
number of filter taps. However filters designed using elliptic functions, also
called Cauer filters, have the poorest phase linearity of the most common
IIR filter design functions. The ripple in the passband and stopband are
equal with elliptic filters.

The phase response is the difference in phase, at a particular frequency, between an input sinewave and the filter's output sinewave at that frequency.
The phase response, sometimes called phase delay, is usually depicted by a
curve showing the filter's phase shift versus the frequency.

An allpass filter is an IIR filter whose magnitude response is unity over its
entire frequency range, but whose phase response is variable. Allpass filters
are typically appended in a cascade arrangement following a standard IIR
filter.

The attenuation is the amplitude loss, usually measured in dB, incurred by
a signal after passing through a digital filter. Filter attenuation is the ratio,
at a given frequency, of the signal amplitude at the output of the filter over
the signal amplitude at the input of the filter, defined as

$$\text{attenuation} = 20 \log_{10} \left(\frac{a_{out}}{a_{in}} \right) \ \text{dB}$$

3.4   Digital Filters from Analog Filters

Digital filters can also be introduced by starting from a analog filter. Consider, for example, the RL low-pass filter described by the first order linear
differential equation

$$\frac{L}{R} \frac{di}{dt} + i = \frac{v}{R}$$

with the initial condition $i(t = 0) = i_0$. A low-pass filter is one which does
not affect low frequencies and rejects high frequencies. We set

$$\tau := \frac{L}{R}$$

(time constant of the circuit),

$$y := i$$

and
$$x := \frac{v}{R} \, .$$

Then the differential equation takes the form

$$\tau \frac{dy}{dt} + y = x \, .$$

We assume that y is sampled at intervals T_s which are small compared to the time constant τ. Then the time derivative of y can be approximated by

$$\frac{dy}{dt} \approx \frac{y_n - y_{n-1}}{T_s}$$

where y_n is the n-th measured value of y, and y_{n-1} the previous one. Thus we can replace the differential equation by the difference equation

$$\tau \frac{y_n - y_{n-1}}{T_s} + y_n = x_n \, .$$

Solving with respect to y_n yields the first order digital filter

$$y_n = \frac{T_s}{T_s + \tau} x_n + \frac{\tau}{T_s + \tau} y_{n-1} \, .$$

Since T_s is much smaller than τ we can simplify this difference equation to

$$y_n = \frac{T_s}{\tau} x_n + y_{n-1} \, .$$

Thus if we have the transfer function $H(s)$ of an analog filter defined in the frequency domain we want to approximate it with a digital filter $H_d(z)$. There are a number of different techniques employed to transform an analog filter into a digital equivalent. For example an analog second-order, low pass filter could have the transfer function

$$H(s) = \frac{\omega^2}{s^2 + 2\eta\omega s + \omega^2}$$

where $\omega = 30 rad/s$, $\eta = 0.6$ and the signal is sampled at 100 Hz. One of the approaches is to find a function $s(z)$ in the variable z, that closely approximates the differential operator, and construct

$$H_d(z) = H(s(z)) \, .$$

The transformation
$$s(z) = \frac{2}{T} \frac{z - 1}{z + 1}$$

is called the *Tustin's bilinear transformation*, where T is the sampling interval and z the unitary time shift operator. This transformation is closely related to the *trapezoidal integration rule* and is valid within the limits in which integration can be substituted by its trapezoidal approximation, which is often the case if the function involved are smooth and the sampling time short enough. Tustin's transformation has the merits of involving relatively simple algebraic operations and mapping stable continuous filters into stable digital filters. Its drawback is that, as the sampling rate decreases, it introduces phase distortion, which can only partially be corrected with prewarping.

There is another technique to convert an analog filter to a digital filter, namely the *impulse invariant method*. The impulse invariant method maps the Laplace transform of $H(s)$ into a discrete-time system using the standard z-transform. The digital filter designed by the impulse-invariant method is required to have an impulse response exactly equal to equally spaced samples of the impulse response of the prototype analog filter. If the analog filter has a transfer function $F(s)$ with an impulse response $f(t)$, the impulse response of the digital filter $h(n)$ is required to match the samples of $f(t)$. For samples at intervals of T seconds the impulse response is

$$h(n) = f(t)|_{t=Tn} = f(Tn) .$$

Thus in the impulse invariant method the impulse response of the digital filter $h(n)$ is made (approximately) equal to the impulse response of an analog filter $f(t)$ evaluated at $t = nT$, where T is an (arbitrary) sampling period. The transfer function of the digital filter is the z-transform of the impulse response of the filter

$$H(z) = \sum_{n=0}^{\infty} h(n)z^{-n} .$$

The *transfer function* of the prototype analog filter is always a rational function

$$F(s) = \frac{B(s)}{A(s)}$$

where $B(s)$ is the numerator polynomial with roots that are zeros of $F(s)$, and $A(s)$ is the denominator with roots that are the poles of $F(s)$. If $F(s)$ is expanded in terms of partial fraction we have

$$F(s) = \sum_{j=1}^{N} \frac{K_j}{s + s_j} .$$

The impulse response of this filter is the inverse Laplace transform. Thus

$$f(t) = \sum_{j=1}^{N} K_j e^{-s_j t} .$$

Sampling this impulse response every T seconds yields

$$f(nT) = \sum_{j=1}^{N} K_j e^{-s_j nT} = \sum_{j=1}^{N} K_j \left(e^{-s_j T} \right)^n .$$

Thus

$$H(z) = \sum_{n=0}^{\infty} \left(\sum_{j=1}^{N} K_j \left(e^{-s_j T} \right)^n \right) z^{-n} = \sum_{j=1}^{N} \frac{K_j z}{z - e^{-s_j T}} .$$

Obviously this is a rational function of z and is the transfer function of the digital filter, which has samples of the prototype analog filter as its impulse response. The impulse invariant method has its requirements set in the time domain. Let us now look at the frequency domain. If the frequency response of the analog filter is denoted by $F(i\omega)$ and the frequency response of the digital filter designed by the impulse invariant method is $H(\omega)$, it can be shown that

$$H(\omega) = \frac{1}{T} \sum_{k=-\infty}^{\infty} F\left(i\left(\omega - \frac{2\pi k}{T} \right) \right) .$$

The frequency response of the digital filter is a periodically repeated version of the frequency response of the analog filter.

3.5 Matlab Filter Implementation

Matlab provides all the tools for digital filters. For example, consider the simplest low-pass filter

$$y(n) = x(n) + x(n - 1)$$

where $n = 1, 2, \ldots, N$ with $N = 10$. Here A is the vector of filter feedback coefficients and B is the vector of filter feedforward coefficients. A Matlab implementation is

```
N = 10;      % length of test input signal
x = [0.5 1.0 1.5 1.0 0.5 0.3 0.2 0.0 0.5 0.7]; % input signal
B = [1,1];   % feedforward coefficients
A = 1;       % feedback coefficients (none)

y = filter(B,A,x);

for i=1:N
   disp(sprintf('x(%d)=%f\ty(%d)=%f',i,x(i),i,y(i)));
end
```

A weighted sum of sinusoids

$$x[n] = a_1 \cdot \sin(w_1 \cdot n + \phi_1) + a_2 \cdot \sin(w_2 \cdot n + \phi_2) + a_3 \cdot \sin(w_3 \cdot n + \phi_3)$$

where $0 \le n \le N - 1$ can be implemented in Matlab as

```
N = 100;
a = [1 1/sqrt(2) 0.5];
w = [1 2 3]*.051*2*pi;
phi = [0 0 0];

x = zeros(N,1);
for n = 0:N-1
    for k = 1:3
        x(n+1) = x(n+1) + a(k)*sin(w(k)*n + phi(k));
    end
end

i = 1:N;
plot(i,x);
```

where we set $\phi_1 = \phi_2 = \phi_3 = 0$, $a_1 = 1$, $a_2 = 1/\sqrt{2}$, $a_3 = 0.5$ and

$$w_1 = 0.051 \cdot 2\pi, \quad w_2 = 0.051 \cdot 4\pi, \quad w_3 = 0.051 \cdot 6\pi \,.$$

3.6   Generating Functions

3.6.1   Introduction

Let

$$x(0), \ x(1), \ x(2), \dots$$

be a sequence. The function

$$G(s) = \sum_{k=0}^{\infty} x(k)s^k$$

is called the *generating function* of the sequence x if the power series has a positive radius of convergence.

The sequence x can be reconstructed from $G(s)$ as

$$\frac{d^k G(s)}{ds^k}\Big|_{s=0} = k!x(k) \,.$$

The generating function does not exist in some cases. For example, let

$$x(k) = k!, \qquad k = 0, 1, 2, \dots \,.$$

Then

$$\sum_{k=0}^{\infty} k! s^k$$

converges only for $s = 0$.

Example. Find the generating function of

$$x(n) = a^n$$

where $a \in \mathbf{R}$ and $a \neq 0$. We have (geometric series)

$$\sum_{n=0}^{\infty} a^n s^n = \frac{1}{1 - as} = G(s)$$

if $|as| < 1$ or $|s| < 1/|a|$.

3.6.2 Linear Difference Equations

Generating functions can be used to solve linear difference equations.

Example. Consider the difference equation

$$(n + 2)x(n + 2) - (n + 3)x(n + 1) + 2x(n) = 0$$

with the initial conditions $x(0) = 1$, $x(1) = 2$ and $n = 0, 1, 2, \ldots$. Let

$$G(s) = \sum_{n=0}^{\infty} x(n)s^n \, .$$

We multiply the difference equation by s^n and then sum from 0 to ∞. Thus

$$0 = \sum_{n=0}^{\infty} (n + 2)x(n + 2)s^n - \sum_{n=0}^{\infty} (n + 3)x(n + 1)s^n + 2\sum_{n=0}^{\infty} x(n)s^n \, .$$

It follows that

$$0 = \sum_{n=2}^{\infty} nx(n)s^{n-2} - \sum_{n=1}^{\infty} (n + 2)x(n)s^{n-1} + 2\sum_{n=0}^{\infty} x(n)s^n \, .$$

Since

$$\frac{dG(s)}{ds} = \sum_{n=1}^{\infty} nx(n)s^{n-1}$$

we have

$$\sum_{n=2}^{\infty} nx(n)s^{n-2} = \frac{1}{s}\left(\frac{dG}{ds} - x(1) \right)$$

and

$$\sum_{n=1}^{\infty}(n+2)x(n)s^{n-1} = \sum_{n=1}^{\infty} nx(n)s^{n-1} + 2\sum_{n=1}^{\infty} x(n)s^{n-1}$$
$$= \frac{dG}{ds} + \frac{2}{s}\left(G(s) - x(0)\right).$$

Thus we arrive at

$$\frac{1}{s}\left(\frac{dG}{ds} - x(1)\right) - \frac{dG}{ds} - \frac{2}{s}\left(G(s) - x(0)\right) + 2G(s) = 0$$

or

$$\frac{dG}{ds} - 2G(s) = \frac{x(1) - 2x(0)}{1 - s}.$$

Inserting the initial conditions $x(0) = 1$ and $x(1) = 2$ yields

$$\frac{dG}{ds} - 2G(s) = 0.$$

This is a first-order linear differential equation with constant coefficients. Since $G(s = 0) = 1$ owing to $x(0) = 1$ we find

$$G(s) = \exp(2s).$$

The expansion of the exponential function yields

$$G(s) = \sum_{n=0}^{\infty} \frac{2^n}{n!}s^n.$$

Thus the solution of the linear difference equation is given by

$$x(n) = \frac{2^n}{n!}.$$

3.6.3   Properties of Generating Functions

Generating functions are linear for the common radius of convergence

$$G(x + y) = G(x) + G(y)$$
$$G(cx) = cG(x).$$

Let $x * y$ denotes the convolution of x and y

$$(x * y)(n) := \sum_{m=0}^{N} x(m)y(n - m).$$

Then
$$G(x * y) = G(x)G(y)$$
for the common radius of convergence of x and y.

Let z be the shift operator
$$zx(k) := x(k+1).$$

Then
$$G(z^n x)(s) = \frac{G(x)(s) - \sum_{j=0}^{n-1} x(j)s^j}{s^n}$$
for $s \neq 0$. This is the *shifting theorem*.

Finally we have $G(x) = G(y)$ if and only if $x = y$.

Chapter 4

Convolution

4.1 Introduction

In discrete signal processing the convolution is of upmost importance in particular for linear digital filters. The discrete convolution and discrete circular convolution are important topics in the discussion of Fast Fourier Transform (FFT) algorithms for reducing multiplications. They also play a central role in the z-transform. Circular convolution is defined for periodic sequences whereas convolution is defined for aperiodic sequences. For speech signals we normally consider one-dimensional discrete convolutions. For image processing we normally consider two-dimensional discrete convolutions. The convolutions for aperiodic sequences plays a central role for the multiplication of polynomials.

The convolution is also defined for continuous functions in the *Banach space* $L^1(\mathbf{R})$. A complete normed vector space is a Banach space. The Banach space $L^1(\mathbf{R})$ is composed of the measurable functions f on $\mathbf{R}$ for which

$$\|f\|_1 := \int_{-\infty}^{+\infty} |f(x)| dx < +\infty \,.$$

This integral defines a norm and $L^1(\mathbf{R})$ is a Banach space provided one identifies functions that are equal almost everywhere (measure zero). The convolution integral of two functions $f, g \in L^1(\mathbf{R})$ is given by

$$(f * g)(x) := \int_{-\infty}^{\infty} f(x - s) g(s) ds \,.$$

We have the property

$$(f * g)(x) = \int_{-\infty}^{\infty} f(x - s) g(s) ds = \int_{-\infty}^{\infty} g(x - s) f(s) ds = (g * f)(x) \,.$$

This means that the convolution is commutative. The definition can be extended to the Banach space $L^1(\mathbf{R}^n)$. The convolution can also be considered in the sense of generalised function. In this case the convolution of any generalised function f with the Dirac δ-function exists and is equal to f.

In the following we only consider discrete convolutions.

4.2 Circular Convolution

The *circular convolution* of two N-point sequences $a(n)$ and $b(n)$, where

$$n = 0, 1, 2, \ldots, N - 1,$$

is the N-point sequence $c(n)$ defined by

$$c(m) = a(n) \odot b(n) := \sum_{n=0}^{N-1} a(n)b(m - n), \qquad m = 0, 1, 2, \ldots, N - 1.$$

Here N-point periodicity means

$$a(n + N) = a(n), \qquad n = 0, 1, 2, \ldots, N - 1.$$

Since

$$c(n + N) = c(n)$$

the sequence $c(n)$ is periodic with period N. Thus the sequences $a(n)$, $b(n)$, and $c(n)$ have the same length, namely N. We can show that

$$c(m) = \sum_{n=0}^{N-1} a(m - n)b(n), \qquad m = 0, 1, \ldots, N - 1.$$

The circular convolution is also called *cyclic convolution* since

$$x(n - m) \equiv x(n - m \,(\mathrm{mod} N)).$$

Sometimes the convolution is normalised by $1/N$.

Example. Consider the sequences with $N = 4$

$$x(0) = 1, \quad x(1) = 2, \quad x(2) = 1, \quad x(3) = 5$$

and

$$y(0) = 2, \quad y(1) = 3, \quad y(2) = 1, \quad y(3) = 4.$$

We calculate $x \odot y$. Since

$$u(m) = \sum_{n=0}^{3} x(n)y(m - n) \quad \mathrm{mod} \quad 4$$

we have

$$u(0) = x(0)y(0) + x(1)y(-1) + x(2)y(-2) + x(3)y(-3) \, .$$

Thus

$$u(0) = x(0)y(0) + x(1)y(3) + x(2)y(2) + x(3)y(1) \, .$$

Analogously

$$u(1) = x(0)y(1) + x(1)y(0) + x(2)y(3) + x(3)y(2)$$

$$u(2) = x(0)y(2) + x(1)y(1) + x(2)y(0) + x(3)y(3)$$

$$u(3) = x(0)y(3) + x(1)y(2) + x(2)y(1) + x(3)y(0) \, .$$

Thus

$$u(0) = 26, \quad u(1) = 16, \quad u(2) = 29, \quad u(3) = 19 \, .$$

The following C++ program implements the circular convolution. It is assumed that the signal starts at 0.

```
// circcon.cpp

#include <iostream>
using namespace std;

void circcon(double* x,double* y,double* u,int N)
{
  for(int m=0;m<N;m++)
  {
  for(int n=0;n<N;n++)
  {
  if((m-n) < 0) u[m]  += x[n]*y[m-n+N];
  else u[m]  += x[n]*y[m-n];
  }
  }
}

int main(void)
{
  int N = 4;
  double* x = new double[N];
  double* y = new double[N];
  double* u = new double[N];
  x[0] = 1.0; x[1] = 2.0; x[2] = 1.0; x[3] = 5.0;
  y[0] = 2.0; y[1] = 3.0; y[2] = 1.0; y[3] = 4.0;
```

```
for(int i=0;i<N;i++)   { u[i] = 0.0; }

circcon(x,y,u,N);

for(int j=0;j<N;j++)
cout << "u[" << j << "] = " << u[j] << endl;

delete[] x;
delete[] y;
delete[] u;
return 0;
}
```

4.3   Noncircular Convolution

The *noncircular convolution* (i.e., aperiodic convolution) of two sequences $a(m)$ $(m = 0, 1, \ldots, L - 1)$ and $b(n)$ $(n = 0, 1, \ldots, M - 1)$ of length L and M, respectively, yields another sequence $c(t)$ of length $N = L + M - 1$

$$c(m) = \sum_{n=0}^{N-1} a(n)b(m - n), \qquad m = 0, 1, \ldots, L + M - 2.$$

Similarly to the circular convolution we can show that the identity

$$\sum_{n=0}^{N-1} a(n)b(m - n) = \sum_{n=0}^{N-1} a(m - n)b(n)$$

holds.

If we define the convolution for sequences with negative and positive terms we have the definition

$$c(m) = \sum_{n=-\infty}^{\infty} a(n)b(m - n).$$

Example 1. Consider the two polynomials

$$p(x) = a_0 + a_1 x + \cdots + a_{L-1} x^{L-1}$$
$$q(x) = b_0 + b_1 x + \cdots + b_{M-1} x^{M-1}.$$

Then the multiplication of the two polynomials $r(x) = p(x) * q(x)$ is a noncircular convolution, where

$$r(x) = c_0 + c_1 x + \cdots + c_{L+M-2} x^{L+M-2}$$

with

$$c_0 = a_0 b_0, \qquad c_1 = a_0 b_1 + a_1 b_0, \qquad c_2 = a_0 b_2 + a_1 b_1 + a_2 b_0, \ \ldots$$

The general term is

$$c_j = \sum_{k=0}^{j} a_k b_{j-k}, \qquad j = 0, 1, \ldots, L + M - 2\,.$$

where we set $a_k = 0$ for $k > L - 1$ and $b_k = 0$ for $k > M - 1$.

Example 2. Consider the sequences

$$x(n) = \begin{cases} 1 & \text{for} \quad n = -1, 0, 1 \\ 0 \, \text{otherwise} \end{cases}$$

$$h(n) = \begin{cases} 1 & \text{for} \quad n = -1, 0, 1 \\ 0 \, \text{otherwise} \end{cases}$$

Then $y(n) = h(n) * y(n)$ is calculated as follows. Since $x(n)$ is 0 for $n < -1$ and $h(n)$ is 0 for $n < -1$ the first nonzero term of $y(n)$ is at -2. Since $x(n)$ is 0 for $n > 1$ and $h(n)$ is 0 for $n < 1$ the last nonzero term of $y(n)$ is at 2. For the nonzero terms we find

$$y(n) = h(n) * x(n) = \sum_{m=-\infty}^{\infty} x(n-m)h(m) = \sum_{m=-2}^{2} x(n-m)h(m)\,.$$

Thus

$$y(-2) = x(-1)h(1) = 1$$
$$y(-1) = x(-1)h(0) + x(0)h(-1) = 2$$
$$y(0) = x(-1)h(1) + x(0)h(0) + x(1)h(-1) = 3\,.$$

For symmetry reason we have $y(1) = 2$ and $y(2) = 1$.

Example 3. Let

$$x(n) = \begin{cases} n + 1 & \text{for} \quad n = 0, 1, 2 \\ 0 & \text{otherwise} \end{cases}$$

and

$$h(n) = a^n u(n)$$

for all $n = 0, 1, 2, \ldots$. Using the formula for the aperiodic convolution we have

$$y(n) = \sum_{k=-\infty}^{\infty} h(k)x(n-k) = \sum_{k=-\infty}^{\infty} a^k u(k)x(n-k) = \sum_{k=0}^{\infty} a^k x(n-k)\,.$$

We note that

$$x(n - k) = \begin{cases} 1 & \text{for} & n = k \\ 2 & \text{for} & k = n - 1 \\ 3 & \text{for} & k = n - 2 \\ 0 & \text{otherwise} \end{cases}$$

Hence the only nonzero terms in the sum are

$$y(n) = a^n u(n) + 2a^{n-1} u(n - 1) + 3a^{n-2} u(n - 2).$$

The circular and noncircular convolution has the following properties

1) Commutative

$$x(n) \odot y(n) = y(n) \odot x(n)$$
$$x(n) * y(n) = y(n) * x(n)$$

2) Associative

$$x(n) \odot (y(n) \odot u(n)) = (x(n) \odot y(n)) \odot u(n)$$
$$x(n) * (y(n) * u(n)) = (x(n) * y(n)) * u(n)$$

3) Distributive

$$x(n) \odot (y(n) + u(n)) = x(n) \odot y(n) + x(n) \odot u(n)$$

$$x(n) * (y(n) + u(n)) = x(n) * y(n) + x(n) * u(n)$$

In signal processing the behaviour of a linear, time-invariant discrete-time system with input signal $x(t)$ and output signal $y(t)$ is described by the convolution sum

$$y(t) = \sum_{k=-\infty}^{\infty} h(k)x(t - k).$$

The signal $h(t)$, assumed known, is the response of the system to a unit-pulse input.

The discrete Fourier transform of a circular convolution

$$(x \odot y)(n) = \sum_{m=0}^{N-1} x(m)y(n - m) = \sum_{m=0}^{N-1} x(n - m)y(m)$$

is the product of the two discrete Fourier transforms.

A Java implementation of the noncircular convolution is given below, where *a.length* finds the length of the array a and || is the logical OR operation. We write the output to the file values.con.

```java
// NonCircular.java

import java.io.*;

class NonCircular
{
  private final static double a[] = { 1.0, 1.0, 1.0 };
  private final static double b[] = { 1.0, 1.0, 1.0 };
  private final static int L = a.length;
  private final static int M = b.length;
  private final static int N = L + M - 1;

  NonCircular()
  {
  double c[] = new double[L+M-1];
  for(int m=0;m<=(L+M-2);m++)
  {
  for(int n=0;n<N;n++)
  {
  c[m] += ((n<L) ? a[n] : 0)*(((m-n)<0 || (m-n)>=M) ? 0 : b[m-n]);
  }
  }
  FileWriter fw;
  try
  {
  fw = new FileWriter("values.con");
  String out = new String();
  out = "c: ";
  for(int i=0;i<c.length;i++)
  { out += c[i] + "; "; }
  fw.write(out + "\n");
  fw.close();
  }
  catch(IOException ex)
  {
  System.err.println(ex);
  return;
  }
  }

  public static void main(String args[])
  { new NonCircular(); }
}
```

The output is

c: 1.0; 2.0; 3.0; 2.0; 1.0;

In image processing we have the *two-dimensional convolution*

$$c(m,n) = a(m,n) \cdot h(m,n) = \sum_{j=0}^{J-1} \sum_{k=0}^{K-1} h(j,k)a(m-j, n-k)$$

where $h(j,k)$ is equal to zero outside the (rectangular) window and $j = 0, 1, \ldots, J-1$, $k = 0, 1, \ldots, K-1$.

Chapter 5

Discrete Fourier Transform

5.1 Introduction

The *Fourier transform* can be defined for signals $x(t)$ which are

1) discrete or continuous time

2) finite or infinite duration

This results in a total of four domains of definition. Obviously the frequency domain for each of these is different.

Case 1. We have

$$X(\omega) = \int_{-\infty}^{\infty} x(t) \exp(i\omega t) dt$$

where the time t is continuous, the domain of t is infinite and $\omega \in (-\infty, \infty)$. Here ω is the continuous *radian frequency* (rad/sec). Furthermore f denotes the continuous frequency in Hertz (Hz), where $\omega = 2\pi f$. Obviously it is assumed that $x(t)$ decreases sufficiently as $t \to \pm\infty$. $x(t)$ is assumed to be in the space $L^1(\mathbf{R}) \cup L^2(\mathbf{R})$. The inverse Fourier transform is given by

$$x(t) = \frac{1}{2\pi} \int_{-\infty}^{\infty} X(\omega) \exp(-i\omega t) d\omega \, .$$

The extension to n dimensions is straightforward. For example, if $x_\alpha(t) = \alpha \exp(-\alpha|t|)/2$ we find

$$X_\alpha(\omega) = \frac{\alpha^2}{\alpha^2 + \omega^2} \, .$$

62

Case 2. For a finite time domain $t \in [0, P]$ but t continuous we have

$$X(k) = \frac{1}{P} \int_0^P x(t) \exp(i\omega_k t) dt$$

where $k = -\infty, \ldots, +\infty$ and ω_k denotes the discrete frequency

$$\omega_k := 2\pi(k/N) f_s$$

with $f_s = 1/T$ the sampling rate and $P = NT$. k is an integer. Owing to $P = NT$ we have

$$\exp(i2\pi k f_s/N) = \exp(i2\pi k/P).$$

Exercise. Find the inverse transformation.

Consider the Hilbert space $L_2[0, P]$. The set of functions

$$\left\{ \frac{1}{\sqrt{P}} \exp(i2\pi t k/P) : \quad k \in \mathbf{Z} \right\}$$

form a basis in the Hilbert space $L_2[0, P]$. This means every function in the Hilbert space $L_2[0, P]$ can be expanded with respect to this basis (so-called *Fourier expansion*). Thus we have

$$x(t) = \sum_{k=-\infty}^{\infty} \langle x(t), \phi_k(t) \rangle \exp(i2\pi t k/P)$$

where $\langle \, , \, \rangle$ denotes the scalar product in the Hilbert space $L_2[0, P]$ and

$$\phi_k(t) = \exp(i2\pi t k/P).$$

Case 3. For continuous frequency $\omega \in (-\pi, \pi)$ and discrete time n we have

$$X(\omega) = \sum_{n=-\infty}^{+\infty} x(n) \exp(i\omega n).$$

Exercise. Find the inverse transformation. Consider the Hilbert space $L_2[-\pi, \pi]$.

Case 2 and case 3 are related to each other in the sense that in case 2 the time is continuous and ω is discrete and in the case 3 the time is discrete and the frequency is continuous.

Case 4. The *discrete Fourier transform* is given by

$$X(k) = \sum_{n=0}^{N-1} x(t_n) \exp(-i\omega_k t_n) \equiv \sum_{n=0}^{N-1} x(t_n) \exp(-i2\pi n k/N)$$

where $k = 0, 1, \ldots, N - 1$ and

$$t_n := nT, \qquad \omega_k := 2\pi \frac{k}{NT}\,.$$

We also write

$$X(k) = \sum_{n=0}^{N-1} x(n) \exp(-i\omega_k n) \equiv \sum_{n=0}^{N-1} x(n) \exp(-i2\pi n k f_s/N)$$

where $k = 0, 1, \ldots, N - 1$.

In the following we only consider this discrete Fourier transform. Mostly the constant $f_s = 1/T$ (T sampling time in sec) is absorbed into k. Thus we write

$$X(k) = \sum_{n=0}^{N-1} x(n) \exp(-i2\pi kn/N)\,.$$

The *inverse discrete Fourier transform* is given by

$$x(n) = \frac{1}{N} \sum_{k=0}^{N-1} X(k) \exp(i2\pi kn/N)\,.$$

To find the inverse Fourier transform we use the identity

$$\sum_{k=0}^{N-1} \exp(i2\pi k(m - n)) = N\delta_{mn}$$

where δ_{mn} denotes the Kronecker delta. As a special case of this identity we have

$$\sum_{k=0}^{N-1} \exp(i2\pi km) = N\delta_{m0}$$

and

$$\sum_{k=0}^{N-1} \exp(i2\pi k) = 0\,.$$

Example. Consider the time series

$$x(n) = \cos(2\pi n/N)$$

where $N = 8$ and $n = 0, 1, 2, \ldots, N-1$. Then the discrete Fourier transform is given by

$$X(k) = \frac{1}{8} \sum_{n=0}^{7} \cos\left(\frac{2\pi n}{8}\right) \exp(-i2\pi kn/8)\,.$$

Using the identity

$$\cos\left(\frac{2\pi n}{8}\right) \equiv \frac{\exp(i2\pi n/8) + \exp(-i2\pi n/8)}{2}$$

we have

$$X(k) = \frac{1}{16} \sum_{n=0}^{7} \left(\exp(i2\pi n(1 - k)/8) + \exp(-i2\pi n(1 + k)/8)\right).$$

Thus we find

$$X(k) = \begin{cases} \frac{1}{2} & \text{for} \quad k = 1 \\ \frac{1}{2} & \text{for} \quad k = 7 \\ 0 & \text{otherwise} \end{cases}$$

Here we used

$$\sum_{n=0}^{7} 1 = 8$$

and

$$\sum_{n=0}^{7} \exp(i2\pi mn/8) = 0$$

for $m = 1, 2, \ldots, 7$.

5.2 Properties of the Discrete Fourier Transform

The properties of the discrete Fourier transform are:

1) Linearity

$$ax(n) + by(n) \rightarrow aX(k) + bY(k)$$

2) Time Shift

$$x(n + p) \rightarrow X(k)\exp(-i2\pi pk)$$

3) Frequency Shift

$$x(n)\exp(i2\pi pn) \rightarrow X(k - p)$$

4) The discrete Fourier transform of a circular convolution

$$(x \odot y)(n) = \sum_{m=0}^{N-1} x(m)y(n - m) = \sum_{m=0}^{N-1} x(n - m)y(m)$$

is the product of the two discrete Fourier transforms.

Most (if not all) of the signals we deal with are real signals. The Fourier transform of real signals exhibits special symmetry which is important in many cases. The transform of a real signal x is therefore

a) Conjugate symmetric (hermitian symmetric)

$$X(-k) = \overline{X(k)}$$

b) Real part symmetric (even)

$$\Re\{X(-k)\} = \Re\{X(k)\}$$

c) Imaginary part antisymmetric (skew symmetric, odd)

$$\Im\{X(-k)\} = -\Im\{X(k)\}$$

d) Magnitude symmetric (even)

$$|X(-k)| = |X(k)|$$

The cross-correlation of x and y in $\mathbf{C}^N$ is defined as

$$(x * y)(n) := \sum_{m=0}^{N-1} \bar{x}(m)y(n+m), \qquad x, y \in \mathbf{C}^N .$$

Using this definition we have the *correlation theorem*

$$(x * y) \leftrightarrow \bar{X}(\omega_k)Y(\omega_k) .$$

The *inner product* of two signals x, y in $\mathbf{C}^N$ is defined as

$$\langle x, y \rangle := \sum_{n=0}^{N-1} x_n \bar{y}_n$$

where $\bar{y}_n$ denotes the complex conjugate of y_n. Using this notation we have

$$\langle x, y \rangle = \frac{1}{N}\langle X, Y \rangle .$$

When we consider the inner product of a signal with itself, we have a special case known as *Parseval's theorem*

$$\|x\|^2 = \langle x, x \rangle = \frac{1}{N}\langle X, X \rangle = \frac{\|X\|^2}{N} .$$

5.3 Windows

In signal processing in particular speech processing *windows* play a central role. The short-time Fourier transform plays a fundamental role in the frequency domain analysis of the speech signal. It is also used to represent, in the frequency domain the time-varying properties of the speech waveform. A useful definition of the time-dependent Fourier transform is

$$S_k(\omega) = \sum_{n=-\infty}^{\infty} w(k-n)s(n)\exp(-i\omega n)$$

where $s(n)$ is the signal and $w(k-n)$ is a real window sequence used to isolate the portion of the input signal that will be analysed at a particular time index, k. During the analysis of the speech signal, the shape and length of the window will affect the frequency representation of speech (or any other signal). Various types of windows have been studied producing window shapes and characteristics suitable for various applications.

The *rectangular window* is defined by

$$w(n) := \begin{cases} 1 & \text{for} \quad 0 \leq n \leq N-1 \\ 0 & \text{otherwise} \end{cases}$$

The *Hamming window* is defined by

$$w(n) := \begin{cases} 0.54 - 0.46\cos(\frac{2\pi n}{N-1}) & \text{for} \quad 0 \leq n \leq N-1 \\ 0 & \text{otherwise} \end{cases}$$

The *Bartlett window* is defined by

$$w(n) := \begin{cases} \frac{2n}{N-1} & \text{for} \quad 0 \leq n \leq (N-1)/2 \\ 2 - \frac{2n}{N-1} & \text{for} \quad (N-1)/2 \leq n \leq N-1 \\ 0 & \text{otherwise} \end{cases}$$

The *Hanning window* is defined by

$$w(n) := \begin{cases} 0.5 - 0.5\cos(\frac{2\pi n}{N-1}) & \text{for} \quad 0 \leq n \leq N-1 \\ 0 & \text{otherwise} \end{cases}$$

The *Blackman window* is defined by

$$w(n) := \begin{cases} 0.42 + 0.5\cos(\frac{2\pi n}{N-1}) + 0.08\cos(\frac{4\pi n}{N-1}) & \text{for} \quad |n| \leq (N-1)/2 \\ 0 & \text{otherwise} \end{cases}$$

The rectangular window has the highest frequency resolution due to the narrowest lobe, but has the largest frequency leakage. On the other hand, the Blackman window has the lowest resolution and the smallest frequency leakage. The additional cosine term in the Blackman window leads to a further reduction in the amplitude of *Gibbs' oscillations*. The passband and stopband oscillations observed are due to slow convergence in the Fourier series, which in turn, is caused by the discontinuity at the passband edge. These are known as Gibbs' oscillations. Due to the high frequency leakage produced by its larger side lobes, rectangular windowed speech looks more noisy. This undesirable high frequency leakage between adjacent harmonics tends to offset the benefits of the flat time domain response (greater frequency resolution) of the rectangular window. As a result, rectangular windows are not usually used in speech spectral analysis.

For good temporal resolution a short window and for good frequency resolution of speech a longer window (narrower main lobe) are required. Since the attenuation of windows is essentially independent of the window duration, increasing the length, N, simply decreases the bandwidth (main lobe). If N is small, e.g. 30 samples, the short-time energy will change very rapidly. If N is too large, on the other hand, e.g. in the order of several pitch periods, the short-time energy will averaged over a long time, and hence will not adequately reflect the changing properties of the speech signal. This implies that there is no satisfactory N value which can be chosen because the duration of a pitch period varies from about 16 samples for a high pitch female or a child, up to 150 samples for a very low pitch male. Therefore, in practice a compromise is made by setting a suitable practical value for N to be between 120-240 samples (i.e. 15-30 ms duration). The size of the window is also being determined by practical considerations. That is, when speech is analysed, some form of parametric information is extracted for transmission, which would require a higher bit rate for a smaller window size (more frequent update rate). In addition, during the analysis of speech it is necessary to have a window length which will represent the harmonic structures fairly accurately (i.e. to have more than one or two pitch periods in each window).

5.4   Fast Fourier Transform

Using the formula

$$X(k) = \sum_{n=0}^{N-1} x(n) \exp(-i2\pi kn/N)$$

to compute the discrete Fourier transform requires N^2 complex additions and multiplications. A simple computation shows that the even frequencies are the coefficients of the discrete Fourier transform of the $N/2$ periodic

signal
$$x_p(n) = x(n) + x(n + N/2)$$
and that the odd frequency coefficients are the coefficients of the discrete Fourier transform of

$$x_i(n) = (x(n) - x(n + N/2)) \exp(-i2\pi n/N).$$

One verifies by induction that the number of operations required by this method to compute the discrete Fourier transform is of the order of

$$KN \log_2(N)$$

where K is a constant which does not depend on N. This is the basic principle of the fast Fourier transform.

The only requirement of the FFT is that the number of points in the sequence must be a power of 2, for example $1024 = 2^{10}$.

5.5 Program

```
// FFT.cpp

#include <iostream>
#include <cmath>        // for sqrt
using namespace std;

// dir = 1 gives the FFT transform
// dir = -1 gives the inverse FFT transform
// n = 2^m is the length of the time series
// x[] is the real part of the signal
// y[] is the imaginary part of the signal
// in place substitution

void FFT(int dir,unsigned long m,double* x,double* y)
{
  unsigned long n, i, i1, j, k, i2, l, l1, l2;
  double c1, c2, tx, ty, t1, t2, u1, u2, z;

  // number of points n = 2^m
  n = 1;
  for(i=0;i<m;i++)
  n *= 2;
  // bit reversal
  i2 = n >> 1;
```

```
j = 0;
for(i=0;i<n-1;i++)
{
if(i < j)
{
tx = x[i];    ty = y[i];
x[i] = x[j]; y[i] = y[j];
x[j] = tx;    y[j] = ty;
}
k = i2;
while(k <= j)
{
j -= k;   k >>= 1;
}
j += k;
} // end for loop

// compute the FFT
c1 = -1.0;   c2 = 0.0;
l2 = 1;
for(l=0;l<m;l++)
{
l1 = l2;
l2 <<= 1;
u1 = 1.0;   u2 = 0.0;
for(j=0;j<l1;j++)
{
for(i=j;i<n;i+=l2)
{
i1 = i + l1;
t1 = u1*x[i1] - u2*y[i1]; t2 = u1*y[i1] + u2*x[i1];
x[i1] = x[i] - t1; y[i1] = y[i] - t2;
x[i] += t1; y[i] += t2;
}
z = u1*c1 - u2*c2;
u2 = u1*c2 + u2*c1;
u1 = z;
}
c2 = sqrt((1.0 - c1)/2.0);
if(dir == 1) c2 = -c2;
c1 = sqrt((1.0 + c1)/2.0);
}

if(dir == 1)
```

```
  {
  for(i=0;i<n;i++)
  {
  x[i] /= n;   y[i] /= n;
  }
  }
} // end function FFT

unsigned long power(unsigned long m)
{
  unsigned long r;
  for(unsigned long i=0;i<m;i++)
  r *= 2;
  return r;
}

int main(void)
{
  unsigned long m = 3;
  const double pi = 3.14159;
  unsigned long n = power(m);
  double* x = new double[n];
  double* y = new double[n];
  unsigned long k;
  for(k=0;k<n;k++)
  {
  x[k] = cos(2.0*pi*k/n); y[k] = 0.0;
  }
  // call FFT
  FFT(1,m,x,y);
  for(k=0;k<n;k++)
  { cout << x[k] << "    " << y[k] << endl; }
  cout << "calling inverse FFT" << endl;
  // call inverse FFT
  FFT(-1,m,x,y);
  for(k=0;k<n;k++)
  { cout << x[k] << "    " << y[k] << endl; }
  delete[] x;
  delete[] y;
  return 0;
}
```

5.6   Discrete Two-Dimensional Fourier Transform

Let $f(n_1, n_2)$ be an $N_1 \times N_2$ two-dimensional periodic discrete signal. The discrete Fourier transform of it is defined as

$$\hat{f}(k_1, k_2) = \sum_{n_1=0}^{N_1-1} \sum_{n_2=0}^{N_2-1} f(n_1, n_2) \exp(-i2\pi(k_1 n_1/N_1 + k_2 n_2/N_2))$$

where $k_1 = 0, 1, \ldots, N_1-1$ and $k_2 = 0, 1, \ldots, N_2-1$. The Fourier transform is a periodic signal of the same periodicity. The inverse transform is given by

$$f(n_1, n_2) = \frac{1}{N_1 N_2} \sum_{k_1=0}^{N_1-1} \sum_{k_2=0}^{N_2-1} \hat{f}(k_1, k_2) \exp(i2\pi(k_1 n_1/N_1 + k_2 n_2/N_2)).$$

If f and g are periodic signals with the same periodicity, the *circulant convolution* of f and g is defined as

$$(f \odot g)(r_1, r_2) := \sum_{n_1=0}^{N_1-1} \sum_{n_2=0}^{N_2-1} f(n_1, n_2) g(r_1 - n_1, r_2 - n_2)$$

which is a periodic signal of the same periodicity. We recall that the circulant convolution is different from the ordinary convolution when f and g are treated as two discrete non-periodic signals. The (ordinary) convolution is defined for two signals f and g of $N_1 \times N_2$ and $A_1 \times A_2$ samples, respectively, as

$$(f * g)(r_1, r_2) := \sum_{n_1=0}^{\infty} \sum_{n_2=0}^{\infty} f(n_1, n_2) g(r_1 - n_1, r_2 - n_2).$$

The size of $f * g$ is $(N_1 + A_1 - 1) \times (N_2 + A_2 - 1)$.

Let

$$F(z_1, z_2) = \sum_{n_1=0}^{N_1-1} \sum_{n_2=0}^{N_2-1} f(n_1, n_2) z_1^{-n_1} z_2^{-n_2}$$

$$G(z_1, z_2) = \sum_{n_1=0}^{A_1-1} \sum_{n_2=0}^{A_2-1} g(n_1, n_2) z_1^{-n_1} z_2^{-n_2}$$

be the two-dimensional z-transform of f and g, respectively (see chapter 7). Then $(f * g)(r_1, r_2)$ is the coefficients of the mono term

$$z_1^{-r_1} z_2^{-r_2}$$

in the product

$$F(z_1, z_2)G(z_1, z_2).$$

Let $\mathcal{F}$ denote the Fourier transform. Then for the circular convolution we have

$$\mathcal{F}(f \odot g) = \mathcal{F}(f)\mathcal{F}(g).$$

This property does not hold for the ordinary convolution.

If f and g are periodic signals of the same periodicity, the *correlation* of f and g is defined as

$$R_{fg}(r_1, r_2) := \sum_{n_1=0}^{N_1-1} \sum_{n_2=0}^{N_2-1} f(n_1 + r_1, n_2 + r_2)g(n_1, n_2)$$

which is a periodic signal of the same periodicity. Similarly to the circulant convolution, we have the discrete correlation property

$$\mathcal{F}(R_{fg}) = \mathcal{F}(f)\mathcal{F}(g)^*$$

where a^* denotes the complex conjugate of a. R_{ff} is called the auto-correlation of f and its Fourier transform is called the power spectrum of f, denoted by S_f.

Chapter 6

Discrete cosine-Transform

6.1 Introduction

Many image compression methods, including JPEG, MPEG, and H.261 standards are based on the discrete cosine transform. JPEG is the image compression standard developed by the Joint Photographic Experts Group. It works best on natural images (scenes). For instance, it compresses the red-green-blue parts of colour images as three separate greyscale images - each compressed to a different extent, if desired. JPEG divides up the image into 8×8 pixel blocks, and then calculates the discrete cosine transform for each block. A quantiser rounds off the discrete cosine transform coefficients according to the quantisation matrix. This step produces the lossy nature of JPEG, but allows for large compression ratios. JPEG's compression uses a variable length code on these coefficients, and then writes the compressed data stream to an output file (`*.jpg`). For decompression JPEG recovers the quantised DCT coefficients from the compressed data stream, takes the inverse discrete transform and displays the image.

The DCT and IDCT are the essential components of many digital image and video compression (coding) systems including:

1) JPEG (still image compression),

2) MPEG-1 (moving image compression),

3) MPEG-2 (moving image compression for digital TV applications), for example, an MPEG-2 video decoder requires an IDCT function,

4) H.261 and H.263 (moving image compression for videoconferencing and videotelephony).

Much of the processing required to encode or decode video using these standards is taken up by calculating the DCT and/or IDCT. An efficient hardware block dedicated to these functions will improve the performance of our digital video system considerably. The inputs are pixel values or coefficients in raster scanned order. The outputs are coefficients or pixel values in *raster scanned order* (may be modified for *zig-zag order* at expense of small increase in gate count).

The discrete cosine transform has a nearly optimal performance in typical images having high correlation in adjacent image pixel. In most practical cases, the transform schemes based on the discrete cosine transform outperform any other orthogonal transform in terms of compression ratio. The cosine transform is closely related to the discrete Fourier transform.

6.2 cosine-Transform

6.2.1 One-Dimensional Case

The discrete one-dimensional cosine transform of the given sequence

$$x(n), \qquad n = 0, 1, 2, \ldots, N-1$$

is defined by

$$C(0) := \frac{1}{\sqrt{N}} \sum_{n=0}^{N-1} x(n)$$

$$C(k) := \sqrt{\frac{2}{N}} \sum_{n=0}^{N-1} x(n) \cos\left(\frac{(2n+1)k\pi}{2N}\right), \qquad k = 1, 2, \ldots, N-1.$$

The inverse one-dimensional cosine transform is given by

$$x(n) = \frac{1}{\sqrt{N}} C(0) + \sqrt{\frac{2}{N}} \sum_{k=1}^{N-1} C(k) \cos\left(\frac{(2n+1)k\pi}{2N}\right).$$

To find the inverse cosine transform we apply the identity

$$\cos(\alpha)\cos(\beta) \equiv \frac{1}{2}\cos(\alpha+\beta) + \frac{1}{2}\cos(\alpha-\beta)$$

with the special case

$$\cos^2(\alpha) \equiv \frac{1}{2}(\cos(2\alpha) + 1).$$

Furthermore we use that

$$\sum_{n=0}^{N-1} \cos\left(\frac{(2n+1)k\pi}{2N}\right) = 0, \qquad k = 1, 2, \ldots, N-1$$

and

$$\frac{1}{\sqrt{N}} \sum_{n=0}^{N-1} C(0) = \sqrt{N}C(0).$$

6.2.2   Two-Dimensional Case

The two-dimensional cosine transform (DCT) helps to separate the image into parts (or spectral sub-bands) of differing importance with respect to the image's visual quality. It transforms a signal or image from the spatial domain to the frequency domain.

Given an input image $x(n_1, n_2)$, i.e. a matrix of size $N_1 \times N_2$ the two-dimensional cosine transform is given by

$$f(k_1, k_2) = 4 \sum_{n_1=0}^{N_1-1} \sum_{n_2=0}^{N_2-1} x(n_1, n_2) \cos\left(\frac{(2n_1+1)k_1\pi}{2N_1}\right) \cos\left(\frac{(2n_2+1)k_2\pi}{2N_2}\right)$$

where $n_1 = 0, 1, \ldots, N_1 - 1$ and $n_2 = 0, 1, \ldots, N_2 - 1$ are the spatial coordinates in the pixel domain. Then k_1, k_2 are the coordinates in the transform domain, where $k_1 = 0, 1, 2, \ldots, N_1 - 1$ and $k_2 = 0, 1, 2, \ldots, N_2 - 1$.

The inverse discrete cosine transform is given by

$$x(n_1, n_2) =$$

$$\frac{1}{N_1 N_2} \sum_{k_1=0}^{N_1-1} \sum_{k_2=0}^{N_2-1} w_1(k_1) w_2(k_2) f(k_1, k_2) \cos\frac{(2n_1+1)k_1\pi}{2N_1} \cos\frac{(2n_2+1)k_2\pi}{2N_2}$$

where the weight functions w_1 and w_2 are given by

$$w_1(k_1) := \begin{cases} \frac{1}{2} \text{ for} & k_1 = 0 \\ 1 \text{ for } 1 \le k_1 \le N_1 - 1 \end{cases}$$

$$w_2(k_2) := \begin{cases} \frac{1}{2} \text{ for} & k_2 = 0 \\ 1 \text{ for } 1 \le k_2 \le N_2 - 1 \end{cases}.$$

In most practical cases for image processing we have $N_1 = N_2 = 8$. The DCT input is an 8×8 array of integers. This array contains each pixel's gray scale level; 8 bit pixels have levels from 0 to 255. The output array of DCT coefficients contains integers; these can range from -1024 to 1023.

For most images, much of the signal energy lies at low frequencies; these appear in the upper left corner of the DCT. The lower right values represent higher frequencies, and are often small - small enough to be neglected with little visible distortion.

Sometimes the normalisation is defined differently such as

$$f(k_1, k_2) =$$

$$\frac{C_{k_1} C_{k_2}}{4} \sum_{n_1=0}^{7} \left(\sum_{n_2=0}^{7} x(n_1, n_2) \cos \left(\frac{(2n_1 + 1)k_1 \pi}{16} \right) \right) \cos \left(\frac{(2n_2 + 1)k_2 \pi}{16} \right)$$

where

$$C_{k_1} = \frac{1}{\sqrt{2}} \quad \text{for} \quad k_1 = 0 \quad \text{otherwise} \quad 1$$

$$C_{k_2} = \frac{1}{\sqrt{2}} \quad \text{for} \quad k_2 = 0 \quad \text{otherwise} \quad 1 \,.$$

The separable nature of the two-dimensional discrete cosine transform is exploited by performing a one-dimensional discrete cosine transform on the eight columns, and then a one-dimensional cosine transform on the eight rows of the result

$$f(k_1, k_2) =$$

$$\frac{C_{k_2}}{2} \sum_{n_1=0}^{7} \left(\frac{C_{k_1}}{2} \sum_{n_2=0}^{7} x(n_1, n_2) \cos \left(\frac{(2n_1 + 1)k_1 \pi}{16} \right) \right) \cos \left(\frac{(2n_2 + 1)k_2 \pi}{16} \right) \,.$$

Several fast algorithms are available for calculating the eight point one-dimensional cosine transform. For example the identity

$$ax + by = a(x + (b/a)y)$$

is used.

We do not implement the inverse discrete cosine transform in the form given above, because this implies 45056 multiplications, 12288 additions and 8192 calls of the cosine function. To implement the inverse discrete cosine transform we try

1) try to multi-use temporary intermediate results.

2) do not use **float** or **double** arithmetic. Instead use an integer arithmetic with virtual decimal point.

3) do not call any cosine function. The formula can be precalculated such that only constants appear as arguments of the cosine. These constants can be computed at compile time.

6.3   Program

In the Java program we implement the one-dimensional cosine transformation with $N = 8$. The values for

$$\cos((2n + 1)k\pi/N)$$

are stored in the two-dimensional array d[k][n], where $k = 0, 1, \ldots, N-1$ and $n = 0, 1, \ldots, N-1$. The input data are x[0], x[1], $\ldots$, x[7].

```
// Cosine.java

class Cosine
{
  public static void main(String args[])
  {
  int N = 8;
  double[][] d = new double[N][N]; // data for cos

  d[0][0] = 1.0;    d[0][1] = 1.0;
  d[0][2] = 1.0;    d[0][3] = 1.0;
  d[0][4] = 1.0;    d[0][5] = 1.0;
  d[0][6] = 1.0;    d[0][7] = 1.0;

  d[1][0] = 0.9807852804032304; d[1][1] = 0.8314696123025452;
  d[1][2] = 0.5555702330196023; d[1][3] = 0.19509032201612833;
  d[1][4] = -0.1950903220161282; d[1][5] = -0.555570233019602;
  d[1][6] = -0.8314696123025453; d[1][7] = -0.9807852804032304;

  d[2][0] = 0.9238795325112867; d[2][1] = 0.38268343236508984;
  d[2][2] = -0.3826834323650897; d[2][3] = -0.9238795325112867;
  d[2][4] = -0.9238795325112868; d[2][5] = -0.38268343236509034;
  d[2][6] = 0.38268343236509; d[2][7] = 0.9238795325112865;

  d[3][0] = 0.8314696123025452; d[3][1] = -0.1950903220161282;
  d[3][2] = -0.9807852804032304; d[3][3] = -0.5555702330196022;
  d[3][4] = 0.5555702330196018; d[3][5] = 0.9807852804032304;
  d[3][6] = 0.19509032201612878; d[3][7] = -0.8314696123025451;

  d[4][0] = 0.7071067811865476; d[4][1] = -0.7071067811865475;
  d[4][2] = -0.7071067811865477; d[4][3] = 0.707106781186474;
  d[4][4] = 0.7071067811865477; d[4][5] = -0.7071067811865467;
  d[4][6] = -0.7071067811865471; d[4][7] = 0.7071067811865466;

  d[5][0] = 0.5555702330196023; d[5][1] = -0.9807852804032304;
```

```
d[5][2] = 0.1950903220161283; d[5][3] = 0.8314696123025456;
d[5][4] = -0.8314696123025451; d[5][5] = -0.19509032201612803;
d[5][6] = 0.9807852804032307; d[5][7] = -0.5555702330196015;

d[6][0] = 0.38268343236508984; d[6][1] = -0.9238795325112868;
d[6][2] = 0.9238795325112865; d[6][3] = -0.3826834323650899;
d[6][4] = -0.38268343236509056; d[6][5] = 0.9238795325112867;
d[6][6] = -0.9238795325112864; d[6][7] = 0.38268343236508956;

d[7][0] = 0.19509032201612833; d[7][1] = -0.5555702330196022;
d[7][2] = 0.8314696123025456; d[7][3] = -0.9807852804032307;
d[7][4] = 0.9807852804032304; d[7][5] = -0.831469612302545;
d[7][6] = 0.5555702330196015; d[7][7] = -0.19509032201612858;

double[] x = new double[N];
double[] C = new double[N];
for(int k=0;k<N;k++) { C[k] = 0.0; }

x[0] = 0.1; x[1] = 0.3; x[2] = 0.6; x[3] = 0.8;
x[4] = 0.7; x[5] = 0.5; x[6] = 0.4; x[7] = 0.2;

for(int n=0;n<N;n++) { C[0] += x[n]; }
C[0] = C[0]/Math.sqrt((double) N);

for(int k=1;k<N;k++)
{
for(int n=0;n<N;n++)
{
C[k] += x[n]*d[k][n];
}
}
for(int k=1;k<N;k++)
{
C[k] = C[k]*Math.sqrt(2.0/((double) N));
}
// display
for(int k=0;k<N;k++)
{
System.out.println("C[" + k + "] = " + C[k]);
}


// inverse transformation
double[] y = new double[N];
for(int n=0;n<N;n++)
```

```
  {
  y[n] = 0.0;
  }
  for(int n=0;n<N;n++)
  {
  for(int k=1;k<N;k++)
  {
  y[n] += C[k]*d[k][n];
  }
  }
  for(int n=0;n<N;n++)
  {
  y[n] = C[0]/Math.sqrt((double) N)
         + y[n]*Math.sqrt(2.0/((double) N));
  }

  // display
  for(int n=0;n<N;n++)
  {
  System.out.println("y[" + n + "] = " + y[n]);
  }
  } // end main
}
```

Chapter 7

Discrete Wavelets

7.1 Introduction

In this section we discuss the one-dimensional discrete wavelet transform (Chui [13], Mallat [39], Daubechies [17]). Within the discrete wavelet transform we distinguish between redundant discrete systems (frames) and orthonormal, semi-orthogonal, and biorthogonal bases of wavelets. In most cases the discrete wavelet transform (or DWT) is an orthogonal function which can be applied to a finite group of data. Functionally, it is very much like the discrete Fourier transform, in that the transforming function is orthogonal, a signal passed twice (i.e. a forward and a backward transform) through the transformation is unchanged, and the input signal is assumed to be a set of discrete-time samples. Both transforms are convolutions. Whereas the basis function of the Fourier transform is sinusoidal, the wavelet basis is a set of functions which are defined by a recursive difference equation for the *scaling function* ϕ (also called *father wavelet*)

$$\phi(x) = \sum_{k=0}^{M-1} c_k \phi(2x - k)$$

where the range of the summation is determined by the specified number of nonzero coefficients M. Here k is the translation parameter. The number of coefficients is not arbitrary and is determined by constraints of orthogonality and normalization. Owing to the periodic boundary condition we have

$$c_k \equiv c_{k+nM}$$

where $n \in \mathbf{N}$. We notice that periodic wavelets are only one possibility to deal with signals defined on an interval. Generally, the area under the scaling function ϕ over all space should be unity, i.e.

$$\int_{\mathbf{R}} \phi(x)dx = 1 .$$

It follows that

$$\sum_{k=0}^{M-1} c_k = 2 .$$

In the Hilbert space $L_2(\mathbf{R})$ with the *scalar product*

$$\langle f, g \rangle := \int_{\mathbf{R}} f(x)\bar{g}(x)dx$$

the scaling function ϕ is orthogonal to its translations; i.e.,

$$\int_{\mathbf{R}} \phi(x)\phi(x-k)dx = 0, \qquad k \in \mathbf{Z} \setminus \{0\} .$$

What is desired is a function ψ which is also orthogonal to its dilations, or scales, i.e.,

$$\int_{\mathbf{R}} \psi(x)\psi(2x-k)dx = 0 .$$

Such a function ψ (called the *mother wavelet*) does exist and is given by (the so-called associated *wavelet function*)

$$\psi(x) = \sum_{k=1}^{M} g_k\phi(2x-k) = \sum_{k=1}^{M}(-1)^k c_{1-k}\phi(2x-k)$$

which is dependent on the solution of ϕ, where $g_k = (-1)^k c_{1-k}$. The sequences c_k and g_k are elements of the Hilbert space $\ell(\mathbf{Z})$. The scalar product of two sequences $a = (\ldots, a_{-1}, a_0, a_1, \ldots)$ and $b = (\ldots, b_{-1}, b_0, b_1, \ldots)$ in the Hilbert space $\ell(\mathbf{Z})$ is defined as

$$\langle a, b \rangle = \sum_{n=-\infty}^{\infty} a_n \bar{b}_n .$$

The following equation follows from the orthonormality of scaling functions

$$\sum_{k} c_k c_{k-2m} = 2\delta_{0m}$$

which means that the above sum is zero for all m not equal to zero, and that the sum of the squares of all coefficients is two. Another equation which can be derived from $\psi(x) \perp \phi(x-m)$ is

$$\sum_{k}(-1)^k c_{1-k} c_{k-2m} = 0 .$$

A way to solve for ϕ is to construct a matrix of coefficient values. This is a square $M \times M$ matrix where M is the number of nonzero coefficients. The matrix is designated L with entries $L_{ij} = c_{2i-j}$. This matrix has an eigenvalue equal to 1, and its corresponding (normalized) eigenvector contains, as its components, the value of the function ϕ at integer values of x. Once these values are known, all other values of the function ϕ can be generated by applying the recursion equation to get values at half-integer x, quarter-integer x, and so on down to the desired dilation. This determines the accuracy of the function approximation.

An example for a mother wavelet ψ is the *Haar function*

$$\psi(x) := \begin{cases} 1 & 0 \leq x < \frac{1}{2} \\ -1 & \frac{1}{2} \leq x < 1 \\ 0 & \text{otherwise} \end{cases}$$

and the scaling function (father wavelet) ϕ is given by

$$\phi(x) := \begin{cases} 1 & 0 \leq x < 1 \\ 0 & \text{otherwise} \end{cases}.$$

We have $\psi(x) = \phi(2x) - \phi(2x - 1)$. The functions

$$\psi_{m,n}(x) := 2^{\frac{m}{2}} \psi(2^m x - n), \quad m, n \in \mathbf{Z}$$

form a basis in the Hilbert space $L_2(\mathbf{R})$. This means that every function $f \in L_2(\mathbf{R})$ can be expanded with respect to this basis. If we restrict m to $m = 0, 1, 2, \ldots$ and

$$n = 0, 1, 2, \ldots, 2^m - 1$$

we obtain a basis in the Hilbert space $L_2[0, 1]$.

This class of wavelet functions is constrained, by definition, to be zero outside of a small interval. This is what makes the wavelet transform able to operate on a finite set of data, a property which is formally called compact support. The recursion relation ensures that a scaling function ϕ is non-differentiable everywhere. Of course this is not valid for Haar wavelets. The following table lists coefficients for two wavelet transforms. The sum of the coefficients is normalized to 2.

Wavelet	c_0	c_1	c_2	c_3
Haar	1.0	1.0		
Daubechies-4	$\frac{1}{4}(1+\sqrt{3})$	$\frac{1}{4}(3+\sqrt{3})$	$\frac{1}{4}(3-\sqrt{3})$	$\frac{1}{4}(1-\sqrt{3})$

Table 7.1: Coefficients for Two Wavelet Functions

7.2   Multiresolution Analysis

A *multiresolution analysis* of a signal $f(t)$ consists of a collection of nested subspaces $\{\,V_j\,\}_{j\in\mathbf{Z}}$ of the Hilbert space $L_2(\mathbf{R})$, satisfying the following set of properties:

(i) for all $(j,k) \in \mathbf{Z}^2$, $f(t) \in V_j \Leftrightarrow f(t - 2^j k)$

(ii) for all $j \in \mathbf{Z}$, $V_j \subset V_{j-1}$

(iii) for all $j \in \mathbf{Z}$ $f(t) \in V_j \Leftrightarrow f(t/2) \in V_{j+1}$

(iv) $\cap_{j\in\mathbf{Z}} V_j = \{0\}$, $\cup_{j\in\mathbf{Z}} V_j$ is dense in the Hilbert space $L_2(\mathbf{R})$

(v) $f(t) \in V_j \Leftrightarrow f(2^j t) \in V_0$

(vi) There exists a function $\phi(t)$ in V_0, called the scaling function, such that the collection $\{\,\phi(t-k),\ k \in \mathbf{Z}\}$ is an unconditional Riesz basis for the subspace V_0.

Let $\mathcal{H}$ be a separable Hilbert space (in our case $L_2(\mathbf{R})$) and $\{\,h_n\,\}_{n\in\mathbf{Z}}$ a countable subset of $\mathbf{H}$. We say that $\{\,h_n\,\}$ is a *Riesz basis* for $\mathcal{H}$ if $\{\,h_n\,\}$ is complete and if there are constants $0 < C_1 \le C_2 < \infty$, for an arbitrary sequence $c := \{c_n\}_{n\in\mathbf{Z}} \in \ell_2(\mathbf{Z})$ such that

$$C_1\|c\| \le \|\sum_{n\in\mathbf{Z}} c_n h_n\| \le C_2\|c\| \,.$$

One can easily see that an orthonormal complete sequence in a Hilbert space is a Riesz basis.

The property (i) means that V_j is invariant under any translation proportional to the scale 2^j. Property (ii) is a causality property which proves that an approximation at a resolution 2^{-j} contains all the necessary information to compute an approximation at a coarser resolution 2^{-j-1}. When the resolution 2^{-j} tends to 0, i.e. $j \to +\infty$, we find that we lose all the details of f. On the other hand, when the resolution 2^{-j} tends to $+\infty$, we find that the signal approximation converges to the original signal $f(t)$.

The set of the scaled and shifted functions

$$\{\phi_{j,k}(t) = 2^{-j/2}\phi(2^{-j}t - k),\ k \in \mathbf{Z}\}$$

constitute a Riesz basis for the space V_j. Performing a multiresolution analysis of the signal f means successively projecting it into each of the approximation subspaces V_j

$$\text{approx}_j(t) = (\text{Proj}_{V_j} f)(t) = \sum_{k \in \mathbf{Z}} a_f(j,k) \phi_{j,k}(t) \,.$$

Since $V_j \subset V_{j-1}$, approx_j is a coarser approximation of f than is approx_{j-1} and therefore, the key idea of the multiresolution analysis consists in examining the loss of information, that is the detail, when going from one approximation to the next, coarser one:

$$\text{detail}_j(t) = \text{approx}_{j-1}(t) - \text{approx}_j(t) \,.$$

The multiresolution analysis shows that the detail signal detail_j can be directly obtained from projections of the signal f onto a collection of subspaces, the W_j, called the wavelet subspaces. We have

$$V_{j+1} = V_j \oplus W_j, \qquad W_j \subset V_{j+1}$$

where $\oplus$ is the orthogonal sum of two linear spaces. Thus we have two mutually orthogonal subspaces, V_j and W_j. Since

$$\text{clos}_{L_2(\mathbf{R})} \left\{ \bigcup_{j=-\infty}^{\infty} V_j \right\} = L_2(\mathbf{R})$$

we obtain the expansion

$$L_2(\mathbf{R}) = \bigoplus_{j=-\infty}^{\infty} W_j \,.$$

Any function in the Hilbert space $L_2(\mathbf{R})$ may be expanded in a generalised Fourier series

$$f(t) = \sum_{j=-\infty}^{\infty} w_j \quad \text{with } w_j \in W_j \text{ for all } j \in \mathbf{Z} \,.$$

There exists a function ψ, called the mother wavelet, to be derived from ϕ, such that its templates $\{\psi_{j,k}(t) = 2^{-j/2}\psi(2^{-j}t - k),\ k \in \mathbf{Z}\}$ constitute a Riesz basis for the subspace W_j

$$\text{detail}_j(t) = (\text{Proj}_{W_j} f)(t) = \sum_{k \in \mathbf{Z}} d_f(j,k) \psi_{j,k}(t) \,.$$

Basically, the multiresolution analysis consists in rewriting the information in f as a collection of details at different resolutions and a low-resolution approximation

$$f(t) = \text{approx}_J(t) + \sum_{j=1}^{j=J} \text{detail}_j(t)$$

$$= \sum_{k \in \mathbf{Z}} a_f(J,k)\phi_{J,k}(t) + \sum_{j=1}^{J}\sum_{k \in \mathbf{Z}} d_f(j,k)\psi_{j,k}(t).$$

The approx_j essentially being coarser and coarser approximations of f means that ϕ needs to be a low-pass function. The details_j, being an information 'differential', indicates rather that ψ is a bandpass function, and therefore a small wave, a wavelet. The multiresolution analysis shows that the mother wavelet ψ must satisfy

$$\int_{\mathbf{R}} \psi(t)dt = 0$$

and that its Fourier transform obeys $|\hat{\psi}(\omega)| \sim \omega^N$, $\omega \to 0$, where N is a positive integer called the number of vanishing moments of the wavelet and ω is the frequency.

Given a scaling function ϕ and a mother-wavelet ψ, the discrete (or non-redundant) wavelet transform is a mapping $L_2(\mathbf{R}) \to \ell_2(\mathbf{Z})$ between the two Hilbert spaces $L_2(\mathbf{R})$ and $\ell_2(\mathbf{Z})$ given by

$$f(t) \to \{\{a_f(J,k),\, k \in \mathbf{Z}\},\, \{d_f(j,k),\, j = 1,\ldots,J,\ k \in \mathbf{Z}\}\}.$$

These coefficients are defined through the inner products of the signal f with two sets of functions

$$a_f(j,k) = \langle f(t), \overset{\circ}{\phi}_{j,k}(t)\rangle$$

$$d_f(j,k) = \langle f(t), \overset{\circ}{\psi}_{j,k}(t)\rangle$$

where $\overset{\circ}{\psi}_{jk}$ (respectively $\overset{\circ}{\phi}_{jk}$) are shifted and dilated templates of $\overset{\circ}{\psi}_0$ (respectively $\overset{\circ}{\phi}_0$), called the dual mother wavelet (respectively the dual scaling function), and whose definition depends on whether one chooses to use an orthogonal, semi-orthogonal or biorthogonal discrete wavelet transform. They can practically be computed by a fast recursive filter-bank-based pyramidal algorithm with an extremely low computational cost.

7.3   Pyramid Algorithm

The *pyramid algorithm* operates on a finite set on N input data

$$x_0,\ x_1,\ \ldots,\ x_{N-1}$$

where N is a power of two; this value will be referred to as the input block size. These data are passed through two *convolution functions*, each of which creates an output stream that is half the length of the original input. These convolution functions are filters, one half of the output is produced by the "low-pass filter"

$$a_i = \frac{1}{2} \sum_{j=0}^{N-1} c_{2i-j+1} x_j, \qquad i = 0, 1, \ldots, \frac{N}{2} - 1$$

and the other half is produced by the "high-pass filter" function

$$b_i = \frac{1}{2} \sum_{j=0}^{N-1} (-1)^j c_{j-2i} x_j, \qquad i = 0, 1, \ldots, \frac{N}{2} - 1$$

where N is the input block size, c_j are the coefficients,

$$\mathbf{x} = (x_0, x_1, \ldots, x_{N-1})$$

is the input sequence, and

$$\mathbf{a} = (a_0, a_1, \ldots, a_{N/2-1}), \qquad \mathbf{b} = (b_0, b_1, \ldots, b_{N/2-1})$$

are the output sequences. In the case of the lattice filter, the low- and high-pass outputs are usually referred to as the odd and even outputs, respectively. In many situations, the odd or low-pass output contains most of the information content of the original input signal. The even, or high-pass output contains the difference between the true input and the value of the reconstructed input if it were to be reconstructed from only the information given in the odd output. In general, higher order wavelets (i.e. those with more nonzero coefficients) tend to put more information into the odd output, and less into the even output. If the average amplitude of the even output is low enough, then the even half of the signal may be discarded without greatly affecting the quality of the reconstructed signal. An important step in wavelet-based data compression is finding wavelet functions which cause the even terms to be nearly zero. However, note that details can only be neglected for very smooth time series and smooth wavelet filters, a situation which is not satisfied for chaotic time signals.

The Haar wavelet represents a simple interpolation scheme. After passing these data through the filter functions, the output of the low-pass filter consists of the average of every two samples, and the output of the high-pass filter consists of the difference of every two samples. The high-pass filter contains less information than the low pass output. If the signal is reconstructed by an inverse low-pass filter of the form

$$x_j^L = \sum_{i=0}^{N/2-1} c_{2i-j+1} a_i, \qquad j = 0, 1, \ldots, N-1$$

then the result is a duplication of each entry from the low-pass filter output. This is a wavelet reconstruction with 2× data compression. Since the perfect reconstruction is a sum of the inverse low-pass and inverse high-pass filters, the output of the inverse high-pass filter can be calculated. This is the result of the inverse high-pass filter function

$$x_j^H = \sum_{i=0}^{N/2-1} (-1)^j c_{j-1-2i} b_i, \qquad j = 0, 1, \ldots, N - 1.$$

The perfectly reconstructed signal is

$$x = x^L + x^H$$

where x is the vector with elements x_j. Using other coefficients and other orders of wavelets yields similar results, except that the outputs are not exactly averages and differences, as in the case using the Haar coefficients.

Let us consider an example. Most discrete signals are filtered using linear difference equations, for example

$$y[n] = ay[n - 1] + (1 - a)x[n], \qquad n = 0, 1, \ldots$$

where $x[n]$ is the input signal, $y[n]$ the output, $y[-1] = 0$, $x[0] = 0$, and a $(0 < a < 1)$ is the filter parameter. Notice that $y[n]$ depends upon previously computed values of the filter output. Thus the chosen filter is an infinite response filter. It is well-known that filtered chaotic signals can exhibit increases in observed fractal dimensions, for example the Liapunov dimension. We study the Liapunov exponent of filtered chaotic one-dimensional maps using wavelets [54]. Our input signal is given as the solution of the logistic map

$$x[t + 1] = 4x[t](1 - x[t])$$

where $x[0] \in [0, 1]$ and $t = 0, 1, \ldots$. The properties of the logistic map are well-known ([55]). For almost all initial values we find that the Liapunov exponent of the logistic map is given by $\ln(2)$. We apply the Haar wavelet to filter the time series $(x_0, x_1, \ldots, x_{N-1})$ resulting from the logistic map in the chaotic regime. The filter decomposes the signal into the moving average coefficients $\{ a_i \}$ and details $\{ b_i \}$ with $i = 0, 1, \ldots, N/2 - 1$. Owing to Broomhead et al [9] the complete set of coefficients $\{ a_i, b_i \}$ have the same Liapunov exponent as the original time series. The reason is that Haar (and Daubechies) wavelets are finite impulse response filters and that the convolution is performed only once. Therefore we deal with a non-recursive finite impulse filter. Using the time series given by the logistic map we evaluate x_j^L, x_j^H using equations given above. We have

$$x_j^L = x_{j+1}^L$$

for j even and

$$x_j^H = -x_{j+1}^H$$

for j even. We use the series x_j^L for the calculation of the Liapunov exponent. Notice that in the case of the logistic equation the even output resulting from Haar wavelets, i.e. the details, contain nearly as much information as the odd output, i.e. the averages. We remove the duplication of each entry of x_j^L and calculate the Liapunov exponent of this time series. Thus the size of the time series is $N/2$. An algorithm to find the Liapunov exponent from time series is described in chapter 2. The Liapunov exponent is much larger than $\ln(2)$ for this time series, i.e. the time series becomes more chaotic.

Using the coefficients for the Daubechies-4 wavelet we find similar results, i.e., the Liapunov exponent is much larger than $\ln(2)$. Furthermore, for other one-dimensional chaotic maps we also find similar results.

```cpp
// waveletliapunov.cpp

#include <iostream>
#include <cmath>        // for fabs, log
using namespace std;

void find(double* a,int size,int point,double& min,int& pos)
{
   int i = 0;
   if(point == 0) { min = fabs(a[i]-a[1]); }
   if(point != 0) { min = fabs(a[i]-a[point]); }
   pos = i;
   double distance;

   for(i=1;i<(size-1);i++)
   {
   if(i != point)
   {
   distance = fabs(a[i]-a[point]);
   if(distance < min)
   {
   min = distance;
   pos = i;
   } // end if
   } // end if
   } // end for
}
```

```c
int main(void)
{
  const double pi = 3.14159;
  // generate time series
  int n = 16384; // length of time series
  int m = n/2;
  int k;
  double* x = new double[n];
  int t;
  x[0] = 1.0/3.0;  // initial value of time series
  for(t=0;t<(n-1);t++)
  { x[t+1] = 4.0*x[t]*(1.0-x[t]); } // time series

  // Haar wavelet
  double* c = new double[n];
  for(k=0;k<n;k++) c[k] = 0.0;
  c[0] = 1.0; c[1] = 1.0;

  double* a = new double[m];
  for(k=0;k<m;k++) a[k] = 0.0;
  double* b = new double[m];
  for(k=0;k<m;k++) b[k] = 0.0;

  int i, j;
  for(i=0;i<m;i++)
  {
  for(j=0;j<n;j++)
  {
  if(2*i-j+1 < 0) a[i] += c[2*i-j+1+n]*x[j];
  else a[i] += c[2*i-j+1]*x[j];
  }
  a[i] = 0.5*a[i];
  }

  for(i=0;i<m;i++)
  {
  for(j=0;j<n;j++)
  {
  if(j-2*i < 0)
  b[i] += pow(-1.0,j)*c[j-2*i+n]*x[j];
  else b[i] += pow(-1.0,j)*c[j-2*i]*x[j];
  }
  b[i] = 0.5*b[i];
  }
```

```
// inverse transform
double* xL = new double[n];
double* xH = new double[n];
for(j=0;j<n;j++) xL[j] = 0.0;
for(j=0;j<n;j++) xH[j] = 0.0;

for(j=0;j<n;j++)
{
for(i=0;i<m;i++)
{
if(2*i-j+1 < 0) xL[j] += c[2*i-j+1+n]*a[i];
else xL[j] += c[2*i-j+1]*a[i];
}
}

for(j=0;j<n;j++)
{
for(i=0;i<m;i++)
{
if(j-2*i < 0) xH[j] += pow(-1.0,j)*c[j-2*i+n]*b[i];
else xH[j] += pow(-1.0,j)*c[j-2*i]*b[i];
}
}
// input signal reconstructed
double* y = new double[n];
for(k=0;k<n;k++) y[k] = xL[k] + xH[k];
// end wavelet block

// timeseries
int count = 0;
t = 0;
double* series = new double[m];
while(t < n)
{
series[count] = xL[t];
count++;
t += 2;
}
// Liapunov block
double* d = new double[m-1];
double* d1 = new double[m-1];
int point = 1;
int pos;
```

```
double min;

for(t=0;t<(m-1);t++)
{
find(series,m,t,min,pos);
d[t] = fabs(series[t]-series[pos]);
d1[t] = fabs(series[t+1]-series[pos+1]);
}

double sum = 0.0;
for(t=0;t<(m-1);t++) { sum += log(d1[t]/d[t]); }

double lambda = sum/((double) (m-1));
cout << "lambda = " << lambda << endl;
delete[] x; delete[] d;  delete[] d1;
return 0;
}
```

7.4   Biorthogonal Wavelets

As described before, dilations and translations of the scaling function ϕ leading to $\{\phi_{jk}\}$ constitute a basis for the subspaces V_j and, similarly $\{\psi_{jk}(t)\}$ for the subspaces W_j. We define a dual multiresolution analysis with dual subspaces $\{\widetilde{V}_j\}$ and $\{\widetilde{W}_j\}$ generated from a dual scaling function $\widetilde{\phi}$ and a dual mother wavelet $\widetilde{\psi}$, respectively. This is done so that instead of

$$\langle \phi_{jk}, \phi_{jl} \rangle = \delta_{kl}, \qquad \langle \psi_{jk}, \psi_{j'l} \rangle = \delta_{jj'}\delta_{kl}, \qquad \langle \phi_{jk}, \psi_{jl} \rangle = 0$$

as in an orthogonal case, where $\langle \, , \, \rangle$ is the scalar product in the Hilbert space $L_2(\mathbf{R})$, we have

$$\langle \widetilde{\phi}_{jk}, \phi_{jl} \rangle = \delta_{kl}, \qquad \langle \widetilde{\psi}_{jk}, \psi_{j'l} \rangle = \delta_{jj'}\delta_{kl},$$

and

$$\langle \widetilde{\psi}_{jk}, \phi_{jl} \rangle = 0, \qquad \langle \widetilde{\phi}_{jk}, \psi_{jl} \rangle = 0$$

where $\widetilde{\phi}_{jk}(t) := 2^{j/2}\widetilde{\phi}(2^j t - k)$ and $\widetilde{\psi}_{jk} = 2^{j/2}\widetilde{\psi}(2^j t - k)$. These sets constitute bases for the dual subspaces $\{\widetilde{V}_j\}$ and $\{\widetilde{W}_j\}$. The conditions displayed above are referred to as biorthogonality conditions and ψ and $\widetilde{\psi}$ biorthogonal wavelets. In terms of subspaces, the above biorthogonality conditions can be expressed as

$$V_j \perp \widetilde{W}_j, \quad \widetilde{V}_j \perp W_j, \quad \text{and} \quad W_j \perp \widetilde{W}_{j'} \text{ for } j \neq j'.$$

By definition, a scaling function ϕ and a mother wavelet ψ satisfy the dilation equation and the wavelet equation. Consequently

$$\phi(t) = \sqrt{2} \sum_{k \in \mathbf{Z}} h_k \phi(2t - k), \qquad \psi(t) = \sqrt{2} \sum_{k \in \mathbf{Z}} g_k \phi(2t - k)$$

and

$$\widetilde{\phi}(t) = \sqrt{2} \sum_{k \in \mathbf{Z}} \widetilde{h}_k \widetilde{\phi}(2t - k), \qquad \widetilde{\psi}(t) = \sqrt{2} \sum_{k \in \mathbf{Z}} \widetilde{g}_k \widetilde{\phi}(2t - k).$$

The coefficients in the above equations can be obtained by taking the scalar product in the Hilbert space $L_2(\mathbf{R})$ with the appropriate dual function. For example,

$$h_k = \langle \widetilde{\phi}_{1,k}, \phi \rangle = \sqrt{2} \int_{\mathbf{R}} \overline{\widetilde{\phi}(2t - k)} \phi(t) dt$$

$$g_k = \langle \widetilde{\phi}_{1,k}, \psi \rangle = \sqrt{2} \int_{\mathbf{R}} \overline{\widetilde{\phi}(2t - k)} \psi(t) dt.$$

The roles of the two functions ϕ and $\widetilde{\phi}$ or ψ and $\widetilde{\psi}$ can be interchanged. Or if we take the dual of the above equations we obtain the following relations

$$\widetilde{h}_k = \langle \phi_{1,k}, \widetilde{\phi} \rangle = \sqrt{2} \int_{\mathbf{R}} \overline{\phi(2t - k)} \widetilde{\phi}(t) dt$$

$$\widetilde{g}_k = \langle \phi_{1,k}, \widetilde{\psi} \rangle = \sqrt{2} \int_{\mathbf{R}} \overline{\phi(2t - k)} \widetilde{\psi}(t) dt.$$

The Cohen-Daubechies-Feauveau biorthogonal linear *spline wavelets* ([14], [19]) have compact support and are known to have optimal time localisation for a given number of null moments (frequency localization). An important property of the spline wavelet is that they have zero moments up to order m, i.e.

$$\int_{\mathbf{R}} t^\ell \psi(t) dt = 0, \quad \text{for } \ell = 0, 1, \ldots, m.$$

Spline wavelets are extremely regular and unlike other wavelets, they are symmetric in time. A special case of the Cohen-Daubechies-Feauveau wavelet is implemented in the following Java program. The time series d[k], k = 0, 1, ... , 64 is generated from the logistic map.

```java
// CDF1.java

public class CDF1
{
  public static void main(String[] arg)
  {
```

```java
double[] d = new double[65]; // length for data 2^n + 1
                             // n integer
d[0] = 1.0/3.0;  // initial value logistic map
for(int k=1;k<d.length;++k)
  { d[k] = 4.0*d[k-1]*(1.0-d[k-1]); } // logistic map

CDF1 cdf = new CDF1();
cdf.transform(d);
// print transformed data
System.out.println("transformed data:");
for(int k=0;k<d.length;++k)
{
System.out.println("d["+k+"] = " + d[k]);
}
cdf.invTransform(d);
System.out.println("reconstructed data:");
for(int k=0;k<d.length;++k)
{
System.out.println("d["+k+"] = "+d[k]);
}
} // end main

public CDF1() { }  // default constructor

final static double[] s =
 { 0.03314563036811941,-0.06629126073623882,
   -0.17677669529663687, 0.41984465132951254,
   0.9943689110435824, 0.41984465132951254,
   -0.17677669529663687, -0.06629126073623882,
   0.03314563036811941 };
final static double[] w = { -0.5, 1.0, -0.5 };
final static double[][] sLeft =
 {{ 1.0275145414117017, 0.7733980419227863,
   -0.22097086912079608, -0.3314563036811941,
   0.16572815184059705 },
  { -0.22189158107546605, 0.4437831621509321,
     0.902297715576584, 0.5800485314420897,
   -0.25687863535292543, -0.06629126073623882,
   0.03314563036811941 },
  { 0.07549838028293866, -0.15099676056587732,
   -0.0957540432856783, 0.34250484713723395,
   1.0330388131397217, 0.41984465132951254,
   -0.17677669529663687, -0.06629126073623882,
   0.03314563036811941 },
```

```
    { -0.013810679320049755, 0.02762135864009951,
      0.011048543456039804, -0.04971844555217912,
      -0.18506310288866673, 0.41984465132951254,
      0.9943689110435824, 0.41984465132951254,
      -0.17677669529663687, -0.06629126073623882,
      0.03314563036811941 }};

final static double[][] sRight =
 {{ 0.03314563036811941, -0.06629126073623882,
    -0.17677669529663687,  0.41984465132951254,
     0.9943689110435824,   0.41984465132951254,
    -0.18506310288866673, -0.04971844555217912,
     0.011048543456039804, 0.02762135864009951,
    -0.013810679320049755 },
  { 0.03314563036811941, -0.06629126073623882,
    -0.17677669529663687, 0.41984465132951254,
     1.0330388131397217, 0.34250484713723395,
    -0.0957540432856783, -0.15099676056587732,
     0.07549838028293866 },
  { 0.03314563036811941, -0.06629126073623882,
    -0.25687863535292543, 0.5800485314420897,
     0.902297715576584, 0.4437831621509321,
    -0.22189158107546605 },
  { 0.16572815184059705, -0.3314563036811941,
    -0.22097086912079608, 0.7733980419227863,
     1.0275145414117017 }};

final static double[] sPrimary =
 { 0.35355339059327373, 0.7071067811865475,
   0.35355339059327373 };
final static double[] wPrimary =
 { 0.0234375, 0.046875, -0.125,
   -0.296875, 0.703125, -0.296875,
   -0.125, 0.046875, 0.0234375 };

final static double[][] sPrimaryLeft =
 {{ 0.7071067811865475, 0.35355339059327373 }};

final static double[][] sPrimaryRight =
 {{ 0.35355339059327373, 0.7071067811865475 }};

final static double[][] wPrimaryLeft =
 {{ -0.546875, 0.5696614583333334,
    -0.3138020833333333, -0.103515625,
```

```
      0.10677083333333333, 0.043619791666666664,
      -0.01953125, -0.009765625 },
   { 0.234375, -0.087890625,
    -0.41015625, 0.673828125,
    -0.2421875, -0.103515625,
     0.03515625, 0.017578125 }};

final static double[][] wPrimaryRight =
 {{  0.017578125, 0.03515625,
     -0.103515625, -0.2421875,
      0.673828125, -0.41015625,
     -0.087890625,  0.234375 },
   { -0.009765625, -0.01953125,
      0.043619791666666664, 0.10677083333333333,
     -0.103515625, -0.3138020833333333,
      0.5696614583333334, -0.546875 }};

public void transform(double[] v)
{
for(int last=v.length;last>=15;last=(last+1)/2)
{
transform(v,last);
}
} // end method transform

public void invTransform(double[] v)
{
int last;
for(last=v.length;last>=15;last=last/2+1) { ; }
for(;2*last-1<=v.length;last=2*last-1) {
  invTransform(v,last);
}
} // end method invTransform

public static void transform(double[] v,int last)
{
double[] ans = new double[last];
int half = (last+1)/2;
if(2*half-1 != last) {
    throw new IllegalArgumentException("Illegal subband : "
      + last + " within array of length " + v.length);
}
// lowpass
for(int k=0;k<sLeft.length;k++) {
```

```
      for(int l=0;l<sLeft[k].length;l++) {
         ans[k] += sLeft[k][l]*v[l];
   }
   }
   for(int k=sLeft.length;k<half-sRight.length;k++) {
      for(int l=0;l<s.length;l++) {
         ans[k] += s[l]*v[2*k+1-sLeft.length];
      }
   }
   for(int k=0;k<sRight.length;k++) {
      for(int l=0;l<sRight[k].length;l++) {
         ans[k+half-sRight.length] +=
            sRight[k][l]*v[last-sRight[k].length+l];
   }
   }
   // highpass
   for(int k=0;k<half-1;k++) {
      for(int l=0;l<w.length;l++) {
         ans[k+half] += w[l]*v[2*k+1];
      }
      }
   System.arraycopy(ans,0,v,0,last);
   } // end method transform

   public static void invTransform(double[] v,int last)
   {
   double[] ans = new double[2*last-1];
   // scale coefficients
   for(int k=0;k<sPrimaryLeft.length;k++) {
      for(int l=0;l<sPrimaryLeft[k].length;l++) {
         ans[l] += sPrimaryLeft[k][l]*v[k];
   }
   }
   for(int k=sPrimaryLeft.length;k<last-sPrimaryRight.length;k++)
   {
   for(int l=0;l<sPrimary.length;l++) {
      ans[2*k-1+l] += sPrimary[l]*v[k];
   }
   }
   for(int k=0;k<sPrimaryRight.length;k++) {
      for(int l=0;l<sPrimaryRight[k].length;l++) {
         ans[l-sPrimaryRight[k].length+ans.length] +=
         sPrimaryRight[k][l]*v[k+last-sPrimaryRight.length];
      }
```

```
}
// wavelet coefficients
for(int k=0;k<wPrimaryLeft.length;k++) {
  for(int l=0;l<wPrimaryLeft[k].length;l++) {
    ans[l] += wPrimaryLeft[k][l]*v[k+last];
  }
}
for(int k=wPrimaryLeft.length;k<last-1-wPrimaryRight.length;k++)
{
for(int l=0;l<wPrimary.length;l++) {
  ans[2*(k-1)-1+l] += wPrimary[l]*v[k+last];
}
}
for(int k=0;k<wPrimaryRight.length;k++) {
  for(int l=0;l<wPrimaryRight[k].length;l++) {
    ans[l-wPrimaryRight[k].length+ans.length] +=
    wPrimaryRight[k][l]*v[k+2*last-1-wPrimaryRight.length];
  }
}
System.arraycopy(ans,0,v,0,ans.length);
} // end method invTransform
} // end class
```

7.5   Two-Dimensional Wavelets

There are several methods to build bases on functional spaces in dimension greater than 1. The simplest one uses separable wavelets. Let us consider $d = 2$. The simplest way to build two-dimensional wavelet bases is to use separable products (tensor products) of a one-dimensional wavelet ψ and scaling function ϕ. This provides the following scaling function

$$\Phi(x_1, x_2) = \phi(x_1)\phi(x_2)$$

and there are three wavelets

$$\psi^{(1)}(x_1, x_2) = \phi(x_1)\psi(x_2)$$
$$\psi^{(2)}(x_1, x_2) = \psi(x_1)\phi(x_2)$$
$$\psi^{(3)}(x_1, x_2) = \psi(x_1)\psi(x_2).$$

In the general case with n dimensions we get $2^n - 1$ wavelets using this method. There are also non-separable two-dimensional wavelets.

Assume that we have a scaling function Φ and wavelets

$$\Psi := \{\, \psi^{(i)} \,:\, i = 1, 2, 3 \,\}$$

constructed by tensor products described above of a one-dimensional orthogonal wavelet system. If we define

$$\psi_{\mathbf{j},k}^{(i)}(\mathbf{x}) := 2^k \psi^{(i)}(2^k \mathbf{x} - \mathbf{j}), \qquad i = 1, 2, 3$$

where $k \in \mathbf{Z}$, and $\mathbf{j} \in \mathbf{Z}^2$, then any function f in the Hilbert space $L_2(\mathbf{R}^2)$ can be written as the expansion

$$f(\mathbf{x}) = \sum_{\mathbf{j},k,\psi} \langle f, \psi_{\mathbf{j},k} \rangle \psi_{\mathbf{j},k}(\mathbf{x})$$

where the sums range over all $\mathbf{j} \in \mathbf{Z}^2$, all $k \in \mathbf{Z}$, and all $\psi \in \Psi$. Here $\langle\,,\,\rangle$ denotes the scalar product in the Hilbert space $L_2(\mathbf{R}^2)$, i.e.

$$\langle f, \psi_{\mathbf{j},k}^{(i)} \rangle = c_{\mathbf{j},k}^{(i)} = \int_{\mathbf{R}^2} f(\mathbf{x}) \psi_{\mathbf{j},k}^{(i)}(\mathbf{x}) d\mathbf{x}\,.$$

Thus we have

$$f(\mathbf{x}) = \sum_{\mathbf{j},k} \langle f, \psi_{\mathbf{j},k}^{(1)} \rangle \psi_{\mathbf{j},k}^{(1)}(\mathbf{x}) + \sum_{\mathbf{j},k} \langle f, \psi_{\mathbf{j},k}^{(2)} \rangle \psi_{\mathbf{j},k}^{(2)}(\mathbf{x}) + \sum_{\mathbf{j},k} \langle f, \psi_{\mathbf{j},k}^{(3)} \rangle \psi_{\mathbf{j},k}^{(3)}(\mathbf{x})\,.$$

Instead of considering the sum over all dyadic levels k, one can sum over $k \geq K$ for a fixed integer K. For this case we have the expansion

$$f(\mathbf{x}) = \sum_{\mathbf{j} \in \mathbf{Z}^2, k \geq K, \psi \in \Psi} c_{\mathbf{j},k,\psi} \psi_{\mathbf{j},k}(\mathbf{x}) + \sum_{\mathbf{j} \in \mathbf{Z}^2} d_{\mathbf{j},K} \Phi_{\mathbf{j},K}(\mathbf{x})$$

where

$$c_{\mathbf{j},k,\psi} = \int_{\mathbf{R}^2} f(\mathbf{x}) \psi_{\mathbf{j},k}(\mathbf{x}) d\mathbf{x}, \qquad d_{\mathbf{j},K} = \int_{\mathbf{R}^2} f(\mathbf{x}) \Phi_{\mathbf{j},K}(\mathbf{x}) d\mathbf{x}\,.$$

When we study finite domains, e.g., the unit square I, then two changes must be made to this basis for all of $L_2(\mathbf{R}^2)$ to obtain an orthonormal basis for $L_2(I)$. Let

$$\mathbf{Z}^2 := \{(j_1, j_2) \,:\, j_1, j_2 \in \mathbf{Z}\}\,.$$

First, one considers only nonnegative scales $k \geq 0$, and not all shifts $\mathbf{j} \in \mathbf{Z}^2$, but only those shifts for which $\psi_{\mathbf{j},k}$ intersects I nontrivially. Second one must adapt the wavelets that overlap the boundary of I in order to preserve orthogonality on the domain. Consider a function f defined on the unit square $I := [0,1)^2$, which is extended periodically to all of $\mathbf{R}^2$ by

$$f(\mathbf{x} + \mathbf{j}) = f(\mathbf{x}), \quad \mathbf{x} \in I, \quad \mathbf{j} \in \mathbf{Z}^2\,.$$

One can construct periodic wavelets on $L_2(I)$ that can be used to decompose periodic functions f on $L_2(I)$. For example, for $\psi \in \Psi$, $k \geq 0$ and $\mathbf{j} \in \{0, 1, \ldots, 2^k - 1\}^2$ one sets

$$\psi_{\mathbf{j},k}^{(p)}(\mathbf{x}) := \sum_{\mathbf{n} \in \mathbf{Z}^2} \psi_{\mathbf{j},k}(\mathbf{x} + \mathbf{n}), \qquad \mathbf{x} \in I\,.$$

One constructs $\Phi^{(p)}$ in the same way; we have $\Phi^{(p)}(\mathbf{x}) = 1$ for all $\mathbf{x}$, since

$$\{\, \Phi(\cdot - \mathbf{j}) \,:\, \mathbf{j} \in \mathbf{Z}^2 \,\}$$

forms a partition of unity. One now has a periodic orthogonal wavelet system on $L_2(I)$ such that

$$f(\mathbf{x}) = \langle f, \Phi^{(p)} \rangle + \sum_{\mathbf{j},k,\psi} \langle f, \psi_{\mathbf{j},k}^{(p)} \rangle \psi_{\mathbf{j},k}^{(p)}(\mathbf{x}) \,.$$

In practice we are given only a finite amount of data, so we cannot calculate the above formula for all $k \geq 0$ and all translations $h \in I$. Assume that we have 2^m rows of 2^m pixels, each of which is the average of f on a square of size $2^{-m} \times 2^{-m}$. Then using the orthogonal wavelets constructed by Daubechies we can calculate these formulae for $k < m$ and average over 2^{2m} different pixel translations $\mathbf{j}/2^m$, $\mathbf{j} = (j_1, j_2)$, $0 \leq j_1, j_2 < 2^m$, instead of averaging over $h \in I$. We obtain

$$f(\mathbf{x}) = \int_I f(\mathbf{y})d\mathbf{y} + \sum_{\substack{0 \leq k < m \\ \mathbf{j},\psi}} 2^{2(k-m)} \int_I f(\mathbf{y})\psi_k \left(\mathbf{y} - \frac{\mathbf{j}}{2^m} \right) d\mathbf{y} \psi_k \left(\mathbf{x} - \frac{\mathbf{j}}{2^m} \right).$$

For each dyadic level k we need to compute 3×2^{2m} terms, one for each pixel and one for each $\psi \in \Psi$.

Chapter 8

z-Transform

8.1 Introduction

The z-transform simplifies the analysis of linear time-invariant discrete-time (LTID) systems [7]. A system is *time-invariant* iff

$$y(n) = T[x(n)] \leftrightarrow y(n - n_0) = T[x(n - n_0)].$$

The z-transform converts equations with integrals and derivatives into algebraic equations. The z-transform method of analysing discrete-time systems is comparable to the Laplace transform method of analysing continuous-time systems. The applications the z-transform include:

i) describe discrete-time signals and systems so that we can infer their degree of stability,

ii) compute and visualise the frequency response of discrete-time systems,

iii) design discrete-time filter applications.

Definition. Given a discrete sequence $x(n)$ the *bilateral z-transform* is defined by

$$X(z) := \sum_{n=-\infty}^{\infty} x(n) z^{-n}$$

where z is a complex variable, i.e.

$$z = \Re z + i\Im z.$$

Hence $X(z)$ is just a weighted sum. The z-transform is only defined for values of z where the series converges. The bilateral z-transform is capable

101

of analysing both causal and non-causal systems.

Example. Given the sequence

$$x(0) = 1, \quad x(1) = 3, \quad x(2) = 4, \quad x(3) = 1$$

and $x(n) = 0$ otherwise. We obtain

$$X(z) = 1 + 3z^{-1} + 4z^{-2} + z^{-3}.$$

If $z = i$ we obtain

$$X(z = i) = 1 + \frac{3}{i} + \frac{4}{i \cdot i} + \frac{1}{i \cdot i \cdot i} = -3 - 2i.$$

We also use the notation $Z(x(n))$ for $X(z)$ in the following.

Definition. The *unilateral z-transform* is defined by

$$X(z) := \sum_{n=0}^{\infty} x(n)z^{-n}$$

i.e. the input signal starts at $n = 0$. The unilateral z-transform is capable of analysing only causal systems with causal inputs (starting at $n = 0$).

The *inverse z-transform* is given by

$$x(n) = \frac{1}{2\pi i} \oint X(z)z^{n-1}dz$$

where $\oint$ denotes integration around a circular path in the complex plane centered at the origin.

We mention that

$$\frac{1}{2\pi i} \oint \frac{1}{z}dz = 1$$

and

$$\frac{1}{2\pi i} \oint \frac{1}{z^n}dz = 0, \qquad \text{for} \quad n = 2, 3, \dots$$

The first formula can be proved as follows. Let

$$z(r, \alpha) = r \exp(i\alpha), \qquad r > 0, \quad 0 \le \alpha < 2\pi.$$

Then

$$dz = ri \exp(i\alpha)d\alpha.$$

Thus

$$\frac{1}{2\pi i} \oint \frac{1}{z}dz = \frac{1}{2\pi} \int_{\alpha=0}^{2\pi} d\alpha = 1.$$

Analogously we can prove the second formula.

Example. Using the expression given in the example above

$$X(z) = 1 + 3z^{-1} + 4z^{-2} + z^{-3}$$

and the complex integration we obtain the original sequence.

For the z-transform the infinite *geometric sum formula* and the finite geometric sum formula play an important role. Let c be a complex number with

$$|c| < 1.$$

Then

$$\sum_{n=0}^{\infty} c^n = \frac{1}{1-c}.$$

The finite geometric sum formula can be found as follows

$$\sum_{n=0}^{N-1} c^n \equiv \sum_{n=0}^{\infty} c^n - \sum_{n=N}^{\infty} c^n \equiv \sum_{n=0}^{\infty} c^n - c^N \sum_{n=0}^{\infty} c^n.$$

Using the result for the infinite geometric series we obtain

$$\sum_{n=0}^{N-1} c^n = \frac{1 - c^N}{1 - c}.$$

While the infinite geometric sum formula requires that the magnitude of the complex number c be strictly less than unity, the finite geometric sum is valid for any value of c.

From the formula given above it follows that

$$\sum_{n=0}^{\infty} a^n c^n = \sum_{n=0}^{\infty} (ac)^n = \frac{1}{1 - ac}$$

where $|ac| < 1$.

8.2 Simple Examples

Example 1. Let $x(n) = \delta(n)$, where

$$\delta(n) := \begin{cases} 1 & \text{for} \quad n = 0 \\ 0 \text{ otherwise} \end{cases}$$

Here $\delta(n)$ is called the *impulse sequence*. Then

$$X(z) = 1.$$

Example 2. Let $x(n) = u(n)$, where

$$u(n) := \begin{cases} 1 & \text{for} \quad n = 0, 1, 2, \dots \\ 0 \text{ otherwise} \end{cases}$$

Here $u(n)$ is called the *unit step sequence*. Then

$$X(z) = \sum_{n=-\infty}^{\infty} x(n)z^{-n} = \sum_{n=0}^{\infty} z^{-n}.$$

Thus

$$X(z) = \sum_{n=0}^{\infty} (z^{-1})^n = \frac{1}{1 - z^{-1}}, \qquad |z^{-1}| < 1$$

where we used that

$$\sum_{k=0}^{\infty} x^k = \frac{1}{1 - x}, \qquad |x| < 1.$$

Example 3. An extension of the sequence in example 2 is

$$x(n) = a^n u(n).$$

Then we find

$$X(z) = \sum_{n=-\infty}^{\infty} x(n)z^{-n} = \sum_{n=0}^{\infty} a^n z^{-n}.$$

Thus

$$X(z) = \sum_{n=0}^{\infty} (az^{-1})^n = \frac{1}{1 - az^{-1}}, \qquad |z| > |a|.$$

Example 4. The causal sinusoidal sequence is given by

$$x(n) = \sin(\omega_0 n)u(n).$$

Using the *Euler identity*

$$\sin(\alpha) \equiv \frac{e^{i\alpha} - e^{-i\alpha}}{2i}$$

we have

$$x(n) = \sin(n\omega_0)u(n) = \frac{1}{2i}(e^{in\omega_0} - e^{-in\omega_0})u(n).$$

Thus

$$X(z) = \frac{1}{2i} \sum_{n=0}^{\infty} e^{in\omega_0} z^{-n} - \frac{1}{2i} \sum_{n=0}^{\infty} e^{-in\omega_0} z^{-n} = \frac{1/2i}{1 - e^{i\omega_0} z^{-1}} - \frac{1/2i}{1 - e^{-i\omega_0} z^{-1}} .$$

We arrive at

$$X(z) = \frac{\sin(\omega_0) z^{-1}}{1 - 2\cos(\omega_0) z^{-1} + z^{-2}}, \qquad |z^{-1}| < 1 .$$

Example 5. Similarly for

$$x(n) = \cos(n\omega_0) u(n)$$

we find

$$X(z) = \frac{1 - \cos(\omega_0) z^{-1}}{1 - 2\cos(\omega_0) z^{-1} + z^{-2}}, \qquad |z^{-1}| < 1$$

where we used the Euler identity

$$\cos(\alpha) \equiv \frac{e^{i\alpha} + e^{-i\alpha}}{2} .$$

Example 6. For

$$h(n) = r^n \cos(n\omega_0) u(n)$$

we find

$$H(z) = \frac{1 - r\cos(\omega_0) z^{-1}}{1 - 2r\cos(\omega_0) z^{-1} + r^2 z^{-2}} .$$

Example 7. For

$$h(n) = r^n \sin(n\omega_0) u(n)$$

we find

$$H(z) = \frac{r\sin(\omega_0) z^{-1}}{1 - 2r\cos(\omega_0) z^{-1} + r^2 z^{-2}} .$$

As an exercise show that z-transform of $nu(n)$ is given by $z/(z-1)^2$.

8.3 Radius of Convergence

The z-transform does not necessarily exist for all values of z in the complex plane. For the z-transform to exist, the summation must converge. Therefore, the z-transform is defined where it exists. The region of convergence of the z-transform is the range of values of z for which $X(z)$ is finite.

Example 1. Let

$$x(n) := \begin{cases} a^n & \text{for} \quad n = 0, 1, 2, \ldots \\ 0 & \text{otherwise} \end{cases}$$

Then

$$X(z) = \sum_{n=-\infty}^{\infty} x(n)z^{-n} = \sum_{n=0}^{\infty} a^n z^{-n} = \sum_{n=0}^{\infty} (az^{-1})^n .$$

This is a geometric series which converges to

$$X(z) = \frac{1}{1 - az^{-1}} = \frac{z}{z - a}$$

for

$$|az^{-1}| < 1 .$$

This means $|z| > |a|$. Thus the radius of convergence includes all values of z with magnitude greater than $|a|$, i.e. all values outside a circle of radius $|a|$ in the z-plane.

Example 2. Let

$$x(n) := \begin{cases} b^n & \text{for} \quad n = 0, -1, -2, \ldots \\ 0 & \text{otherwise} \end{cases}$$

Then

$$X(z) = \sum_{n=-\infty}^{\infty} x(n)z^{-n} = \sum_{n=-\infty}^{0} b^n z^{-n} = \sum_{n=0}^{\infty} (b^{-1}z)^n .$$

This is a geometric series which converges to

$$X(z) = \frac{1}{1 - b^{-1}z} = \frac{b}{b - z}$$

for

$$|b^{-1}z| < 1 .$$

This means $|z| < |b|$. Thus the radius of convergence lies inside a circle of radius $|b|$ in the complex plane.

Example 3. Let
$$x(n) = a^n u(n) - b^n u(-n - 1)$$

where $|a| < 1$ and $|b| > 1$. Then

$$X(z) = \sum_{n=0}^{\infty} a^n z^{-n} - \sum_{n=-\infty}^{-1} b^n z^{-n} = \sum_{n=0}^{\infty} a^n z^{-n} - \sum_{m=0}^{\infty} b^{-m} z^m + 1 .$$

It follows that

$$X(z) = \frac{1}{1 - az^{-1}} - \frac{1}{1 - b^{-1}z} + 1 = \frac{1}{1 - az^{-1}} + \frac{1}{1 - bz^{-1}} .$$

The radius of convergence is $|a| < |z|$ and $|z| < |b|$.

Example 4. Radius of convergence for finite series

$$X(z) := \begin{cases} \sum_{n=0}^{M_1} x(n)z^{-n} & \text{right side} \\ \sum_{n=0}^{M_2} x(n)z^{-n} & \text{left side} \end{cases}$$

The series converges everywhere except $z = 0$ and/or $z = \infty$.

8.4 Properties of the z-Transform

The z-transform has the following properties:

Linearity

$$w(n) = ax(n) + by(n) \Rightarrow W(z) = aX(z) + bY(z)$$

where

$$ROC_x \cap ROC_y \subset ROC_w \,.$$

Notice that it may not be $ROC_w = ROC_x \cap ROC_y$ since poles may be cancelled in the summation. The proof is as follows

$$Z(ax(n) + by(n)) = \sum_{n=0}^{\infty} (ax(n) + by(n))z^{-n}$$

$$= a\sum_{n=0}^{\infty} x(n)z^{-n} + b\sum_{n=0}^{\infty} y(n))z^{-n}$$

$$= aZ(x(n)) + bZ(y(n)) \,.$$

Example. Let

$$x(n) = (4a^n + 3)u(n) \,.$$

Then

$$X(z) = 4Z(a^n u(n)) + 3Z(u(n)) = 4\frac{1}{1 - az^{-1}} + 3\frac{1}{1 - z^{-1}} \,.$$

Delay/Advance

$$w(n) = x(n - d) \Rightarrow W(z) = z^{-d}X(z)$$
$$w(n) = x(n + d) \Rightarrow W(z) = z^{d}X(z) \,.$$

The proof is as follows. We have

$$Z(x(n - m)) = \sum_{n=0}^{\infty} x(n - m)z^{-n} \,.$$

The index of summation can be changed such that when n is replaced by $n + m$, we find

$$Z(x(n - m)) = \sum_{n=0}^{\infty} x(n - m)z^{-n} = z^{-m} \sum_{n=0}^{\infty} x(n)z^{-n} .$$

Thus

$$Z(x(n - m)) = z^{-m}X(z) .$$

Example. Given the sequence

$$x(0) = 0, \quad x(1) = 0, \quad x(2) = 1, \quad x(3) = 2, \quad x(4) = 1$$

with $x(n) = 0$ otherwise. Then

$$X(z) = z^{-2}(1 + 2z^{-1} + z^{-2}) .$$

Multiplication by an Exponential

$$w(n) = a^n x(n) \rightarrow W(z) = X(a^{-1}z) .$$

The proof is as follows. We have

$$Z(a^n x(n)) = \sum_{n=-\infty}^{\infty} a^n x(n)z^{-n} = \sum_{n=-\infty}^{\infty} x(n)(a^{-1}z)^{-n} .$$

The last expression is the z-transform of $x(n)$ with z replaced by $a^{-1}z$. Therefore

$$Z(a^n x(n)) = X(a^{-1}z) .$$

Example. Let

$$x(n) = 2u(n) \rightarrow X(z) = \frac{2}{1 - z^{-1}} .$$

Then

$$x(n) = 2a^n u(n) \rightarrow X(z) = \frac{2}{1 - (z/a)^{-1}} = \frac{2}{1 - az^{-1}} .$$

Convolution

$$w(n) = x(n) * y(n) \rightarrow W(z) = X(z)Y(z)$$

The proof uses the Cauchy sum formula

$$(\sum_{n=0}^{\infty} x(n)z^{-n})(\sum_{n=0}^{\infty} x(n)z^{-n}) = \sum_{n=0}^{\infty}(\sum_{k=0}^{n} x(k)y(n - k))z^{-n}$$

$$= \sum_{n=0}^{\infty}(\sum_{k=0}^{n} x(n - k)y(k))z^{-n} .$$

Analogously we have the theorem for the bilateral z-transform.

Example. Let $H(z) = 1 + z^{-1}$ and the input sequence is

$$X(z) = 1 + 2z^{-1} + z^{-2}.$$

Then the output sequence is

$$(1 + z^{-1})(1 + 2z^{-1} + z^{-2}) = 1 + 3z^{-1} + 3z^{-2} + z^{-3}.$$

Example. Let

$$x(n) = a^n u(n)$$

and

$$y(n) = \delta(n) - b\delta(n - 1)$$

and $w(n) = x(n) * y(n)$. Then

$$X(z) = \frac{1}{1 - az^{-1}}, \qquad |z| > |a|$$
$$Y(z) = 1 - bz^{-1}, \qquad |z| > 0$$

and therefore

$$W(z) = \frac{1 - bz^{-1}}{1 - az^{-1}}, \qquad |z| > |a|.$$

Multiplication of Sequence

$$w(n) = x(n)y(n) \rightarrow W(z) = \frac{1}{2\pi i} \oint \frac{Y(z/v)X(v)}{v} dv.$$

Complex Conjugation

$$y(n) = x^*(n) \rightarrow Y(z) = X^*(z^*).$$

Differentiation of the z-transform

Differentiating the one-sided z-transform and multiplying by $1/z$ gives

$$z^{-1}\frac{dX}{dz^{-1}} = z^{-1}\sum_{n=0}^{\infty} nx(n)(z^{-1})^{n-1} = \sum_{n=0}^{\infty} nx(n)z^{-n}.$$

Therefore

$$Z(nx(n)) = z^{-1}\frac{dX}{dz^{-1}}.$$

Initial value theorem (only if $x(n)$ is causal)

$$x(0) = \lim_{z \to \infty} X(z).$$

Example. Let

$$\frac{1}{1 - az^{-1}} \Leftrightarrow a^n u(n).$$

Then

$$\lim_{z \to \infty} \frac{1}{1 - az^{-1}} = 1$$
$$a^n u(n)|_{n=0} = 1.$$

Final value theorem

It only applies if ROC includes all points $|z| > 1$ and all poles of $(z-1)X(z)$ are inside the unit circle. Then

$$\lim_{n \to \infty} x(n) = \lim_{z \to 1} (z - 1)X(z).$$

8.5   Poles and Zeros

For a given linear time-invariant system, the z-transform of the impulse response, $h(n)$, is called the transfer function and denoted by $H(z)$. It is often useful to factorize the transfer function, $H(z)$, into a product of sums

$$H(z) = \frac{N(z)}{D(z)} = k\frac{\prod_{i=1}^{M}(1 - z_i z^{-1})}{\prod_{j=1}^{N}(1 - p_j z^{-1})} = k\frac{(1 - z_1 z^{-1})(1 - z_2 z^{-1})\cdots}{(1 - p_1 z^{-1})(1 - p_2 z^{-1})\cdots}.$$

The *zeros* of $H(z)$ are the values of z for which

$$N(z) = 0.$$

The *poles* of $H(z)$ are the values of z for which

$$D(z) = 0.$$

Example. Consider

$$H(z) = \frac{(z - 2)(z + 1)}{z}.$$

The poles are given by $z = 0$ and the zeros are given by $z = 2$, $z = -1$.

Example. Consider

$$H(z) = \frac{1 + 3z^{-1} + 2z^{-2}}{1 - z^{-1} - 12z^{-2}}.$$

The numerator and the denominator can be factorized providing

$$H(z) = \frac{(1 + z^{-1})(1 + 2z^{-1})}{(1 + 3z^{-1})(1 - 4z^{-1})}.$$

Thus the zeros are $z = -1$ and $z = -2$ and the poles are $z = -3$ and $z = 4$.

8.6 Inverse z-Transform

One method to find the inverse z-transform was already introduced in section 7.1 using integration in the complex plane. If the function $X(z)$ is available as a power series in z^{-n} then its inverse can be found by inspection.

Example. Let

$$X(z) = 1 + 2z^{-1} - z^{-2} + 3z^{-3}.$$

Then

$$x(n) = \{\, 1,\, 2,\, -1,\, 3 \,\}.$$

In many cases the function $X(z)$ is the ratio of two polynomials. Other methods are polynomial division and partial fraction expansion.

One very useful method of solving the inverse z-transform is by taking partial fractions of $X(z)$. Each partial fraction will hopefully be in a form where simply looking up the table of z-transforms will give the time domain sequence. To find out the poles and zeros of a rational polynomial, factor

$$X(z) = \frac{(z - z_1)(z - z_2) \cdots (z - z_m)}{(z - p_1)(z - p_2) \cdots (z - p_n)}$$

and write it as

$$X(z) = \frac{A_1}{z - p_1} + \frac{A_2}{z - p_2} + \cdots + \frac{A_n}{z - p_n}$$

where $m < n$.

Example. Let

$$X(z) = \frac{z}{(z - 2)(z - 1)}.$$

From

$$X(z) = \frac{A_1}{z - 2} + \frac{A_2}{z - 1}$$

we obtain $A_1 = 2$ and $A_2 = -1$. Therefore

$$X(z) = \frac{2}{z - 2} - \frac{1}{z - 1}.$$

Both of these terms can be found from tables for z-transform. We find

$$x(n) = 2^n u(n-1) - u(n-1) \,.$$

8.7 Linear Difference Equations

The z-transform can be used to solve linear difference equations.

Example 1. Consider the following linear difference equation

$$x(n+2) + 3x(n+1) + 2x(n) = 0, \qquad x(0) = 0, \quad x(1) = 1 \,.$$

The z-transform of $x(n+2)$, $x(n+1)$ and $x(n)$ are given by

$$Z(x(n+2)) = z^2 X(z) - z^2 x(0) - zx(1)$$
$$Z(x(n+1)) = zX(z) - zx(0)$$
$$Z(x(n)) = X(z) \,.$$

Taking the z-transform of both sides of the given linear difference equation, we obtain

$$z^2 X(z) - z^2 x(0) - zx(1) + 3zX(z) - 3zx(0) + 2X(z) = 0 \,.$$

Inserting the initial conditions $x(0) = 0$ and $x(1) = 1$ yields

$$z^2 X(z) - z + 3zX(z) + 2X(z) = 0 \,.$$

Solving with respect to $X(z)$ gives

$$X(z) = \frac{z}{z^2 + 3z + 2} = \frac{z}{(z+1)(z+2)} \,.$$

Thus

$$X(z) = \frac{z}{z+1} - \frac{z}{z+2} = \frac{1}{1+z^{-1}} - \frac{1}{1+2z^{-1}} \,.$$

Since

$$Z(a^n) = \frac{1}{1-az^{-1}}$$

we obtain for the solution of the linear difference equation

$$x(n) = (-1)^n - (-2)^n \,.$$

Example 2. Consider the following linear difference equation

$$x(n+2) - 3x(n+1) + 2x(n) = u(n)$$

where

$$x(n) = 0 \quad \text{for } n \leq 0,$$
$$u(0) = 1$$
$$u(n) = 0 \quad \text{for } n > 0 \text{ and } n < 0.$$

Inserting $n = -1$ into the linear difference equation and using these conditions we find

$$x(1) = 0.$$

Taking the z-transform of the linear difference equation together with the initial conditions $x(0) = 0$, $x(1) = 0$, we find

$$(z^2 - 3z + 2)X(z) = U(z).$$

Since

$$U(z) = \sum_{n=0}^{\infty} z^{-n}$$

we have $U(z) = 1$. Thus

$$X(z) = \frac{1}{z^2 - 3z + 2} = \frac{-1}{z - 1} + \frac{1}{z - 2}.$$

Using the relationship

$$Z(x(n+1)) = zX(z) - zx(0) = zX(z)$$

where we used $x(0) = 0$ we obtain

$$Z(x(n+1)) = zX(z) = -\frac{z}{z-1} + \frac{z}{z-2} = -\frac{1}{1-z^{-1}} + \frac{1}{1-2z^{-1}}.$$

Since

$$Z(1^n) = \frac{1}{1 - z^{-1}}, \qquad Z(2^n) = \frac{1}{1 - 2z^{-1}}$$

we obtain the solution of the difference equation

$$x(n+1) = -1 + 2^n, \qquad n = 0, 1, 2, \ldots$$

8.8 z-Transform and System Function

The linear system acts through the z-transform of its unit-sample response $h(n)$, or its system function $H(z)$. The z-transform of the output $Y(z)$ is called the *response function*, while that of the input $X(z)$ is the *excitation transform*. In other words, the response transform is equal to the product of the excitation transform and the system function. As mentioned above the system function is defined as the z-transform of the unit-sample response. We can also determine the system function in terms of the coefficients in the linear difference equation. The finite order difference equation describing the linear time-invariant system is given by (see chapter 2)

$$y(n) = \sum_{k=1}^{M} a_k y(n-k) + \sum_{k=-N_F}^{N_P} b_k x(n-k).$$

Taking the z-transform of the output sequence, we have

$$Y(z) = \sum_{n=-\infty}^{\infty} y(n) z^{-n} = \sum_{n=-\infty}^{\infty} \left[\sum_{k=1}^{M} a_k y(n-k) + \sum_{k=-N_F}^{N_P} b_k x(n-k) \right] z^{-n}.$$

Changing the order of summation, we obtain

$$Y(z) = \sum_{k=1}^{M} a_k \left[\sum_{n=-\infty}^{\infty} y(n-k) z^{-n} \right] + \sum_{k=-N_F}^{N_P} b_k \left[\sum_{n=-\infty}^{\infty} x(n-k) z^{-n} \right].$$

Applying the relation for the z-transform of a delayed sequence, we have

$$Y(z) = \sum_{k=1}^{M} a_k z^{-k} Y(z) + \sum_{k=-N_F}^{N_P} b_k z^{-k} X(z).$$

Since $Y(z)$ and $X(z)$ do not depend on k, they can be factored out to give

$$Y(z) \left(1 - \sum_{k=1}^{M} a_k z^{-k} \right) = X(z) \sum_{k=-N_F}^{N_P} b_k z^{-k}.$$

Applying the definition for the system function $H(z)$ we find

$$H(z) = \frac{Y(z)}{X(z)} = \frac{\sum_{k=-N_F}^{N_P} b_k z^{-k}}{1 - \sum_{k=1}^{M} a_k z^{-k}}.$$

The numerator allows both positive and negative exponent values of z, corresponding to future and past values of the input. The denominator, however, does not contain positive exponent values, indicating that only current and past values of the output are accessible.

Example. For the three-sample averager, the difference equation is

$$y(n) = \frac{1}{3}(x(n+1) + x(n) + x(n-1)).$$

Taking the z-transform, we have

$$Y(z) = \frac{1}{3}(zX(z) + X(z) + z^{-1}X(z)).$$

The system function is then

$$H(z) = \frac{Y(z)}{X(z)} = \frac{z}{3} + \frac{1}{3} + \frac{1}{3}z^{-1}.$$

8.9 An Application

In tone generation one outputs samples of a sinusoidal waveform to the *pulse width modulation* module at the system sampling rate. This method is relatively simple but is limited to single tones and may require large amounts of memory depending on the number of samples used per cycle of the waveform and the number of tones that need to be generated. A more efficient method of generating both single and dual-tones signals is to use a difference equation that is derived from the z-transform of a sinusoid as follows. The z-transform of a sinusoid is

$$H(z) = \frac{z^{-1}\sin(\omega T)}{1 - 2z^{-1}\cos(\omega T) + z^{-2}}$$

where the period $\omega = 2\pi f$ and $T = 1/f_s$ is the sampling period. If this is interpreted as the transfer function

$$H(z) = \frac{Y(z)}{X(z)}$$

then the difference equation can be found taking the inverse z-transform and applying the associated shift theorem as follows. Since

$$\frac{Y(z)}{X(z)} = \frac{z^{-1}\sin(\omega T)}{1 - 2z^{-1}\cos(\omega T) + z^{-2}}$$

we obtain

$$Y(z)(1 - 2z^{-1}\cos(\omega T) + z^{-2}) = X(z)z^{-1}\sin(\omega T).$$

Thus

$$Y(z) = z^{-1}X(z)\sin(\omega T) + 2z^{-1}Y(z)\cos(\omega T) - z^{-2}Y(z).$$

Taking the inverse z-transform of this equation we find

$$y(n) = (\sin(\omega T))x(n-1) + 2(\cos(\omega T))y(n-1) - y(n-2).$$

If we set
$$a := \sin(\omega T), \qquad b := \cos(\omega T)$$
the linear difference equation can be written

$$y(n) = ax(n-1) + 2by(n-1) - y(n-2)$$

where $n = 1, 2, \ldots$ and a and b are constant coefficients. If we input an impulse to the system

$$x(n) := \begin{cases} 1 & \text{for} \quad n = 0 \\ 0 \, \text{otherwise} \end{cases}$$

then the output of the system will be a discrete-time sinusoidal sequence. We set for the initial values of y

$$y(0) = 0, \quad y(-1) = 0\,.$$

Thus we obtain $y(1) = a$ and

$$y(n) = 2by(n-1) - y(n-2)$$

for $n = 2, 3, \ldots$. For example, if the sampling rate is

$$f_s = 8\text{kHz}$$

$(T = 1/f_s)$ and the tone frequency is

$$f = 800\text{Hz}$$

and since $\omega = 2\pi f$ we have

$$a := \sin(\omega T) = \sin(2\pi 0.8/8) = \sin(2\pi 0.1) \approx 0.58778$$
$$b := \cos(\omega T) = \cos(2\pi 0.8/8) = \cos(2\pi 0.1) \approx 0.80901\,.$$

Pulse width modulation is a technique to provide an output logic 1 for a period of time and a logic 0 for the balance of time. Pulse Width Modulation is a modulation in which the duration of pulses is varied in accordance with some characteristic of the modulating signal. Pulse Width Modulation is also called pulse duration modulation or pulse length modulation. Pulse Width Modulation is used in diverse areas such as controlling the speed of DC motors, and the analog transition of digital audio using the 1-bit DAC of a CD player.

Chapter 9

Discrete Hidden Markov Processes

9.1 Introduction

A *Markov chain* is a finite state machine with probabilities for each transition, that is, a probability that the next state is s_j given that the current state is s_i. Equivalently, a Markov chain is described by a weighted, directed graph in which the weights correspond to the probability of that transition. In other words, the weights are nonnegative and the total weight of the outgoing edges is positive. If the weights are normalised, the total weight, including self-loops is 1.

The *hidden Markov model* ([47], [48], [11]) is a finite state machine with probabilities for each transition, that is, a probability that the next state is s_j given that the current state is s_i. The states are not directly observable. Instead, each state produces one of the observable outputs with certain probability.

Computing a model given sets of sequences of observed outputs is very difficult, since the states are not directly observable and transitions are probabilistic. Although the states cannot, by definition, be directly observed, the most likely sequence of sets for a given sequence of observed outputs can be computed in $O(nT)$, where n is the number of states and T is the length of the sequence. Thus a hidden Markov model is a Markov chain, where each state generates an observation. We only see the observations, and the goal is to infer the hidden state sequence.

Hidden Markov models are very useful for time-series modelling, since the discrete state-space can be used to approximate many non-linear, non-Gaussian systems.

In a statistical framework, an inventory of elementary probabilistic models of basic linguistic units (e.g., phonemes) is used to build word representations. A sequence of acoustic parameters, extracted from a spoken utterance, is seen as a realization of a concatenation of elementary processes described by hidden Markov models.

A hidden Markov model is a composition of two stochastic processes, a hidden Markov chain, which accounts for temporal variability, and an observable process, which accounts for spectral variability. This combination has proven to be powerful enough to cope with the most important sources of speech ambiguity, and flexible enough to allow the realization of recognition systems with dictionaries of hundred of thousands of words.

Applications of the hidden Markov model are

in mobile robots, where

$$\text{states} = \text{location}, \qquad \text{observations} = \text{sensor input}$$

in biological sequencing

$$\text{states} = \text{protein structure}, \qquad \text{observations} = \text{amino acids}$$

In biological sequencing the objective of the algorithm is: Given the structure of a protein, such as insulin, find the amino acids that make up that protein. There are 20 amino acids.

in speech recognition

$$\text{states} = \text{phonemes}, \qquad \text{observations} = \text{acoustic signal}$$

Given a speech signal, find the most probable sequence of words

$$\text{words} = \text{argmax} P(\text{words—speech})$$

Two formal assumptions characterize hidden Markov models as used in speech recognition. The first-order Markov hypothesis states that history has no influence on the chain's future evolution if the present is specified, and the output independence hypothesis states that neither chain evolution nor past observation influences the present observation if the last chain transition is specified.

In general, there are many different possible sequences:

```
an ice cream
and nice cream
and nice scream
```

A statistical language model can be used to choose the most probable interpretation:

assign probabilities to all possible sequences of words

select most probable sequence from those proposed by the speech analyser

In the contemporary speech research community, the hidden Markov model is a dominant tool used to model a speech utterance. The utterance to be modeled may be a phone, a syllable, a word, or, in principle, an intact sentence or entire paragraph. In small vocabulary systems, the hidden Markov model tends to be used to model words, whereas in a large vocabulary conversational speech recognition system the hidden Markov model is usually used to model sub-word units such as phones or syllables. There are two major tasks involved in a typical automatic speech recognition system.

First, given a series of training observations and their associated transcriptions, how do we estimate the parameters of the hidden Markov models which represent the words or phones covered in the transcriptions? Second, given a set of trained hidden Markov models and an input speech observation sequence, how do we find the maximum likelihood of this observation sequence and the corresponding set of hidden Markov models which produce this maximum value? This is the speech recognition problem.

We first introduce Markov chains and then, as an extension, hidden Markov processes.

9.2 Markov Chains

In this section we introduce Markov chains and give a number of examples. First we introduce some definitions.

Definition. A vector $\mathbf{p} = (p_0, p_1, \ldots, p_{N-1})$ is called a *probability vector* if the components are nonnegative and their sum is 1, i.e.,

$$\sum_{j=0}^{N-1} p_j = 1 \,.$$

Example 1. The vector

$$\mathbf{p} = (1/4, 1/8, 0, 5/8)$$

is a probability vector.

Example 2. The nonzero vector $(2, 3, 5, 0, 1)$ is not a probability vector. However since all numbers are nonnegative it can be normalised to get a probability vector. Since the sum of the components is equal to 11 we obtain the probability vector

$$\mathbf{p} = (2/11, 3/11, 5/11, 0, 1/11).$$

Definition. An $N \times N$ square matrix $A = (a_{ij})$ is called a *stochastic matrix* if each of its rows is a probability vector, i.e. if each entry of A is nonnegative and the sum of the entries in each row is 1.

Example. The following matrix is a stochastic matrix

$$A = \begin{pmatrix} 0 & 1 & 0 & 0 \\ 1/2 & 1/6 & 1/3 & 0 \\ 0 & 1/3 & 0 & 2/3 \\ 1/4 & 1/4 & 1/4 & 1/4 \end{pmatrix}.$$

We can easily prove that if A_1 and A_2 are stochastic matrices, then the matrix product $A_1 A_2$ is also a stochastic matrix. Furthermore $A_1 \otimes A_2$ is also a $(N^2 \times N^2)$ stochastic matrix, where $\otimes$ denotes the *Kronecker product*.

Definition. A stochastic matrix A is called *regular* if all the entries of some power A^n are positive.

Example 1. The stochastic matrix

$$A = \begin{pmatrix} 0 & 1 \\ 1/2 & 1/2 \end{pmatrix}$$

is regular since

$$A^2 = \begin{pmatrix} 1/2 & 1/2 \\ 1/4 & 3/4 \end{pmatrix}$$

is positive in every entry.

Example 2. The stochastic matrix

$$A = \begin{pmatrix} 1 & 0 \\ 1/2 & 1/2 \end{pmatrix}$$

is not regular since

$$A^2 = \begin{pmatrix} 1 & 0 \\ 3/4 & 1/4 \end{pmatrix}.$$

Definition. A *fixed point* **q** (row vector of length N) of a regular stochastic matrix A is defined by

$$\mathbf{q}A = \mathbf{q}.$$

Example. Consider the regular stochastic matrix

$$A = \begin{pmatrix} 0 & 1 & 0 \\ 0 & 0 & 1 \\ 1/2 & 1/2 & 0 \end{pmatrix}.$$

The vector **q** can be written as $\mathbf{q} = (x, y, 1 - x - y)$ with the constraints $x \in [0, 1]$ and $y \in [0, 1]$. Then the solution to the fixed point equation $\mathbf{q}A = \mathbf{q}$ is given by

$$\mathbf{q} = (1/5, 2/5, 2/5).$$

The fundamental property of regular stochastic matrices is contained in the following theorem.

Theorem. Let A be a regular stochastic matrix. Then

(i) A has a unique fixed probability vector **q**, and the components of **q** are all positive.

(ii) the sequence of matrices A, A^2, A^3, ... of powers of A approaches the matrix B whose rows are each the fixed point **q**.

(iii) if **p** is any probability vector, then the sequence of vectors

$$\mathbf{p}A, \ \mathbf{p}A^2, \ \mathbf{p}A^3, \ldots$$

approaches the fixed point **q**.

Next we consider *Markov chains*. We consider a sequence of trials whose outcome, say

$$o_0, o_1, o_2, \ldots, o_{T-1}$$

satisfy the following two properties:

(i) Each outcome belongs to a finite set of outcomes

$$\{ q_0, q_1, q_2, \ldots, q_{N-1} \}$$

called the *state space* of the system. If the outcome on the t-th trial is q_i, then we say that the system is in state q_i at time t or at the t-th step.

(ii) The outcome of any trial depends at most upon the outcome of the immediately preceding trial and not upon any other previous outcomes; with each pair of states (q_i, q_j) there is given the probability a_{ij} that q_j occurs immediately after q_i occurs.

Such a stochastic process is called a finite Markov chain. The numbers a_{ij}, called the *transition probabilities* can be arranged in the square $N \times N$ matrix

$$A = \begin{pmatrix} a_{00} & a_{01} & \cdots & a_{0N-1} \\ a_{10} & a_{11} & \cdots & a_{1N-1} \\ \cdots & \cdots & \ddots & \cdots \\ a_{N-10} & a_{N-11} & \cdots & a_{N-1N-1} \end{pmatrix}$$

called the *transition matrix*. The transition matrix A of a Markov chain is a stochastic matrix.

Example. A typical example of a Markov chain is a *random walk*. Given the set (state space)

$$\{\, 0,\, 1,\, 2,\, 3,\, 4,\, 5\,\}$$

where 0 is the origin and 5 the end point. A woman is at any of these points. She takes a unit step to the right with probability p or to the left with probability $q = 1 - p$, unless she is at the origin where she takes a step to the right to 1 or the point 5 where she takes a step to the left to 4. Let o_t denote her position after t steps. This is a Markov chain with the state space given by the set above. Thus 2 means that the woman is at the point 2. The transition matrix A is

$$A = \begin{pmatrix} 0 & 1 & 0 & 0 & 0 & 0 \\ q & 0 & p & 0 & 0 & 0 \\ 0 & q & 0 & p & 0 & 0 \\ 0 & 0 & q & 0 & p & 0 \\ 0 & 0 & 0 & q & 0 & p \\ 0 & 0 & 0 & 0 & 1 & 0 \end{pmatrix}.$$

Next we discuss the question: What is the probability, denoted by $a_{ij}^{(t)}$, that the system changes from the state q_i to the state q_j in exactly t steps? Let A be the transition matrix of a Markov chain process. Then the t-step transition matrix is equal to the t-th power of A; that is $A^{(t)} = A^t$. The $a_{ij}^{(t)}$ are the elements of the matrix $A^{(t)}$.

Example. Consider again the random walk problem discussed above. Suppose the woman starts at the point 2. To find the probability distribution after three steps we do the following calculation. Since

$$\mathbf{p}^{(0)} = (0, 0, 1, 0, 0, 0)$$

we find

$$
\begin{aligned}
\mathbf{p}^{(1)} &= \mathbf{p}^{(0)} A = (0, q, 0, p, 0, 0) \\
\mathbf{p}^{(2)} &= \mathbf{p}^{(1)} A = (q^2, 0, 2pq, 0, p^2, 0) \\
\mathbf{p}^{(3)} &= \mathbf{p}^{(2)} A = (0, q^2 + 2pq^2, 0, 3p^2q, 0, p^3) \,.
\end{aligned}
$$

Thus the probability after three steps to be at the point 1 is $q^2 + 2pq^2$. If $p = q = 1/2$ we obtain $1/2$. Notice that

$$
\mathbf{p}^{(3)} A \equiv \mathbf{p}^{(0)} A^3 \,.
$$

A state q_i of a Markov chain is called *absorbing* if the system remains in the state q_i once it enters there. Thus a state q_i is absorbing if and only if the i-th row of the transition matrix A has a 1 on the main diagonal and obviously zeros everywhere else in the row.

Example. Consider the following transition matrix

$$
A = \begin{pmatrix}
1/4 & 0 & 1/4 & 1/4 & 1/4 \\
0 & 1 & 0 & 0 & 0 \\
1/2 & 0 & 1/4 & 1/4 & 0 \\
0 & 1 & 0 & 0 & 0 \\
0 & 0 & 0 & 0 & 1
\end{pmatrix} \,.
$$

The states q_1 and q_4 are each absorbing (notice that we count from 0), since each of the second and fifth rows has a 1 on the main diagonal.

The transition probabilities of a Markov chain can be represented by a diagram, called the *transition diagram*, where a positive probability a_{ij} is denoted by an arrow from the state q_i to the state q_j.

9.3 Discrete Hidden Markov Processes

The following notation is used.

N is the number of states in the model. M is the total number of distinct observation symbols in the alphabet. If the observations are continuous then M is infinite. We only consider the case for M finite. T is the length of the sequence of observations (training set), where

$$
t = 0, 1, \ldots, T - 1 \,.
$$

Thus there exist N^T possible state sequences.

Let
$$\Omega_q := \{ q_0, q_1, \ldots, q_{N-1} \}$$
be the finite set of possible states. Let
$$V := \{ v_0, v_1, \ldots, v_{M-1} \}$$
be the finite set of possible observation symbols.

q_t is the random variable denoting the state at time t (state variable).

o_t is the random variable denoting the observation at time t (output variable).

$O = (o_0, o_1, \ldots, o_{T-1})$ is the sequence of actual observations.

The set of state transition probabilities is $A = (a_{ij})$, where $i, j = 0, 1, \ldots, N-1$
$$a_{ij} = p(q_{t+1} = j | q_t = i)$$
where p is the state-transition probability, i.e. the probability of being in state j at time $t + 1$ given that we were in state i at time t. We assume that the a_{ij}'s are independent of time t. Obviously we have the conditions

$$a_{ij} \geq 0 \quad \text{for} \quad i, j = 0, 1, \ldots, N - 1$$

$$\sum_{j=0}^{N-1} a_{ij} = 1 \quad \text{for} \quad i = 0, 1, \ldots, N - 1.$$

Thus A is an $N \times N$ matrix.

Example. If we have six states, the transition matrix in speech recognition could look as follows
$$A = \begin{pmatrix} 0.3 & 0.5 & 0.2 & 0 & 0 & 0 \\ 0 & 0.4 & 0.3 & 0.3 & 0 & 0 \\ 0 & 0 & 0.4 & 0.2 & 0.4 & 0 \\ 0 & 0 & 0 & 0.7 & 0.2 & 0.1 \\ 0 & 0 & 0 & 0 & 0.5 & 0.5 \\ 0 & 0 & 0 & 0 & 0 & 1.0 \end{pmatrix}.$$

The conditional probability distribution of the observation at time t, o_t, given the state j is
$$b_j(k) = p(o_t = v_k | q_t = j)$$
where $j \in \{0, 1, \ldots, N-1\}$ and $k \in \{0, 1, \ldots, M-1\}$, i.e. p is the probability of observing the symbol v_k given that we are in state j. Let $B := \{ b_j(k) \}$. We have
$$b_j(k) \geq 0$$

for $j \in \{0, 1, \ldots, N-1\}$ and $k \in \{0, 1, \ldots, M-1\}$ and

$$\sum_{k=0}^{M-1} b_j(k) = 1$$

for $j = 0, 1, \ldots, N-1$.

The initial state distribution $\pi = \{\pi_i\}$

$$\pi_i = p(q_0 = i)$$

where $i = 0, 1, \ldots, N-1$, i.e. π_i is the probability of being in state i at the beginning of the experiment ($t = 0$).

Thus we arrive at the definition:

A hidden Markov model (HMM) is a five-tuple (Ω_q, V, A, B, π).

Let $\lambda := (A, B, \pi)$ denote the parameters for a given hidden Markov model with fixed Ω_q and V.

The three problems for hidden Markov models are:

1) Given the observation sequence

$$O = (o_0, o_1, \ldots, o_{T-1})$$

and a model $\lambda = (A, B, \pi)$. Find $P(O|\lambda)$: the probability of the observations given the model.

2) Given the observation sequence

$$O = (o_0, o_1, \ldots, o_{T-1})$$

and a model $\lambda = (A, B, \pi)$. Find the most likely state sequence given the model and observations. In other words, given the model $\lambda = (A, B, \pi)$ how do we choose a state sequence $\mathbf{q} = (q_0, q_1, \ldots, q_{T-1})$ so that $P(O, \mathbf{q}|\lambda)$, the joint probability of the observation sequence $O = (o_0, o_1, \ldots, o_{T-1})$ and the state sequence given the model is maximised.

3) Adjust λ to maximise $P(O|\lambda)$. In other words how do we adjust the hidden Markov model parameters $\lambda = (A, B, \pi)$ so that $P(O|\lambda)$ (or $P(O, \mathbf{v}|\lambda)$) is maximised.

Example. As an example consider the Urn-and-Ball model. We assume that there are N urns (number of states) in a room. Within each urn is a number of coloured balls, for example

$$\{\, \text{red, blue, green, yellow, white, black}\,\}\,.$$

Thus the number M of possible observations is 6. The physical process for obtaining observations is as follows. Randomly we choose an initial urn. From this urn, a ball is chosen at random, and its colour is recorded as the observation. The ball is then replaced in the urn from which is was selected. A new urn is then selected according to the random selection procedure associated with the current urn (thus there is a probability that the same urn is selected again), and the ball selection is repeated. This process generates a finite observation sequence of colours, which we would like to model as the observable output of a discrete hidden Markov model. For example

$$O = (\text{blue, green, red, red, white, black, blue, yellow})\,.$$

Thus the number of observation is $T = 8$. It is obvious that the simplest hidden Markov model that corresponds to the urn-and-ball process is one in which each state corresponds to a specific urn, and for which a ball colour probability is defined for each state. The choice of urns is dictated by the state-transition matrix of the discrete hidden Markov model. Note that the ball colours in each urn may be the same, and the distinction among various urns is in the way the collection of coloured balls is composed. Therefore, an isolated observation of a particular colour ball does not tell which urn it is drawn from.

Example. We consider a discrete hidden Markov model representation of a coin-tossing experiment. Thus we have $M = 2$. We assume that the number of states is $N = 3$ corresponding to three different coins. The probabilities are

```
          state 0    state 1    state 2
====================================
P(Head)    0.5        0.75       0.25
P(Tail)    0.5        0.25       0.75
====================================
```

We set `Head = 0` and `Tail = 1`. Thus

$$b_0(0) = 0.5, \qquad b_1(0) = 0.75, \qquad b_2(0) = 0.25$$

$$b_0(1) = 0.5, \qquad b_1(1) = 0.25, \qquad b_2(1) = 0.75\,.$$

Assume that all state-transition probabilities are 1/3 and assume the initial state probability of 1/3. Assume we observe the sequence ($T = 10$)

$$O = (H, H, H, H, T, H, T, T, T, T).$$

Since all state transitions are equiprobable, the most likely state sequence is the one for which the probability of each individual observation is a maximum. Thus for each Head, the most likely state is 1 and for each Tail the most likely state is 2. Consequently the most likely state sequence is

$$\mathbf{q} = (1, 1, 1, 1, 2, 1, 2, 2, 2, 2).$$

The probability of O and $\mathbf{q}$ given the model is

$$P(O, \mathbf{q}|\lambda) = (0.75)^{10} \left(\frac{1}{3}\right)^{10}.$$

Next we calculate the probability that the observation came completely from state 0, i.e.

$$\hat{\mathbf{q}} = (0, 0, 0, 0, 0, 0, 0, 0, 0, 0).$$

Then

$$P(O, \hat{\mathbf{q}}|\lambda) = (0.50)^{10} \left(\frac{1}{3}\right)^{10}.$$

The ratio R of $P(O, \mathbf{q}|\lambda)$ to $P(O, \hat{\mathbf{q}}|\lambda)$ is given by

$$R = \frac{P(O, \mathbf{q}|\lambda)}{P(O, \hat{\mathbf{q}}|\lambda)} = \left(\frac{3}{2}\right)^{10} = 57.67.$$

Thus the state sequence $\mathbf{q}$ is much more likely than the state sequence $\hat{\mathbf{q}}$.

9.4 Forward-Backward Algorithm

Given the model $\lambda = (A, B, \pi)$. How do we calculate $P(O|\lambda)$, the probability of occurrence of the observation sequence

$$O = (o_0, o_1, \ldots, o_{T-1})?$$

The most straightforward way to find $P(O|\lambda)$ is to find $P(O|\mathbf{q}, \lambda)$ for a fixed state sequence. Then we multiply it by $P(\mathbf{q}|\lambda)$ and then sum up over all possible state sequences. We have

$$P(O|\mathbf{q}, \lambda) = \prod_{t=0}^{T-1} P(o_t|q_t, \lambda)$$

where we have assumed statistical independence of observations. Thus we find

$$P(O|\mathbf{q}, \lambda) = b_{q_0}(o_0)b_{q_1}(o_1)\ldots b_{q_{T-1}}(o_{T-1}) \, .$$

The probability of such a state sequence $\mathbf{q}$ can be written as

$$P(\mathbf{q}|\lambda) = \pi_{q_0} a_{q_0 q_1} a_{q_1 q_2} \ldots a_{q_{T-2} q_{T-1}} \, .$$

The joint probability of O and $\mathbf{q}$, i.e., the probability that O and $\mathbf{q}$ occur simultaneously, is simply the product of the above two expressions, i.e.

$$P(O, \mathbf{q}|\lambda) = P(O|\mathbf{q}, \lambda)P(\mathbf{q}|\lambda) \, .$$

The probability of O (given the model) is obtained by summing this joint probability over all possible state sequences $\mathbf{q}$. Thus

$$P(O|\lambda) = \sum_{\text{all } \mathbf{q}} P(O|\mathbf{q}, \lambda)P(\mathbf{q}|\lambda) \, .$$

Thus we find

$$P(O|\lambda) = \sum_{q_0, q_1, \ldots, q_{T-1}} \pi_{q_0} b_{q_0}(o_0) a_{q_0 q_1} b_{q_1}(o_1) \ldots a_{q_{T-2} q_{T-1}} b_{q_{T-1}}(o_{T-1}) \, .$$

The interpretation of the computation is as follows. At time $t = 0$ we are in state q_0 with probability π_{q_0} and generate the symbol o_0 (in this state) with probability $b_{q_0}(o_0)$. The time is incremented by 1 (i.e. $t = 1$) and we make a transition to state q_1 from state q_0 with probability $a_{q_0 q_1}$ and generate symbol o_1 with probability $b_{q_1}(o_1)$. This process continues in this manner until we make the last transition (at time $T - 1$) from state q_{T-2} to state q_{T-1} with probability $a_{q_{T-2} q_{T-1}}$ and generate symbol o_{T-1} with probability $b_{q_{T-1}}(o_{T-1})$.

We see that the summand of this equation involves $2T - 1$ multiplications and there exists N^T distinct possible state sequences. Hence a direct computation of this equation will involve of the order of $2TN^T$ multiplications. Even for small numbers, for example $N = 5$ and $T = 100$, this means approximately 10^{72} multiplications.

Fortunately a much more efficient technique exists to solve problem 1. It is called *forward-backward procedure*.

The forward procedure is as follows. Consider the forward variable $\alpha_t(i)$ defined as

$$\alpha_t(i) := P(o_0 o_1 \ldots o_t, q_t = i|\lambda)$$

where $i = 0, 1, \ldots, N - 1$. Thus $\alpha_i(t)$ is the probability of the partial observation sequence up to time t and the state i at time t, given the model.

It can be shown that $\alpha_t(i)$ can be computed as follows:

Initialisation:
$$\alpha_0(i) = \pi_i b_i(o_0)$$

where $i = 0, 1, \ldots, N - 1$.

Recursion: For $t = 0, 1, \ldots, T - 2$ and $j = 0, 1, \ldots, N - 1$ we have

$$\alpha_{t+1}(j) = \left(\sum_{i=0}^{N-1} \alpha_t(i) a_{ij} \right) b_j(o_{t+1})$$

where $j = 0, 1, \ldots, N - 1$ and $t = 0, 1, \ldots, T - 2$.

Probability: We have

$$P(\mathbf{O}|\lambda) = \sum_{i=0}^{N-1} \alpha_{T-1}(i) \,.$$

The initialisation step involves N multiplications. In the recursion step the summation involves N multiplications plus one for the out of bracket $b_j(o_{t+1})$ term. This has to be done for $j = 0$ to $N - 1$ and $t = 0$ to $T - 2$, making the total number of multiplications in step 2, $(N-1)N(T+1)$. Step 3 involves no multiplications only summations. Thus the total number of multiplications is

$$N + N(N + 1)(T - 1)$$

i.e., of the order $N^2 T$ as compared to $2TN^T$ required for the direct method. For $N = 5$ and $T = 100$ we need about 3000 computations for the forward method as compared to 10^{72} required by the direct method - a saving of about 69 orders of magnitude.

The forward algorithm is implemented in the following Java program.

```
// Forward.java

public class Forward
{
    public static void main(String[] args)
    {
    int T = 10; // Number of observations
    int M = 2;  // number of observation symbols
    int N = 3;  // Number of states

    int[] obser = new int[T];
```

```
obser[0] = 0; obser[1] = 0; obser[2] = 0; obser[3] = 0;
obser[4] = 1; obser[5] = 0; obser[6] = 1; obser[7] = 1;
obser[8] = 1; obser[9] = 1;

double[][] b = new double[N][M];
b[0][0] = 0.5; b[1][0] = 0.75; b[2][0] = 0.25;
b[0][1] = 0.5; b[1][1] = 0.25; b[2][1] = 0.75;

double[][] A  = new double[N][N];
A[0][0] = 1.0/3.0; A[0][1] = 1.0/3.0; A[0][2] = 1.0/3.0;
A[1][0] = 1.0/3.0; A[1][1] = 1.0/3.0; A[1][2] = 1.0/3.0;
A[2][0] = 1.0/3.0; A[2][1] = 1.0/3.0; A[2][2] = 1.0/3.0;

double[] alphaold = new double[N];
double[] alphanew = new double[N];

// initialisation
int temp = obser[0];

for(int i=0;i<N;i++)
{ alphaold[i] = (1.0/3.0)*b[i][temp]; }

// iteration
for(int t=0;t<=T-2;t++)
{
temp = obser[t+1];
for(int j=0;j<N;j++)
{
double sum = 0.0;
for(int i=0;i<N;i++)
{
sum += alphaold[i]*A[i][j];
} // end for loop i
alphanew[j] = sum*b[j][temp];
} // end for loop j
for(int k=0;k<N;k++)
{
alphaold[k] = alphanew[k];
}
} // end for loop t

// probability
double P = 0.0;
for(int i=0;i<N;i++) { P += alphanew[i]; }
```

```
    System.out.println("P = " + P);
    } // end main
}
```

In a similar manner we may define a backward variable $\beta_t(i)$ as

$$\beta_t(i) := P(o_{t+1}o_{t+2}\ldots o_{T-1}, q_t = i|\lambda)$$

where $i = 0, 1, \ldots, N-1$. Thus $\beta_i(t)$ is the probability of the observation sequence from $t+1$ to $T-1$ given the state i at time t and the model λ. It can be shown that $\beta_t(i)$ can be computed as follows

$$\beta_{T-1}(i) = 1$$

where $i = 0, 1, \ldots, N-1$. For $t = T-2, T-1, \ldots, 1, 0$ and $i = 0, 1, \ldots, N-1$ we have

$$\beta_t(i) = \sum_{j=0}^{N-1} a_{ij} b_j(o_{t+1})\beta_{t+1}(j).$$

Thus

$$P(O|\lambda) = \sum_{i=0}^{N-1} \pi_i b_i(o_0)\beta_0(i).$$

The computation of $P(O|\lambda)$ using $\beta_t(i)$ also involves of the order of N^2T calculations. Hence both the forward and backward method are equally efficient for the computation of $P(O|\lambda)$.

9.5   Viterbi Algorithm

The Viterbi algorithm is an algorithm to compute the optimal (most likely) state sequence $(q_0, q_1, \ldots, q_{T-1})$ in a hidden Markov model given a sequence of observed outputs. In other words we have to find a state sequence such that the probability of occurrence of the observation sequence

$$(o_0, o_1, \ldots, o_{T-1})$$

from this state sequence is greater than that from any other state sequence. Thus our problem is to find $\mathbf{q}$ that will maximise $P(O, \mathbf{q}|\lambda)$.

In order to give an idea of the Viterbi algorithm, as applied to the optimum state estimation problem, a reformulation of the problem will be useful. Consider the expression for $P(O, \mathbf{q}|\lambda)$

$$\begin{aligned} P(O, \mathbf{q}|\lambda) &= P(O|\mathbf{q}, \lambda)P(\mathbf{q}|\lambda) \\ &= \pi_{q_0} b_{q_0}(o_0) a_{q_0 q_1} b_{q_1}(o_1) \ldots a_{q_{T-2}q_{T-1}} b_{q_{T-1}}(o_{T-1}). \end{aligned}$$

We define

$$U(q_0, q_1, \ldots, q_{T-1}) := -\left(\ln(\pi_{q_0} b_{q_0}(o_0)) + \sum_{t=1}^{T-1} \ln(a_{q_{t-1}q_t} b_{q_t}(o_t))\right).$$

It follows that

$$P(O, \mathbf{q}|\lambda) = \exp(-U(q_0, q_1, \ldots, q_{T-1})).$$

Consequently the problem of optimal state estimation, namely

$$\max_{q_t} P(O, q_0, q_1, \ldots, q_{T-1}|\lambda)$$

becomes equivalent to

$$\min_{q_t} U(q_0, q_1, \ldots, q_{T-1}).$$

This reformulation now enables us to view terms like

$$-\ln(a_{q_i q_j} b_{q_j}(o_t))$$

as the cost associated in going from state q_i to state q_j at time t.

The Viterbi algorithm to find the optimum state sequence can now be described as follows: Suppose we are currently in state i and we are considering going to state j next. We say that the weight on the path from state i to state j is

$$-\ln(a_{ij} b_j(o_t))$$

i.e., the negative of the logarithm of the probability of going from state i to state j and selecting the observation symbol o_t in state j. Here o_t is the observation symbol selected after visiting state j. This is the same symbol that appears in the observation sequence

$$O = (o_0, o_1, \ldots, o_{T-1}).$$

When the initial state is selected as state i the corresponding weight is

$$-\ln(\pi_i b_i(o_0)).$$

We call this the initial weight. We define the weight of a sequence of states as the sum of the weights on the adjacent states. This corresponds to multiplying the corresponding probabilities. Now finding the optimum sequence is merely a matter of finding the path (i.e. a sequence of states) of minimum weight through which the given observation sequence occurs.

9.6 Baum-Welch Algorithm

As described above the third problem in hidden Markov models deals with training the hidden Markov model such a way that if a observation sequence having many characteristics similar to the given one be encountered later it should be able to identify it. There are two methods that can be used:

The Segmental K-means Algorithm: In this method the parameters of the model $\lambda = (A, B, \pi)$ are adjusted to maximise $P(O, \mathbf{q}|\lambda)$, where $\mathbf{q}$ here is the optimum sequence as given by the solution to the problem 2.

Baum-Welch Algorithm: Here parameters of the model $\lambda = (A, B, \pi)$ are adjusted so as to increase $P(O|\lambda)$ until a maximum value is reached. As described before calculating $P(O|\lambda)$ involves summing up $P(O, \mathbf{q}|\lambda)$ over all possible state sequences.

9.7 Distances Between HMMs

If we want to compare two hidden Markov models then we need a measure of distance between two hidden Markov models. Such a measure is based on the *Kullback-Leibler distance* between two probability distribution function.

Let $\rho_1(x)$ and $\rho_2(x)$ be two probability density functions (or probability mass functions) then the Kullback-Leibler distance measure can be used to find out how close the two probability distributions are. The Kullback-Leibler distance measure is defined as follows:

Definition. The Kullback-Leibler distance measure $I(\rho_1, \rho_2)$ for determining how close the probability density function $\rho_2(x)$ is to $\rho_1(x)$ with respect to $\rho_1(x)$ is

$$I(\rho_1, \rho_2) := \int_{-\infty}^{\infty} \rho_1(x) \ln\left(\frac{\rho_1(x)}{\rho_2(x)}\right) dx.$$

If $\rho_1(x)$ and $\rho_2(x)$ are probability mass functions then

$$I(p_1, p_2) := \sum_{\text{all } x} \rho_1(x) \ln\left(\frac{\rho_1(x)}{\rho_2(x)}\right).$$

Note that the Kullback-Leibler distance measure is not symmetric

$$I(\rho_1, \rho_2) \neq I(\rho_2, \rho_1)$$

in general. If our objective is to simply compare ρ_1 and ρ_2 we can define a symmetric distance measure as

$$I_s(\rho_1, \rho_2) := \frac{1}{2}(I(\rho_1, \rho_2) + I(\rho_2, \rho_1)).$$

It is the use of the Kullback-Leibler distance measure which leads to the definition of the distance measure between two hidden Markov models. For hidden Markov models, the probability function is very complex, and practically it can be only computed via a recursive procedure - the forward/backward or upward/downward algorithm ([47]). Thus there is no simple closed form expression for the Kullback-Leibler distance for these models. Commonly, the Monte-Carlo method is used to numerically approximate the integral given above.

9.8   Application of HMMs

We look at some of the details of applying the HMM algorithms to speech recognition [48]. These include selecting the size of unit to model and connecting models together to make words and phrases.

A Hidden Markov Model is a statistical model of a sequence of feature vector observations. In building a recogniser with HMMs we need to decide what sequences will correspond to what models. In the very simplest case, each utterance could be assigned an HMM: for example, one HMM for each digit in a digit recognition task. To recognise an utterance, the probability metric according to each model is computed and the model with the best fit to the utterance is chosen. However, this approach is inflexible and requires that new models be trained if new words are to be added to the recogniser. A more general approach is to assign some kind of sub-word unit to each model and construct word and phrase models from these. The most obvious sub-word unit is the phoneme. If we assign each phoneme to an HMM we would need around 45 models for English; an additional model is also created for silence and background noise. Using this approach, a model for any word can be constructed by chaining together models for the component phonemes.

Each phoneme model will be made up of a number of states; the number of states per model is another design decision which needs to be made by the system designer. Each state in the model corresponds to some part of the input speech signal; we would like the feature vectors assigned to each state to be as uniform as possible so that the Gaussian model can be accurate. A common approach is to use three states for each phoneme model; intuitively this corresponds to one state for the transition into the phoneme, one for the middle part and one for the transition out of the phoneme. Similarly the topology of the model must be decided. The three states might be linked in a chain where transitions are only allowed to higher numbered states or to themselves. Alternatively each state might be all linked to all others, the so called ergodic model. These two structures are common but many other combinations are possible.

When phoneme based HMMs are being used, they must be concatenated to construct word or phrase HMMs. For example, an HMM for cat can be constructed from the phoneme HMMs for /k/ /a/ and /t/. If each phoneme HMM has three states the cat HMM will have nine states. Some words have alternate pronunciations and so their composite models will have a more complex structure to reflect these alternatives. An example might be a model for lives which has two alternatives for the pronunciation of 'i'.

While phoneme based models can be used to construct word models for any word they do not take into account any contextual variation in phoneme production. However we can use units larger than phonemes or use context dependent models. The most common solution is to use triphone models where there is one distinct phoneme model for every different left and right phoneme context. Thus there are different models for the /ai/ in /k-ai-t/ and in /h-ai-t/. Now, a word model is made up from the appropriate context dependant triphone models: 'cat' would be made up from the three models [/sil-k-a/ /k-a-t/ /a-t-sil/].

While the use of triphones solves the problem of context sensitivity it presents another problem. With around 45 phonemes in English there are $45^3 = 91125$ possible triphone models to train. Not all of these occur in speech due to phonotactic constraints. The problem of not having enough data to effectively train these models becomes important. One technique is state tying but another is to use only word internal triphones instead of the more general cross word triphones. Cross word triphones capture coarticulation effects across word boundaries which can be very important for continuous speech production. A word internal triphone model uses triphones only for word internal triples and diphones for word final phonemes; cat would become:

[sil /k-a/ /k-a-t/ /a-t/ sil]

This will clearly be less accurate for continuos speech modelling but the number of models required is smaller (none involve silence as a context) and so they can be more accurately trained on a given set of data.

There are many free parameters in an HMM. Fortunately, we can reduce the number to allow better training. We discuss two of them: state tying and diagonal covariance matrices.

A single HMM contains a number of free parameters whose values must be determined from training data. For a fully connected three state model there are nine transition probabilities plus the parameters (means and co-variance matrices) of three Gaussian models. If we use 24 input parameters (12 Mel-frequency cepstral coefficients plus 12 delta Mel-frequency cepstral coefficients) then the mean vector has 24 free parameters and the covariance matrix has $24^2 = 576$ free parameters making 609 in all. Multiply this by 45 phoneme models and there are 27,405 free parameters to estimate from training data; using context sensitive models there are many more. With this many free parameters, a very large amount of training data will be required to get reliable statistical estimates. In addition, it is unlikely that the training data will be distributed evenly so that some models in a triphone based recogniser will receive only a small number of training tokens while others will receive many.

One way of addressing this problem is to share states between triphone models. If the context sensitive triphone models consist of three states (for example) then we might assume that for all /i/ vowel models (/i/ in all contexts) the middle state might be very similar and so can be shared between all models. Similarly, the initial state might be shared between all /i/ models preceded by fricatives. Sharing states between models means that the Gaussian model associated with the state is trained on the data assigned to that state in both models: more data can be used to train each Gaussian making them more accurate. The limit of this kind of operation is to have all /i/ models share all states, in which case we have reduced the models to context insensitive models again. In practice, states are shared between a significant number of models based on phonetic similarity of the preceding and following contexts.

The covariance matrix associated with each Gaussian inside each state measures both the amount of variance along each dimension in the parameter space and the amount of co-variance between parameters. In two dimensions this co-variance gives us the orientation and 'stretch' of the ellipse shape. One simplification is to ignore the co-variance part of the matrix and only compute and use the individual dimension variances. In doing this we retain only the diagonal part of the co-variance matrix, setting all of the off-diagonal elements to zero. While this simplification does lose information it means a significant reduction in the number of parameters that need to be estimated. For this reason it is used in some HMM implementations.

Choosing to build phoneme or triphone based models means that to recognise words or phrases we must make composite HMMs from these subword building blocks. A model for the word cat can be made by joining together phoneme models for /k/ /a/ and /t/. If each phoneme model has three states then this composite model has nine states but can be treated just like any other HMM for the purposes of matching against an input observation sequence.

To recognise more than one word we need to construct models for each word. Rather than have many separate models it is better to construct a network of phoneme models and have paths through the network indicate the words that are recognised. The phonemes can be arranged in a tree, each leaf of the tree corresponds to a word in the lexicon.

An example lexical tree which links together phoneme models in a network such that alternate paths through the network represent different words in the lexicon. The tree of phoneme models ensures that any path through the network corresponds to a real word. Each open circle represents a single HMM which might consist of three states. Each solid circle corresponds to a word boundary. Cases of multiple pronunciations (for 'A') and homonyms ('hart' and 'heart') can be seen in this network. If triphones models are being used this network would be expanded.

For connected word recognition this network can be extended to link words together into phrases such that the legal paths through the network correspond to phrases that we want to recognise. The question is: what phrases are to be allowed? The answer lies in what is called a language model. This should define possible word sequences either via definite patterns such as grammar rules or via statistical models. The language model defines the shape of the network of HMMs. In most cases this network will be extremely complicated. While it is useful to think of a static, pre-constructed network being searched by the Viterbi algorithm, in a real recogniser the network is constructed as it is searched.

Assuming that we have designed our individual phoneme or triphone HMMs then the first step is to initialise the free parameters in the models. These parameters are the transition probabilities between states and the means and covariance matrices of the Gaussian models associated with each state. The next step will be to begin supervised training where we will force align the models with speech samples and update the model parameters to better fit that segmentation. If we begin with a poor set of parameters (for example, by choosing random values for each parameter) the forced alignment will be unlikely to assign appropriate phonemes to each model and so the model will be unlikely to improve itself. HMM training can be thought of as a search for the lowest point on a hilly landscape; if we begin from a point close to the lowest point we may well find it but if we begin from a point close to a higher dip, we may get stuck there and be unable to see the better solution over the horizon. The standard way to initialise the Gaussian models in each state is to use a small amount of hand segmented data and align it to each model. In a three state model, each state might be given four vectors of a twelve vector input sequence corresponding to one token. In this way the Gaussians are initialised to approximate the distributions for each phoneme. Transition probabilities are less troublesome and are usually initialised to equal values.

The raw data are speech recordings for which word transcriptions are available. The supervised training procedure looks at each utterance in turn, constructs an HMM corresponding to that utterance from the sub-word constituent models, recognises the utterance with the HMM and finally updates the statistical estimates needed for training. After all of the utterances have been treated in this way, the parameters of the constituent models are updated according to the statistics collected. This process is repeated until the changes to the HMM parameters on each iteration are very small.

9.9   Program

The C++ program implements the hidden Markov model, where N is the number of states ($N = 3$ in `main`), M is the total number of distinct observations (only $M = 2$ possible) and T is the number of observations. We use the `string` class of C++ for the observation sequence.

```
// hmmt1.cpp

#include <iostream>
#include <string>
#include <cmath>       // for log
using namespace std;

class Data {
  private:
    double **transitions;
    double **emissions;
    double *pi_transitions;

  public:
    Data(int,int);   // constructor

    double get_transition(int i,int j)
    { return transitions[i][j]; }

    double get_emission(int i,int j)
    { return emissions[i][j]; }
```

```
        double get_pi_transition(int i)
        { return pi_transitions[i]; }

        void set_transition(int i,int j,double v)
        { transitions[i][j] = v; }

        void set_emission(int i,int j,double v)
        { emissions[i][j] = v; }

        void set_pi_transition(int i,double v)
        { pi_transitions[i] = v; }
};

Data::Data(int n=0,int m=0)
{
  transitions = new double*[n+1];
  for(int i=0;i<n+1;i++) transitions[i] = new double[n+1];

  emissions = new double*[n+1];
  for(int i=0;i<n+1;i++) emissions[i] = new double[m+1];

  pi_transitions = new double[n+1];
} // end class Data

class HMM {
  private:
    int N, M, T;
    string o;    // observation
    double** alpha_table;
    double** beta_table;
    double* alpha_beta_table;
    double* xi_divisor;
    Data* current;
    Data* reestimated;

  public:
    HMM(int,int);   // constructor

    void error(const string s)
    { cerr << "error: " << s << '\n'; }

    void init(int s1,int s2,double value)
    { current->set_transition(s1,s2,value); }
```

```
    void pi_init(int s,double value)
    { current->set_pi_transition(s,value); }

    void o_init(int s,const char c,double value)
    { current->set_emission(s,index(c),value); }

    double a(int s1,int s2)
    { return current->get_transition(s1,s2); }

    double b(int state,int pos)
    { return current->get_emission(state,index(o[pos-1])); }

    double b(int state,int pos,string o)
    { return current->get_emission(state,index(o[pos-1])); }

    double pi(int state)
    { return current->get_pi_transition(state); }

    double alpha(const string s);
    double beta(const string s);
    double gamma(int t,int i);
    int index(const char c);
    double viterbi(const string s,int *best_sequence);
    double** construct_alpha_table();
    double** construct_beta_table();
    double* construct_alpha_beta_table();
    double xi(int t,int i,int j);
    void reestimate_pi();
    void reestimate_a();
    void reestimate_b();
    double* construct_xi_divisor();
    void maximize(string training,string test);
    void forward_backward(string s);
};

HMM::HMM(int n=0,int m=0)
{
  N = n; M = m;
  current = new Data(n,m);
  reestimated = new Data(n,m);
}

double HMM::alpha(const string s)
{
```

```
    string out;
    double P = 0.0;
    out = s;
    int T1 = out.length();
    double* previous_alpha = new double[N+1];
    double* current_alpha = new double[N+1];

    // Initialization:
    for(int i=1;i<=N;i++) previous_alpha[i] = pi(i)*b(i,1,out);

    // Induction:
    for(int t=1;t<T1;t++) {
      for(int j=1;j<=N;j++) {
        double sum = 0.0;
        for(int i=1;i<=N;i++) {
        sum += previous_alpha[i]*a(i,j);
        }
        current_alpha[j] = sum*b(j,t+1,out);
      }
      for(int c=1;c<=N;c++)
        previous_alpha[c] = current_alpha[c];
    }

    // Termination:
    for(int i=1;i<=N;i++) P += previous_alpha[i];
    return P;
}

double HMM::beta(const string s)
{
    double P = 0.0;
    o = s;
    int T = o.length();
    double* next_beta = new double[N+1];
    double* current_beta = new double[N+1];

    // Initialization:
    for(int i=1;i<=N;i++) next_beta[i] = 1.0;

    // Induction:
    double sum;
    for(int t=T-1;t>=1;t--) {
      for(int i=1;i<=N;i++) {
        sum = 0.0;
```

```
      for(int j=1;j<=N;j++) {
      sum += a(i,j)*b(j,t+1)*next_beta[j];
      }
      current_beta[i] = sum;
    }
    for(int c=1;c<=N;c++)
      next_beta[c] = current_beta[c];
  }

  // Termination:
  for(int i=1;i<=N;i++) P += next_beta[i]*pi(i)*b(i,1);
  return P;
}

double HMM::gamma(int t,int i)
{
  return
   (alpha_table[t][i]*beta_table[t][i])/alpha_beta_table[t];
}

int HMM::index(const char c) {
  switch(c) {
  case 'H': return 0;
  case 'T': return 1;
  default: error("no legal input symbol!");
  return 0;
  }
}

double HMM::viterbi(const string s,int best_path[])
{
  double P_star = 0.0;
  string o = s;
  int *help = new int;
  int T = o.length();
  double* previous_delta = new double[N+1];
  double* current_delta = new double[N+1];
  int** psi = new int*[T+1];
  for(int i=0;i<=T;i++) psi[i] = new int[N+1];

  // Initializitaion:
  for(int i=1;i<=N;i++)
  { previous_delta[i] = pi(i)*b(i,1); psi[1][i] = 0; }
```

```
  double tmp, max;

  // Recursion:
  for(int t=2;t<=T;t++) {
    for(int j=1;j<=N;j++) {
      max = 0.0;
      for(int i=1;i<=N;i++) {
        tmp = previous_delta[i]*a(i,j);
        if(tmp >= max) { max = tmp; psi[t][j] = i; }
      }
      current_delta[j] = max*b(j,t);
    }
    for(int c=1;c<=N;c++)
      previous_delta[c] = current_delta[c];
  }

  // Termination:
  for(int i=1;i<=N;i++) {
    if(previous_delta[i] >= P_star) {
      P_star = previous_delta[i];
      best_path[T] = i;
    }
  }

  // Extract best sequence:
  for(int t=T-1;t>=1;t--)
    best_path[t] = psi[t+1][best_path[t+1]];

  best_path[T+1] = -1;
  return P_star;
}

double** HMM::construct_alpha_table()
{
  double** alpha_table = new double*[T+1];
  for(int i=0;i<=T+1;i++) alpha_table[i] = new double[N+1];

  // Initialization:
  for(int i=1;i<=N;i++) alpha_table[1][i] = pi(i)*b(i,1);

  // Induction:
  for(int t=1;t<T;t++) {
    for(int j=1;j<=N;j++) {
      double sum = 0.0;
```

```
      for(int i=1;i<=N;i++) {
       sum += alpha_table[t][i]*a(i,j);
       }
      alpha_table[t+1][j] = sum*b(j,t+1);
    }
  }
  return alpha_table;
}

double** HMM::construct_beta_table()
{
  double** beta_table = new double*[T+1];
  for(int i=0;i<=T+1;i++) beta_table[i] = new double[N+1];

  // Initialization:
  for(int i=1;i<=N;i++) beta_table[T][i] = 1.0;

  double sum;

  // Induction:
  for(int t=T-1;t>=1;t--) {
    for(int i=1;i<=N;i++) {
      sum = 0.0;
      for(int j=1;j<=N;j++) {
       sum += a(i,j)*b(j,t+1)*beta_table[t+1][j];
       }
      beta_table[t][i] = sum;
    }
  }

  // Termination:
  for(int i=1;i<=N;i++)
    beta_table[1][i] = beta_table[1][i]*pi(i)*b(i,1);

  return beta_table;
}

double* HMM::construct_alpha_beta_table()
{
  double* alpha_beta_table = new double[T+1];

  for(int t=1;t<=T;t++) {
    alpha_beta_table[t] = 0;
    for(int i=1;i<=N;i++) {
```

```
      alpha_beta_table[t] += alpha_table[t][i]*beta_table[t][i];
    }
  }
  return alpha_beta_table;
}

double* HMM::construct_xi_divisor()
{
  xi_divisor = new double[T+1];
  double sum_j;

  for(int t=1;t<T;t++) {
    xi_divisor[t] = 0.0;
    for(int i=1;i<=N;i++) {
      sum_j = 0.0;
      for(int j=1;j<=N;j++) {
      sum_j += (alpha_table[t][i]*a(i,j)*b(j,t+1)
              *beta_table[t+1][j]);
      }
      xi_divisor[t] += sum_j;
    }
  }
  return xi_divisor;
}

double HMM::xi(int t,int i,int j)
{
  return ((alpha_table[t][i]*a(i,j)*b(j,t+1)
          *beta_table[t+1][j])/(xi_divisor[t]));
}

void HMM::reestimate_pi()
{
  for(int i=1;i<=N;i++) {
    reestimated->set_pi_transition(i,gamma(1,i));
  }
}

void HMM::reestimate_a()
{
  double sum_xi, sum_gamma;

  for(int i=1;i<=N;i++) {
    for(int j=1;j<=N;j++) {
```

```
      sum_xi = 0.0; sum_gamma = 0.0;
      for(int t=1;t<T;t++) { sum_xi += xi(t,i,j); }
      for(int t=1;t<T;t++) { sum_gamma += gamma(t,i); }
      reestimated->set_transition(i,j,(sum_xi/sum_gamma));
    }
  }
}

void HMM::reestimate_b()
{
  double sum_gamma, tmp_gamma, sum_gamma_output;
  for(int j=1;j<=N;j++) {
    for(int k=0;k<M;k++) {
      sum_gamma = 0.0; sum_gamma_output = 0.0;
      for(int t=1;t<=T;t++) {
        tmp_gamma = gamma(t,j);
        if(index(o[t-1]) == k) {
        sum_gamma_output += tmp_gamma;
        }
        sum_gamma += tmp_gamma;
      }
      reestimated->set_emission(j,k,sum_gamma_output/sum_gamma);
    }
  }
}

void HMM::forward_backward(string o)
{
  T = o.length();
  alpha_table = construct_alpha_table();
  beta_table = construct_beta_table();
  alpha_beta_table = construct_alpha_beta_table();
  xi_divisor = construct_xi_divisor();
  reestimate_pi();
  reestimate_a();
  reestimate_b();

  // deletion
  for(int t=1;t<=T;t++) delete[] alpha_table[t];
  delete[] alpha_table;

  for(int t=1;t<=T;t++)
  delete[] beta_table[t];
  delete[] beta_table;
```

```
    delete[] alpha_beta_table;
    delete[] xi_divisor;

    Data* tmp_value = current;
    current = reestimated;
    reestimated = tmp_value;
}

void HMM::maximize(string o,string test)
{
    double diff_entropy, old_cross_entropy, new_cross_entropy;
    int c = 1;
    int t = test.length();
    old_cross_entropy = -((log10(alpha(test))/log10(2))/t);
    cout << "Re-estimation:\n";
    cout << "initial cross_entropy: " << old_cross_entropy
         << "\n";

    do {
     forward_backward(o);
     new_cross_entropy = -(log10(alpha(test))/log10(2))/t;
     diff_entropy = (old_cross_entropy-new_cross_entropy);
     old_cross_entropy = new_cross_entropy;
     c++;
    } while(diff_entropy > 0.0);

    cout << "No of iterations: " << c << "\n";
    cout << "resulting cross_entropy: "
         << old_cross_entropy << "\n";
}

int main(void)
{
    HMM hmm(3,2);
    hmm.pi_init(1,0.33333333);
    hmm.pi_init(2,0.33333333);
    hmm.pi_init(3,0.33333333);
    hmm.init(1,1,0.33333333);
    hmm.init(1,2,0.33333333);
    hmm.init(1,3,0.33333333);
    hmm.init(2,1,0.33333333);
    hmm.init(2,2,0.33333333);
    hmm.init(2,3,0.33333333);
    hmm.init(3,1,0.33333333);
```

```
hmm.init(3,2,0.33333333);
hmm.init(3,3,0.33333333);
hmm.o_init(1,'H',0.5);
hmm.o_init(2,'H',0.75);
hmm.o_init(3,'H',0.25);
hmm.o_init(1,'T',0.5);
hmm.o_init(2,'T',0.25);
hmm.o_init(3,'T',0.75);

string training = "HTTHTTTHHTTHTTTHHTTHTTTHHTTHTTT"
                  "HHTTHTTTHHTTHTTTHHTTHTTTHHTTHTTTH";
string test = "HTHTTHTHTTHTHTHTHTHTTHHTHTHTTHTHTTHHT";

cout << "\nInput:  " << training << "\n\n";
cout << "Probability (forward): "
    << hmm.alpha(training) << "\n";
cout << "Probability (backward): "
    << hmm.beta(training) << "\n\n";
int *best_path = new int[256];
cout << "Best-path-probability: "
    << hmm.viterbi(training,best_path) << "\n\n";
cout << "Best path: ";
for(int t=1;best_path[t+1]!=-1;t++)
  cout << best_path[t] << "," ;
cout << best_path[t] << "\n\n";
hmm.maximize(training,test);
cout << "Probability (forward): "
    << hmm.alpha(training) << "\n";
cout << "Best-path-probability : "
    << hmm.viterbi(training,best_path) << "\n";
return 0;
}
```

Chapter 10

Linear Prediction Analysis

10.1   Introduction

Typically speech recognition starts with the digital sampling of speech. The next stage is acoustic signal processing. Most techniques include spectral analysis; e.g. linear predictive coding analysis, mel frequency cepstral coefficients, cochlea modelling and many more. The next stage is recognition of phonemes, groups of phonemes and words. This stage can be done by many processes such as dynamic time warping, hidden Markov modelling, neural networks, expert systems and combinations of these techniques ([46], [48]).

LPC stands for *linear predictive coding* ([18],[46], [45]). CELP stands for *code excited linear prediction*. They are compression algorithms used for low bit rate (2400 and 4800 bps) speech coding. LPC is a powerful speech analysis technique for representing good quality speech for low bit rate transmission or storage. It provides extremely accurate estimates of speech parameters, and is relatively efficient for computation.

An LPC coder fits speech to a simple, analytic model of the vocal tract, then throws away the speech and ships the parameters of the best-fit model. An LPC decoder uses those parameters to generate synthetic speech that is usually more-or-less similar to the original. The result is intelligible, but sounds like a machine is talking. A CELP coder does the same LPC modelling but then computes the errors between the original speech and the synthetic model and transmits both model parameters and a very compressed representation of the errors. The compressed representation is an index into a code book shared between coders and decoders. This is why it is called "code excited". A CELP does much more work than an LPC coder, usually about an order of magnitude more. Of course this results in a much better quality speech.

10.2   Human Speech Production

The vocal tract consists of the throat, the tongue, the nose, and the mouth. It is defined as the speech producing path through the vocal organs. The process of producing speech can be summarised as air from the lungs being pushed through the vocal tract and out through the mouth to generate speech. It is the generation or articulation of speech in the vocal tract that LPC models.

As a person speaks, the vocal tract is constantly changing shape at a very slow rate to produce different sounds which flow together to create words. The higher the volume of air that flows from the lungs and through the vocal tract, the louder the sound. If the vocal cords vibrate and the rate that vocal cords vibrate affect speech production.

A key concept in speech production is phonemes, a limited set of individual sounds. There are two categories of phonemes that are considered in LPC

a) *voiced sounds*   and   b) *unvoiced sounds.*

Voiced sound are usually vowels. They are generated by air from the lungs being forced over the vocal cords. As a result the vocal cords vibrate in a somewhat periodic pattern that produces a series of air pulses or glottal pulses. The rate at which the vocal tract vibrates is what determines the *pitch* (pitch frequency, fundamental frequency) of the sound produced. Woman and young children tend to have high pitch (fast vibration) while adult males tend to have low pitch (slow vibration). These air pulses that are created by the vibrations finally pass along the vocal tract where some frequencies resonate.

Unvoiced sound (fricatives and plosive) are usually consonants. They are produced when air is forced through the vocal tract in a turbulent flow. During this process the vocal cords do not vibrate, instead they stay open until the sound is produced. Pitch is an unimportant attribute of the unvoiced speech since there is no vibration of the vocal cords and no glottal pulses.

The shape of the vocal tract changes relatively slow on the scale of 10 msec to 100 msec. The amount of air coming from our lung determines the loudness of our voice.

A *phone* is a single speech sound (vowel or consonant). According to Webster's dictionary, a phone is a speech sound considered as a physical event without regard to its place in the sound system of a language. The acoustic signals are converted by a listener into a sequence of words and sentences. The most familiar language units are words. They can be thoughts of as a sequence of smaller linguistic units, phoneme, which are the fundamental units of phonology. *Phonemes* are the units of the system of sounds of a language. A *dipthong* is a two vowels sound that run together to form a single phoneme. There are roughly 40-49 phonemes in the English language. A phoneme is not a single sound but a set of sounds sharing similar characteristics. The elements in the set is called *allophones*. Every phoneme consists of several allophones, i.e., several different ways of pronunciation. The ARPABET symbols lists the phonemes.

Phonemes can be combined into larger units called *syllables*. A syllable usually consists of a vowel surrounded by one or more consonants. In English there are approximately 10 000 syllables. An even larger unit is the word, which normally consists of sequences of several phonemes that combine into one or more syllables. The structure of sentences is described by the grammar of a language. Grammar includes phonology, morphology, syntax and semantics.

For example, consider the word `segmentation`. Its representation according to each of the above subword unit sets is

```
word          segmentation
phoneme       s eh g m ax n t ey sh ix n
diphone       s s_eh eh_g g_m m_ax ax_n n_t t_ey ey_sh sh_ix
              ix_n n
syllable      seg men ta tion
demisyllable  s_eh eh_g m_ax ax_n t_ey ey_sh sh_ix ix_n
```

Phoneme recognition is a simple form of speech recognition. We can recognise a speech sample phoneme by phoneme. The phoneme-recognition system learns only a comparatively small set of minimal syllables or phonemes. More advanced systems learn and recognise words, phrases, or sentences, which are more numerous by orders of magnitude than phonemes. Words and phrases can also undergo more complex forms of distortion and time warping. In principle we can recognise phonemes and speech with vector-quantisation methods. These methods search for a small but representative set of prototypes, which can then be used to match sample patterns with nearest-neighbour techniques. In neural-network phoneme recognition, a sequence of discrete phonemes from a continuous speech sample produces a series of neuronal responses. Kohonen's [33] supervised neural phoneme-recognition system successfully classifies 21 Finnish phonemes. The stochastic competitive-learning system behaves as an adaptive vector-quantisation system.

10.3 LPC Modelling

The LPC model is derived from a mathematical approximation of the vocal tract represented as a varying diameter tube. It has two key components: i) analysis or encoding, ii) synthesis or decoding.

The LPC model is based on the source-filter model which separates the source from the filter. The source information has to be: Is the segment voiced or unvoiced? What is the pitch period of the segment? The filter information has to be: What parameters are needed to build a filter that models the vocal tract for the current segment? Thus the basic principles are: LPC starts with the assumption that the speech signal is produced by a buzzer at the end of a tube. The glottis (the space between the vocal cords) produces the buzz, which is characterized by its intensity (loudness) and frequency (pitch). The vocal tract (the throat and mouth) forms the tube, which is characterized by its resonances, which are called *formants*.

LPC performs a spectral analysis of an input signal by sectioning the signal into frames. Frames are time-ordered snapshots of the signal. The name Linear Predictive Coding is derived from the fact that output samples are predicted by a linear combination of filter parameters and previous samples. Any prediction algorithm has the possibility of being wrong so an LPC analysis also returns an error estimation. The error estimation may be used as an indication of a voiced or unvoiced frame. Values greater than .2 generally indicate an unvoiced frame. An LPC analysis consists of a frame number, the root-mean-square (rms) of the residual of analysis (krmsr), the rms of the original signal (krmso), the normalised error signal (kerr), and the pitch in Hertz (kcps).

LPC analyses the speech signal by estimating the formants, removing their effects from the speech signal, and estimating the intensity and frequency of the remaining buzz. The process of removing the formants is called *inverse filtering*, and the remaining signal is called the *residue*.

The numbers which describe the formants and the residue can be stored or transmitted somewhere else. LPC synthesises the speech signal by reversing the process: use the residue to create a source signal, use the formants to create a filter (which represents the tube), and run the source through the filter, resulting in speech.

The basic problem of the LPC system is to determine the formants from the speech signal. The basic solution is a difference equation, which expresses each sample of the signal as a linear combination of previous samples. Such an equation is called a linear predictor, which is why this is called Linear Predictive Coding.

In the following figures we show the human speech production, speech production by a machine and a simplified source filter of speech production [48].

Figure 10.1. The Human Speech Production

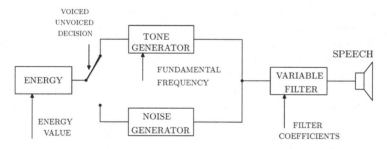

Figure 10.2. Speech Production by a Machine

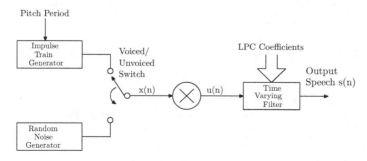

Figure 10.3. Simplified Source Filter of Speech Production

Voiced sounds are similar to periodic waveforms. They have high average energy levels which means that they have very large amplitudes. Voiced sounds also have distinct resonant of formant frequencies. Unvoiced sounds often have very chaotic and random waveforms. They have less energy and therefore smaller amplitudes then voiced sounds. Unvoiced sounds also have higher frequencies then voiced sounds.

Since speech signals vary with time, this process is done on short chunks of the speech signal, which are called *frames* or *windows*. Usually 30 to 50 frames per second give intelligible speech with good compression. The input signal is sampled at a rate of 8000 samples per second. This input signal is then broken up into segments or blocks which are each analysed and transmitted to the receiver. The samples in each second of speech signal are broken into, for example, 180 sample segments - each representing 22.5 milliseconds of the input speech signal. Sometimes blocks of 240 samples each representing 30 milliseconds of the input speech signal are used.

LPC provides a good model of the speech signal. This is especially true for the quasi steady state voiced regions of speech in which the all-pole model of LPC provides a good approximation to the vocal tract spectral envelope. During unvoiced and transient regions of speech, the LPC model is less effective than for voiced regions, but it still provides an acceptably useful model for speech-recognition purposes. The way in which LPC is applied to the analysis of speech signals leads to a reasonable source-vocal tract separation. As a result, a parsimonious representation of the vocal tract characteristics (which we know are directly related to the speech sound being produced) becomes possible. LPC is an analytically tractable model. The method of LPC is mathematically precise and is simple to implement in either software or hardware. The computation involved in LPC processing is considerably less than that required for an all-digital implementation of the bank-of-filters model. The LPC model works well in recognition applications. Experience has shown that the performance of speech recognisers, based on LPC front ends, is comparable to or better than that of recognisers based on filter-bank ends.

To summarise: The LPC algorithm extracts two set of parameters characterizing the voice. The first one characterizes the sounds as voiced or unvoiced. In the former case, the pitch frequency of the voiced sound is also extracted. The second set of parameters characterizes the transfer function that models the effect of the vocal tract on the source signal. The transfer function is all-pole and is therefore represented by the transfer function gain G and the feedback coefficients a_i $(i = 1, 2, \ldots, p)$, where p is the filter order. In many cases the filter order is set to $p = 10$. The algorithm can be divided into the following main processing blocks.

a) Segmentation, windowing and pre-emphasis filtering

b) Autocorrelation computation

c) Levinson-Durbin algorithm

d) Pitch detection.

The speech signal is sampled at a frequency of 8 kHz and is processed in the LPC algorithm in blocks of 240 samples each representing 30 milliseconds of the input speech signal. The processed blocks overlap by 80 samples. Therefore, the LPC algorithm must extract the required parameters characterizing the 240 samples of speech each 20 ms. In the segmentation processing block, the segments of 240 samples are highpass filtered and windowed using a Hamming window. The obtained data samples are used as the input to the autocorrelation and pitch detection blocks. The detection of silent speech blocks is also done in this processing unit. The autocorrelation processing block computes the autocorrelation of the 240 windowed samples for 11 different offsets. The *Levinson-Durbin algorithm* is then used to solve a set of 10 linear equations. The transfer function gain G is also obtained from the Levinson-Durbin algorithm. The Levinson-Durbin algorithm is a recursive algorithm involving various manipulations and in particular the computation of a division. The 240 windowed samples are also processed to find the voiced/unvoiced characteristics of the speech signal. They are first lowpass filtered using a 24 tap FIR filter. The filtered signal is than clipped using a 3-level centre clipping function. The autocorrelation of the clipped signal is then computed for 60 different sequence offsets. From these autocorrelation results the voice/unvoiced parameters of the speech signal are extracted.

10.4 Restrictions of LPC

The coefficients of the difference equation (the prediction coefficients) characterize the formants, so the LPC system needs to estimate these coefficients. The estimate is done by minimising the mean-square error between the predicted signal and the actual signal. This is a straightforward problem, in principle. In practice, it involves (1) the computation of a matrix of coefficient values, and (2) the solution of a set of linear equations. Several methods (autocorrelation, covariance, recursive lattice formulation) may be used to assure convergence to a unique solution with efficient computation.

It is surprising that the signal can be characterized by such a simple linear predictor. In order for this to work, the tube must not have any side branches. In mathematical terms, side branches introduce zeros, which require much more complex equations.

For ordinary vowels, the vocal tract is well represented by a single tube. However, for nasal sounds, the nose cavity forms a side branch. Theoretically, therefore, nasal sounds require a different and more complicated algorithm. In practice, this difference is partly ignored and partly dealt with during the encoding of the residue.

If the predictor coefficients are accurate, and everything else works correctly, the speech signal can be inverse filtered by the predictor, and the result will be the pure source (buzz). For such a signal, it's fairly easy to extract the frequency and amplitude and encode them.

However, some consonants are produced with turbulent airflow, resulting in a hissy sound (fricatives and stop consonants). Fortunately, the predictor equation does not care if the sound source is periodic (buzz) or chaotic (hiss).

This means that for each frame, the LPC encoder must decide if the sound source is buzz or hiss; if buzz, estimate the frequency; in either case, estimate the intensity; and encode the information so that the decoder can undo all these steps. This is how LPC-10e, the algorithm described in federal standard 1015, works: it uses one number to represent the frequency of the buzz, and the number 0 is understood to represent hiss. LPC-10e provides intelligible speech transmission at 2400 bits per second. However, things are not so simple. One reason is that there are speech sounds which are made with a combination of buzz and hiss sources. Examples are the initial consonants in **this** **z**oo and the middle consonant in a**z**ure. Speech sounds like this will not be reproduced accurately by a simple LPC encoder.

Another problem is that any inaccuracy in the estimation of the formants means that more speech information gets left in the residue. The aspects of nasal sounds that do not match the LPC model, for example, will end up in the residue. There are other aspects of the speech sound that do not match the LPC model; side branches introduced by the tongue positions of some consonants, and tracheal (lung) resonances are some examples.

Therefore, the residue contains important information about how the speech should sound, and LPC synthesis without this information will result in poor quality speech. For the best quality results, we could just send the residue signal, and the LPC synthesis would sound great. Unfortunately, the whole idea of this technique is to compress the speech signal, and the residue signal takes just as many bits as the original speech signal, so this would not provide any compression.

Formant synthesiser employs formant resonances and bandwidths to represent the stored spectrum. The vocal tract filter is usually represented by 10-23 spectral parameters. Formant synthesisers have an advantage over LPC systems in that bandwidth can be more easily manipulated and that zeros can be directly introduced into the filter. However, locating the poles and zeros automatically in natural speech is a more difficult task than automatic LPC analysis. The excitation is either a periodic train of impulses (for voiced speech), pseudo-random noise (for unvoiced speech), or periodically shaped noise (for voiced fricatives). These sources are multiplied by a gain (i.e. voice amplitude, aspiration amplitude, and frication amplitude) to adjust the amplitude of the synthetic speech. The vocal tract is usually modelled as a cascade of resonators. Each representing either a formant or the spectral shape of the excitation source. A cascade of resonators are often used for vowel generation.

10.5 Mathematical Model

The model described in section 10.2 and 10.3 is called the LPC model. The model says that the digital speech signal is the output of a digital filter (called the LPC filter) whose input is either a train of impulses or a white noise sequence. The relationship between the physical and mathematical models:

Vocal tract $\;\leftrightarrow\;$ $H(z)$ (LPC filter)

Air $\;\leftrightarrow\;$ $u(t)$ (innovations)

Vocal cord vibration $\;\leftrightarrow\;$ V (voiced)

Vocal cord vibration period $\leftrightarrow$ T (pitch period)

Fricatives and plosives $\leftrightarrow$ UV (unvoiced)

Air volume $\;\leftrightarrow G$ (gain)

The basic idea behind the LPC model is that a given sample at time t, $s(t)$ can be approximated as a linear combination of the past p (in most cases $p = 10$) speech samples, such that

$$s(t) \approx a_1 s(t-1) + a_2 s(t-2) + \cdots + a_p s(t-p)$$

where the coefficients $a_1, a_2, \ldots, a_p$ are assumed to be constant over the speech analysis frame. Let G be the gain of the excitation and $u(t)$ the normalised excitation. Then we obtain the linear difference equation

$$s(t) = \sum_{j=1}^{p} a_j s(t-j) + Gu(t) \,.$$

This equation is the well-known LPC difference equation, which states that the value of the present output, $s(t)$, may be determined by summing the weighted present input, $Gu(t)$, and a weighted sum of the past output samples. Here the normalised excitation source is chosen by a switch whose position is controlled by the voiced/unvoiced character of the speech, which chooses either a quasiperiodic train of pulses as the excitation for voiced sounds, or a random noise sequence for unvoiced sounds.

Hence in LPC analysis the problem can be stated as follows: given measurements of the signal, $s(t)$, determine the parameters a_j, where $j = 1, 2, \ldots, p$. The resulting parameters are then assumed to be the parameters of our model system transfer function.

Using the z-transform we obtain from the difference equation

$$S(z) = \sum_{j=0}^{p} a_j z^{-j} S(z) + GU(z) \,.$$

Thus we obtain the transfer function

$$H(z) = \frac{S(z)}{GU(z)} = \frac{1}{1 - \sum_{j=1}^{p} a_j z^{-j}} \,.$$

In most cases we have $p = 10$. Thus the LPC filter is given by

$$H(z) = \frac{1}{1 - a_1 z^{-1} - a_2 z^{-2} - \cdots - a_{10} z^{-10}} \,.$$

Thus the LPC model can be represented in vector form as

$$\mathbf{A} = (a_1, a_2, a_3, a_4, a_5, a_6, a_7, a_8, a_9, a_{10}, G, V/UV, T) \,.$$

The digital speech signal is divided into frames of size 20 msec. There are 50 frames/second. Thus we have 160 samples for 20 msec. The model says that A is equivalent to

$$\mathbf{s} = (s(0), s(1), \ldots, s(159)) \,.$$

Thus the 160 values of $\mathbf{s}$ are compactly represented by the 13 values of $\mathbf{A}$. There is almost no perceptual difference in $\mathbf{s}$ if for voiced sounds (V): the impulse train is shifted (insensitive to phase change)

for unvoiced sounds (UV): a different white noise sequence is used.

The LPC synthesis is: Given $\mathbf{A}$, generate $\mathbf{s}$. This is done using standard filtering techniques.

The LPC analysis is: Given $\mathbf{s}$, find the best $\mathbf{A}$.

10.6 LPC Analysis

First we describe the algorithms to obtain the coefficients a_j. If α_j represents the estimate of a_j, the error or residual is given by

$$e(t) := s(t) - \sum_{j=1}^{p} \alpha_j s(t-j) \,.$$

It is now possible to determine the estimates by minimising the average mean squared error

$$E(e^2(t)) = E\left(\left(s(t) - \sum_{j=1}^{p} \alpha_j s(t-j)\right)^2\right) \,.$$

Taking the derivative with respect to α_j for $j = 1, 2, \ldots, p$ and set the result to zero yields

$$E\left(\left(s(t) - \sum_{j=1}^{p} \alpha_j s(t-j)\right) s(t-i)\right) = 0, \qquad i = 1, 2, \ldots \,.$$

We have that $e(t)$ is orthogonal to $s(t-i)$ for $i = 1, 2, \ldots, p$. Thus our equation can be rearranged to give

$$\sum_{j=1}^{p} \alpha_j \phi_t(i,j) = \phi_t(i,0), \qquad \text{for } i = 1, 2, \ldots, p$$

where

$$\phi_t(i,j) = E(s(t-i)s(t-j)) \,.$$

In the derivation of this equation a major assumption is that the signal of our model is stationary. For speech this is obviously untrue over a long duration. However, for short segments of speech the stationary assumption is realistic. Thus, our expectations E in the equation can be replaced by finite summations over a short length of speech samples.

We derived the equations for the LPC analysis from the Least Mean Square approach. An equally valid result can also be obtained using the Maximum Likelihood method, and other formulations.

To model the time-varying nature of the speech signal whilst staying within the constraint of our LPC analysis, i.e. stationary signal, it is necessary to limit our analysis to short-time blocks of speech. For example, the speech sample size could be 20 msec (200 samples at a 10-kHz rate) and the analysis is performed using a $p = 14$-th order LPC analysis. This is achieved by replacing the expectations of the equations given above by summations over finite limits, i.e.

$$\phi_t(i,j) = E(s(t-i)s(t-j)) = \sum_m s_t(m-i)s_t(m-j)$$

where $i = 1, 2, \ldots, p$, $j = 0, 1, \ldots, p$. There are two interpretations of this equation. This leads to two methods, the auto-correlation and covariance methods.

For the *auto-correlation method*, the waveform segment, $s_t(m)$, is assumed to be zero outside the interval $0 \le m \le N-1$, where N is the length of the sample sequence. Since, for $N \le m \le N+p$, we are trying to predict zero sample values (which are not actually zero), the prediction error for these samples will not be zero. Similarly, the beginning of the current frame will be affected by the same inaccuracy incurred in the previous frame. Assuming that we are interested in the future prediction performance, the limits for the equation given above can then be expressed as

$$\phi_t(i,j) = \sum_{m=0}^{N+p-1} s_t(m-i)s_t(m-j), \qquad i = 1, \ldots, p, \quad j = 0, 1, \ldots, p.$$

This equation can also be written as

$$\phi_t(i,j) = \sum_{m=0}^{N-1-(i-j)} s_t(m)s_t(m+i-j), \qquad i = 1, \ldots, p, \quad j = 0, 1, \ldots, p.$$

It can be rewritten as

$$\phi_t(i,j) = R_t(|i-j|), \qquad i = 1, \ldots, p, \quad j = 0, 1, \ldots, p$$

where

$$R_t(j) := \sum_{m=0}^{N-1-j} s_t(m)s_t(m+j).$$

Therefore we can write

$$\sum_{j=1}^{p} \alpha_j R_t(|i - j|) = R_t(i), \qquad i = 1, 2, \ldots, p.$$

This equation can be expressed in matrix form as

$$\begin{pmatrix} R_t(0) & R_t(1) & R_t(2) & \cdots & R_t(p-1) \\ R_t(1) & R_t(0) & R_t(1) & \cdots & R_t(p-2) \\ R_t(2) & R_t(1) & R_t(0) & \cdots & R_t(p-3) \\ \cdots & \cdots & \cdots & \cdots & \cdots \\ R_t(p-1) & R_t(p-2) & R_t(p-3) & \cdots & R_t(0) \end{pmatrix} \begin{pmatrix} \alpha_1 \\ \alpha_2 \\ \alpha_3 \\ \cdots \\ \alpha_p \end{pmatrix} = \begin{pmatrix} R_t(1) \\ R_t(2) \\ R_t(3) \\ \cdots \\ R_t(p) \end{pmatrix}.$$

The matrix is a symmetric $p \times p$ matrix and all the elements along a given diagonal are equal. Thus the matrix is a so-called *Toeplitz matrix*.

The linear equation can be solved by the inversion of the $p \times p$ matrix. This is not done due to computational errors such as finite precision tend to accumulate. By exploiting the Toeplitz characteristic, however, very efficient recursive procedures have been developed. The most widely used is *Durbin's algorithm*, which is recursive. The method is as follows

$$E_t^{(0)} = R_t(0)$$

$$k_i = (R_t(i) - \sum_{j=1}^{i-1} \alpha_j^{(i-1)} R_t(i-j))/E_t^{(i-1)}, \quad i = 1, 2, \ldots, p$$

$$\alpha_i^{(i)} = k_i$$
$$\alpha_j^{(i)} = \alpha_j^{(i-1)} - k_i \alpha_{i-j}^{(i-1)}, \quad j = 1, 2, \ldots, i-1$$
$$E_t^{(i)} = (1 - k_i^2) E_t^{(i-1)}.$$

We solve for $i = 1, 2, \ldots, p$ and then set

$$\alpha_j = \alpha_j^{(p)}$$

where $j = 1, 2, \ldots, p$.

For the *covariance method* the opposite approach to the autocorrelation method is taken. Here the interval over which the mean squared error is computed is fixed, i.e.

$$\sum_{m=0}^{N-1} e_t^2(m).$$

Now the equation given above

$$\phi_t(i, j) = E(s(t-i)s(t-j))$$
$$= \sum_m s_t(m-i)s_t(m-j) \qquad i = 1, \ldots, p, \quad j = 0, 1, \ldots, p$$

can be rewritten as

$$\phi_t(i,j) = \sum_{m=0}^{N-1} s_t(m-i)s_t(m-j), \qquad i=1,\ldots,p, \quad j=0,1,\ldots,p.$$

Changing the summation index yields

$$\phi_t(i,j) = \sum_{m=-i}^{N-i-1} s_t(m)s_t(m+i-j), \qquad i=1,\ldots,p, \quad j=0,1,\ldots,p.$$

The expression given by this equation is slightly different from the equivalent expression for the auto-correlation method. It requires the use of samples in the interval $-p \le m \le N-1$. Thus this is not a true auto-correlation function, but rather the cross-correlation between two similar, but not identical, finite length sampled sequences. We can write

$$\sum_{j=1}^{p} \alpha_j \phi_t(i-j) = \phi_t(i), \qquad i=1,\ldots,p.$$

In matrix form we have

$$\begin{pmatrix} \phi_t(1,1) & \phi_t(1,2) & \phi_t(1,3) & \ldots & \phi_t(1,p) \\ \phi_t(2,1) & \phi_t(2,2) & \phi_t(2,3) & \ldots & \phi_t(2,p) \\ \phi_t(3,1) & \phi_t(3,2) & \phi_t(3,3) & \ldots & \phi_t(3,p) \\ \ldots & \ldots & \ldots & \ldots & \ldots \\ \phi_t(p,1) & \phi_t(p,2) & \phi_t(p,3) & \ldots & \phi_t(p,p) \end{pmatrix} \begin{pmatrix} \alpha_1 \\ \alpha_2 \\ \alpha_3 \\ \ldots \\ \alpha_p \end{pmatrix} = \begin{pmatrix} \phi_t(1,0) \\ \phi_t(2,0) \\ \phi_t(3,0) \\ \ldots \\ \phi_t(p,0) \end{pmatrix}.$$

The matrix is not a Toeplitz matrix. Efficient matrix inversion solutions such as Cholesky decomposition can be applied to find the solution.

The solution to the LPC equation involves two basic steps:

(i) computation of a matrix of correlation values, $\phi_t(i,j)$,

and

(ii) solution of a set of linear equations.

Although the two steps are very efficient, another class of auto-correlation based methods, called Lattice Methods, have been developed. These methods combine the two steps to compute the LPC parameters. The basic idea of the Lattice Methods is that during calculation of the intermediate stages of the predictor parameters, knowledge of both the forward and backward prediction errors are incorporated. A major incentive in using the Lattice Method is that the parameters computed are guaranteed to form a stable filter, a feature which neither the autocorrelation method nor the covariance method possesses.

Next we have to find the three other parameters $(V/U, G, T)$. First we do the voiced/unvoiced determination.

Step 1. If the amplitude levels are large then the segment is classified as voiced and if they are small then the segment is considered as unvoiced. This determination requires a preconceived notation about the range of amplitude values and energy levels associated with the two types of sound.

Step 2. This step takes advantage of the fact that: i) voiced speech segments have large amplitudes, ii) unvoiced speech segments have high frequencies, iii) the average values of both types of speech samples is close to zero. These three facts lead to the conclusion that the unvoiced speech waveform must cross the x-axis more often than the waveform of voiced speech. We can therefore count this number to refine our determination.

Step 3. An additional factor that influences this classification is the surrounding segments. The classification of these neighbouring segments is taken into consideration because it is undesirable to have an unvoiced frame in the middle of a group of voiced frames or vice versa.

For the *pitch period estimation* we proceed as follows. For speech signals, the pitch period can be thought of as the period of the vocal cord vibration that occurs during the production of voiced speech. Therefore, the pitch period is only needed for the decoding of voiced segments and is not required for unvoiced segments since they are produced by turbulent air flow not vocal cord vibrations.

In LPC the *average magnitude difference function* (AMDF) is used to determine the pitch period. This function is defined as

$$AMDF(P) := \frac{1}{N} \sum_{t=k_0+1}^{k_0+N} |s(t) - s(t-P)|.$$

Since the pitch period P for humans is limited, the AMDF is evaluated for a limited range of the possible pitch period values. There is an assumption that the pitch period is between 2.5 and 20 milliseconds. If the signal is sampled at a rate of 8000 samples/second then $20 \leq P \leq 160$. For voiced segments we can consider $s(t)$ as a periodic sequence with period P_0. This means that samples that are P_0 apart should have similar values and that the AMDF function will have a minimum at P_0, that is when P is equal to the pitch period.

During the quantisation of the filter coefficients for transmission there is an opportunity for errors in the filter coefficients that can lead to instability in the vocal tract filter and create an inaccurate output signal. Thus during the Levension-Durbin algorithm which computes the filter coefficients a_i, a set of coefficients k_i called reflection coefficients can be used to rebuild the set of filter coefficients a_i and can guarantee a stable filter if their magnitude is strictly less than one.

The encoder sends a single bit to tell if the current segment is voiced or unvoiced. For pitch segments, the pitch period is quantised using a log companded quantiser to one of 60 possible values. If the segment contains voiced speech then a 10-th order filter is used. This means that 11 values are needed: 10 reflection coefficients and the gain. If the segment contains unvoiced speech then a 4-th order filter is used. This means that 5 values are needed: 4 reflection coefficients and the gain. The reflection coefficients are denoted by k_n where $1 \le n \le 10$ for voiced speech filters and $1 \le n \le 4$ for unvoiced filters.

The reflection coefficients k_n cause the vocal tract filter to be especially sensitive to errors if they have a magnitude close to one. The first two reflection coefficients k_1 and k_2 are the most likely coefficients to have magnitudes ≈ 1. LPC-10 uses nonuniform quantisation for k_1 and k_2. First, each coefficient is used to generate a new coefficient g_i of the form

$$g_i = \frac{1 + k_i}{1 - k_i}.$$

These new coefficients, g_1 and g_2, are then quantised using a 5-bit uniform quantiser. All other reflection coefficients are quantised using uniform quantisers. k_3 and k_4 are quantised using 5-bit uniform quantisation. For voiced segments the coefficients k_5 up to k_8 are quantised using a 4-bit uniform quantiser. For voiced segments the coefficient k_9 uses a 3-bit quantiser. For voiced segments the coefficient k_{10} uses a 2-bit uniform quantiser. For unvoiced segments the bits used to represent the reflection coefficients, k_5 through k_{10}, in voiced segment are used for error protection.

Once the reflection coefficients for a filter have been quantised, the only thing left to quantise is the gain. The gain G is calculated using the root mean squared (rms) value of the current segment. The gain is quantised using a 5-bit long log-companded quantiser.

For the transmitting parameters we have

```
1  bit     voiced/unvoiced
6  bits    pitch period (60 values)
10 bits    a_1 and a_2 (5 each)
10 bits    a_3 and a_4 (5 each)
16 bits    a_5, a_6, a_7, a_8 (4 each)
3  bits    a_9
2  bits    a_10
5  bits    gain G
1  bit     synchronization
--------------------------------
54 bits    total bits per frame
```

The verification of LPC bit rate is:

```
sample rate   =  8000 samples/second

samples per segment = 180 samples/segment

segment rate = sample rate/samples per segment
             = (8000 samples/second)/(180 samples/second)
             = 44.444... segments/second

segment size = 54 bits/segment

bit rate = segment size * segment rate
         = (54 bits/segment)*(44.44 segments/second)
         = 2400 bits/second
```

10.7 LPC Synthesis

Synthesisers can be classified by how they parameterise the speech for storage and synthesis.

1) Waveform synthesisers concatenate speech units using stored waveforms. This method requires a large memory and a good algorithm to smooth the transitions but it can yield good quality speech.

2) Terminal analog synthesisers (e.g. LPC vocoder) model the speech output of the vocal tract without explicitly taking account of articular movements. This method generates lower quality speech but is more efficient.

3) Articulatory synthesiser directly model the vibrating vocal cords and the movement of tongue, lips, and other articulators. Due to the difficulty of obtaining accurate three-dimensional vocal tract representations and of

modelling the system with a limited set of parameters, this method provides lower-quality speech.

4) Formant synthesisers use a buzz generator to simulate the vocal cords and individual formant resonators to simulate the acoustic resonances of the vocal tract.

In the LPC synthesis (decoding) we generate the excitation signal. The following steps are carried out:

1. Determine if speech segment is voiced or unvoiced from voiced/unvoiced bit. Voiced speech segments use a locally stored pulse consists of 40 samples. Unvoiced speech segments use white noise produced by a pseudorandom number generator.

2. Determine pitch period for voiced speech segments. The pitch period for voiced segments is used to determine whether the 40 sample pulse used as the excitation signal needs to be truncated or extended. If the pulse needs to be extended it is padded with zeros since the definition of a pulse is "... an isolated disturbance, that travels through an otherwise undisturbed medium".

3. The decoder builds a filter to generate the speech when given the excitation signal as input. 10 reflection coefficients are transmitted for voiced segment filters and 4 reflection coefficients are used for unvoiced segments. These reflection coefficients are used to generate the vocal tract parameters. The vocal tract parameters are used to create the filter. The excitement signal is passed through the filter to produce a synthesised speech signal that accurately represents the original speech. Each segment is decoded individually and the sequence of reproduced sound segments is joined together to represent the entire input speech signal.

10.8   LPC Applications

LPC is used in telephone systems, in particular secure telephony.

```
North American Telephone Systems    64 kb/s (uncompressed)
International Telephone Network      32 kb/s (range 5.3-64 kb/s)
Digital Cellular standards          6.7 - 13 kb/s
Regional Cellular standards         3.45 - 13 kb/s
Secure Telephony                    0.8 - 16 kb/s
```

Other applications are

a) Speech-to-Text synthesis can take advantage of the fact that LPC synthesis speech form a model

b) Voice mail and answering machines

c) Multimedia applications store speech for later use and are often concerned about the size of the speech which is directly related to the bit rate.

10.9   Bank-of-Filters Model

The two most common choices of a signal-processing front end for speech recognition are a bank-of-filters model and an LPC model.

The overall structure of the bank-of-filters model is shown in the following figure.

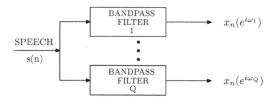

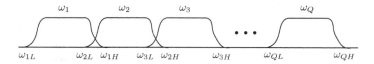

Figure 10.4.   Bank-of-Filter Model

The digital speech signal $s(t)$ is passed through a bank of Q bandpass filters whose coverage spans the frequency range of interest in the signal (e.g.,

$$100 - 3000 \text{ Hz}$$

for telephony-quality signals,

$$100 - 8000 \text{ Hz}$$

for broadband signals). The individual filters can and generally do overlap in frequency. The output of the i-th bandpass filter, $X_t(\exp(i\omega_i))$, where

ω_i is the normalised frequency

$$\omega_i = \frac{2\pi f_i}{F_s}$$

(F_s the sampling frequency) is the short-time spectral representation of the signal $s(t)$ at time t, as seen through the i-th bandpass filter with center frequency ω_i. It can be seen that in the bank-of-filters model each band-pass filter processes the speech signal independently to produce the spectral representation X_t.

A block diagram of the canonic structure of a complete filter-bank front-end analyser is given in the following figure.

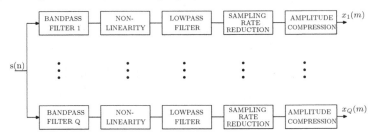

Figure 10.5.   Filter-Bank Front-End Analyser

The sampled speech signal, $s(t)$, is passed through a bank of Q bandpass filters, giving the signals

$$s_i(t) = s(t) * h_i(t) = \sum_{m=0}^{M_i-1} h_i(m)s(t-m)$$

where $i = 1, \ldots, Q$. Here we have assumed that the impulse response of the i-th bandpass filter is $h_i(m)$ with a duration of M_i samples. Therefore, we use the convolution representation of the filtering operation to give an explicit expression for $s_i(t)$, the bandpass-filtered speech signal. Since the purpose of the filter-bank analyser is to give a measurement of the energy of the speech signal in a given frequency band, each of the bandpass signals, $s_i(t)$, is passed through a nonlinearity, such as a full-wave or half-wave rectifier. The nonlinearity shifts the bandpass signal spectrum to the low-frequency band as well as creates high-frequency images. A lowpass filter is used to eliminate the high-frequency images, giving a set of signals, $u_i(t)$, ($i = 1, \ldots, Q$), which represent an estimate of the speech signal energy in each of the Q frequency bands.

Consider the design of a $Q = 16$ channel filter bank for a wideband speech signal where the highest frequency of interest is 8 kHz. Assume we use a sampling rate of $F_s = 20\text{kHz}$ on the speech data to minimise the effects of aliasing in the analog-to-digital conversion. The information (bit rate) rate of the raw speech signal is on the order of 240 kbits per second (20k samples per second times 12 bits per samples). At the output of the analyser, if we use a sampling rate of 50 Hz and we use a 7 bit logarithmic amplitude compressor, we obtain an information rate of 16 channels times 50 samples per second per channel times 7 bits per sample, or 5600 bits per second. Thus, for this simple example we have achieved about a 40-to-1 reduction in the bit rate.

The most common type of filter bank used for speech recognition is the uniform filter bank for which the center frequency, f_i, of the i-th bandpass filter is defined as

$$f_i = \frac{F_s}{N} i, \qquad i = 1, \ldots, Q$$

where F_s is the sampling rate of the speech signal, and N is the number of uniformly spaced filters required to span the frequency range of the speech. The actual number of filters used in the filter bank, Q, satisfies the relation

$$Q \leq N/2$$

with equality when the entire frequency range of the speech signal is used in the analysis. The bandwidth, b_i, of the i-th filter, generally satisfies the property

$$b_i \geq \frac{F_s}{N}$$

with equality meaning that there is no frequency overlap between adjacent channels, and with inequality meaning that adjacent filter channels overlap. If

$$b_i < \frac{F_s}{N}$$

then certain portions of the speech spectrum would be missing from the analysis and the resulting speech spectrum would not be considered very meaningful.

10.10 Mel-Cepstrum

The *mel-cepstrum* is a useful parameter for speech recognition and has widely been used in many speech recognition systems. There exist several methods to obtain mel-cepstral coefficients. The cepstrum $c(t)$ of a real sequence $x(t)$ is defined as

$$c(m) = \frac{1}{2\pi i} \oint_C \log X(z) z^{m-1} dz$$

where

$$\log X(z) = \sum_{m=-\infty}^{\infty} c(m)z^{-m}$$

and $X(z)$ is the z-transform of $x(t)$. Here C is a counterclockwise closed contour in the region of convergence of $\log X(z)$ and encircling the origin of the z-plane. Frequency-transformed cepstrum, so-called mel-cepstrum, is defined as

$$\widetilde{c}(m) = \frac{1}{2\pi i} \oint_C \log X(z)\widetilde{z}^{m-1}d\widetilde{z}$$

$$\log X(z) = \sum_{m=-\infty}^{\infty} \widetilde{c}(m)\widetilde{z}^{-m}$$

where

$$\widetilde{z}^{-1} = \Psi(z) = \frac{z^{-1} - \alpha}{1 - \alpha z^{-1}}, \qquad |\alpha| < 1\,.$$

The phase response $\widetilde{\omega}$ of the all-pass system $\Psi(\exp(i\omega)) = \exp(-i\widetilde{\omega})$ is given by

$$\widetilde{\omega} = \beta(\omega) = \arctan\left(\frac{(1-\alpha^2)\sin\omega}{(1+\alpha^2)\cos\omega - 2\alpha}\right)\,.$$

Thus, evaluating $\widetilde{c}(m)$ on the unit circle of the $\widetilde{z}$-plane, we see that $\widetilde{c}(m)$ is the inverse Fourier transform of $\log X(\exp(i\omega))$ calculated on a warped frequency scale $\widetilde{\omega}$

$$\widetilde{c}(m) = \frac{1}{2\pi} \int_{-\pi}^{\pi} \log \widetilde{X}(\exp(i\widetilde{\omega}))\exp(i\widetilde{\omega}m)d\widetilde{\omega}$$

$$\log \widetilde{X}(\exp(i\widetilde{\omega})) = \sum_{m=-\infty}^{\infty} \widetilde{c}(m)\exp(-i\widetilde{\omega}m)$$

where

$$\widetilde{X}(\exp(i\widetilde{\omega})) = X(\exp(i\beta^{-1}(\widetilde{\omega})))\,.$$

The phase response $\widetilde{\omega} = \beta(\omega)$ gives a good approximation to auditory frequency scales with an appropriate choice of α.

Examples of α

Sampling frequency	8 kHz	10 kHz	12 kHz	16 kHz
mel scale	0.31	0.35	0.37	0.42
Bark scale	0.42	0.47	0.50	0.55

10.11   CELP

Various attempts have been made to encode the residue signal in an efficient
way, providing better quality speech than LPC-10e without increasing the
bit rate too much. The most successful methods use a codebook, a table of
typical residue signals, which is set up by the system designers. In operation, the analyser compares the residue to all the entries in the codebook,
chooses the entry which is the closest match, and just sends the code for
that entry. The synthesiser receives this code, retrieves the corresponding residue from the codebook, and uses that to excite the formant filter.
Schemes of this kind are called Code Excited Linear Prediction (CELP).

For CELP to work well, the codebook must be big enough to include all
the various kinds of residues. However, if the codebook is too big, it will be
time consuming to search through, and it will require large codes to specify
the desired residue. The biggest problem is that such a system would require a different code for every frequency of the source (pitch of the voice),
which would make the codebook extremely large.

This problem can be solved by using two small codebooks instead of one
large one. One codebook is fixed by the designers, and contains just enough
codes to represent one pitch period of residue. The other codebook is adaptive; it starts out empty, and is filled in during operation, with copies of the
previous residue delayed by various amounts. Thus, the adaptive codebook
acts like a variable shift register, and the amount of delay provides the pitch.

This is the CELP algorithm described in federal standard 1016. It provides
good quality, natural sounding speech at 4800 bits per second.

Chapter 11

Neural Networks

11.1 Introduction

Neural networks approximate functions with raw sample data. A neural network's topology and dynamics define a black-box approximator from input to output. An unknown function $f : X \rightarrow Y$ $(X \subset \mathbf{R}^n, Y \subset \mathbf{R}^m)$ produces the observed sample pairs $(\mathbf{x}_0, \mathbf{y}_0)$, $(\mathbf{x}_1, \mathbf{y}_1)$, ... The sample data modify parameters (so-called weights) in the neural estimator and brings the neural system's input-output responses closer to the input-output response of the unknown estimand f. The approximation accuracy tends to increase as the sample size increases. In psychological terms, the neural network learns from experience ([25],[27],[28],[33],[38],[55]).

Nowhere in the neural-estimation process need the neural engineer articulate, write down, or guess at the mathematical shape of the unknown function f. Neural estimation is model-free. Model-free estimation remains the central advantage of neurocomputing. Different neural engineers can estimate the same unknown function with the sample data but with different neural models and still produce black boxes with similar input-output responses.

A neural network, which is also called a connection model, a neural net, or a parallel distributed processing model, is basically a dense interconnection of simple, nonlinear, computation elements. It is assumed that there are N inputs, labeled x_1, x_2, ..., x_N, which are summed with weights w_1, w_2, ..., w_N, thresholded, and then nonlinearly compressed to give the output y defined as

$$y = f \left(\sum_{i=1}^{N} w_i x_i - \theta \right)$$

where θ is an internal threshold or offset. We often set $x_0 = 1$ and $w_0 = -\theta$. The function f is a nonlinearity of one of the types given below:

1. *hard limiter*

$$f(x) = \begin{cases} +1 \text{ for } x \geq 0 \\ -1 \text{ for } x < 0 \end{cases}$$

or

2. *sigmoid functions* $(f_\beta(x) : \mathbf{R} \to [-1, 1])$

$$f_\beta(x) = \tanh(\beta x), \qquad \beta > 0$$

or $(f_\beta(x) : \mathbf{R} \to [0, 1])$

$$f_\beta(x) = \frac{1}{1 + \exp(-\beta x)}, \qquad \beta > 0.$$

The function $f_\beta(x) = \tanh(\beta x)$ satisfies the nonlinear differential equation

$$\frac{df_\beta}{dx} = \beta(1 - f_\beta^2).$$

The function $f_\beta(x) = 1/(1 + \exp(-\beta x))$ satisfies the nonlinear differential equation

$$\frac{df_\beta}{dx} = \beta f_\beta(1 - f_\beta).$$

The sigmoid nonlinearities are used most often because they are continuous and differentiable.

The biological basis of the neural network is a model by McCullough and Pitts of neurons in the human nervous system. This model exhibits all the properties of the neural elements, including excitation potential thresholds for neuron firing (below which there is little or no activity) and nonlinear amplification, which compresses strong input signals.

There are several issues in the design of so-called artificial neural networks, which model various physical phenomena, where we define an artificial neural networks as an arbitrary connection of simple elements. One key issue is network topology - that is, how the simple computational elements are interconnected. There are three standard and well known topologies:

a) single/multilayer perceptrons

b) Hopfield or recurrent networks

c) Kohonen or self-organising networks

In the single/multilayer perceptron, the outputs of one or more computational elements at one layer form the input to a new set of simple computational elements of the next layer. The single layer perceptron has N inputs connected to M outputs in the output layer. A three layer perceptron has two hidden layers between the input and output layers. What distinguishes the layers of the multilayer perceptron is the nonlinearity at each layer that enables the mapping between the input and output variables to possess certain particular classifications/discrimination properties. For example, we can show that a single-layer perceptron given above can separate static patterns into classes with class boundaries characterized by hyperplanes in the $(x_1, x_2, \ldots, x_n)$ space. Similarly, a multilayer perceptron, with at least one hidden layer, can realize an arbitrary set of decision regions in the $(x_1, x_2, \ldots, x_n)$ space.

For example, if the inputs to a multilayer perceptron are the first two speech formants (F_1 and F_2), the network can implement a set of decision regions that partition the $(F_1 - F_2)$ space into the 10 steady state vowels. For voiced phonemes, the signature involves large concentrations of energy called formants. Within each formant, and typically across all active formants, there is a characteristic waxing and waning of energy in all frequencies which is the most salient characteristic of what we call the human voice. This cyclic pattern is caused by the repetitive opening and closing of the vocal cords which occurs at an average of 125 times per second in the average adult male, and approximately twice as fast (250 Hz) in the adult female, giving rise to the sensation of pitch.

A Hopfield network is a recurrent network in which the input to each computational element includes both inputs as well as outputs. Thus with the input and output indexed by discrete time, $x_i(t)$ and $y_i(t)$, and the weight connection of the i-th node and the j-th node denoted by w_{ij}, the basic equation for the i-th recurrent computational element is

$$y_i(t) = f(x_i(t) + \sum_{j=1}^{N} w_{ij} y_j(t-1) - \theta)$$

where $t = 1, 2, \ldots$. The most important property of the Hopfield network is that when $w_{ij} = w_{ji}$ (matrix is symmetric) and when the recurrent computation is performed asynchronously, for an arbitrary constant input, the network will eventually settle down to a fixed point. A *fixed point* is defined as

$$y_i(t) = y_i(t-1)$$

for all i. These fixed points of the map represent stable configurations of the network and can be used in applications that have a fixed set of patterns to be matched in the form of a content addressable or associative memory. The Hopfield network has a set of stable attractors and repellers. Every input vector is either attracted to one of the fixed points or repelled from another of the fixed points. The strength of this type of network is the ability to correctly classify noisy versions of the patterns that form the stable fixed points.

The third popular type of neural network topology is the Kohonen, self-organising feature map, which is a clustering procedure for providing a codebook of stable patterns in the input space that characterize an arbitrary input vector, by a small number of representative clusters.

Neural networks have been given serious considerations for a wide range of problems including speech recognition. The reasons are:

1. They can readily implement a massive degree of parallel computation. Since a neural net is a highly parallel structure of simple, identical, computational elements, it should be clear that they are prime candidates for massively parallel (analog or digital) computation.

2. They intrinsically possess a great deal of robustness or fault tolerance. Since the information embedded in the neural network is spread to every computational element within the network, this structure is inherently among the least sensitive of networks to noise or defects within the structure.

3. The connection weights of the network need not be constrained to be fixed. They can be adapted in real time to improve performance. This is the basis of the concept of adaptive learning, which is inherent in the neural network structure.

4. Owing to the nonlinearity within each computational element, a sufficiently large neural network can approximate (arbitrarily close) any nonlinearity or nonlinear dynamical system. Therefore neural networks provide a convenient way of implementing nonlinear transformations between arbitrary inputs and outputs and are often more efficient than alternative physical implementations of the nonlinearity.

Conventional artificial neural networks are structured to deal with static patterns. However, speech is inherently dynamic in nature. Hence some modifications to the simple structures discussed above are required for all but the simplest of problems.

The simplest neural network structure that incorporates speech pattern dynamics is the time delay neural network computation element. For example the input could be 16 melscale filterbank coefficients. This structure extends the input to each computational element to include N speech frames (i.e. speech vectors that cover a duration of $N\Delta$ seconds, where Δ is the time separation between adjacent speech spectra. By expanding the input to N frames (where N is on the order of 15 with 10 msec frame rate), various types of acoustic-phonetic detectors become practical via the time delay neural network.

Another neural network for speech recognition combines the concept of a matched filter with a conventional neural network to account for the dynamics within speech. The acoustic features of the speech are estimated via conventional neural network architectures. The pattern classifier takes the detected acoustic feature vectors (delayed appropriately) and convolutes them with filters matched to the acoustic features and sums up the results over time. At the appropriate time (corresponding to the end of some speech unit to be detected or recognised), the output units indicate the presence of the speech.

11.2 Competitive Learning and Quantisation

Vector quantisation is one example of competitive learning. A basic competitive learning network has one layer of input nodes and one layer of output nodes. There are no hidden layers. Binary valued outputs are often (but not always) used. There are as many output nodes as there are classes. In competitive networks output units compete for the right to respond. In the method of clustering we divide the data into a number of clusters such that the inputs in the same clusters are in some sense similar. The goal here is to have the network discover structure in the data by finding how the data is clustered. The results can be used for data encoding and compression. One such method for doing this is called vector quantisation. In vector quantisation we assume there is a codebook which is defined by a set of M prototype vectors. M is chosen by the user. For setting up the codebook the initial prototype vectors are chosen arbitrarily. An input belongs to cluster i if i is the index of the closest prototype. Here closest means in the sense of a norm, for example the Euclidean distance. This has the effect of dividing up the input as *Voronoi tessellation*.

We use now this competitive learning to set up a codebook. The algorithm is as follows.

0) Given the vectors $\mathbf{x}_j$ ($j = 0, 1, \ldots, N - 1$) (input data) for which the codebook should be set up.

1) Choose the number of clusters M, where $M < N$.

2) Initialise the prototypes $\mathbf{w}_0$, $\mathbf{w}_1$, $\ldots$, $\mathbf{w}_{M-1}$. A method for doing this is to randomly choose M vectors from the input data.

3) Repeat until stopping condition is satisfied:

a) Randomly pick an input $\mathbf{x}$ from the set of input data.

b) Determine the winning node k by finding the prototype vector that satisfies
$$\|\mathbf{w}_k - \mathbf{x}\| \leq \|\mathbf{w}_i - \mathbf{x}\| \quad \text{for} \quad i = 0, 1, \ldots, M - 1.$$
$\mathbf{w}_k$ is called the *winning prototype weight.*

c) Update only the winning prototype weight according to
$$\mathbf{w}_k(t + 1) = \mathbf{w}_k(t) + \eta(\mathbf{x} - \mathbf{w}_k(t))$$
where η is the *learning rate.* The learning rate is a number between 0 and 1 and decreases for the next iteration, i.e., the learning rate becomes smaller and smaller.

Vector quantisation can be used for lossy data compression. If we are sending information over a phone line, we initially send the codebook vectors and then for each input, we send the index of the class that the input belongs to. For a large amount of data, this can be a significant reduction. If $M = 64$, then it takes only 6 bits to encode the index. If the data itself of floating point numbers (4 bytes) there is an 80% reduction ($100 * (1 - 6/32)$).

Example. Consider the following nine vectors in $\mathbf{R}^2$, i.e. $N = 9$
$$\mathbf{x}_0 = (-1.5, -1.5), \quad \mathbf{x}_1 = (2.0, 2.0), \quad \mathbf{x}_2 = (-2.0, -2.0),$$
$$\mathbf{x}_3 = (1.0, 1.0), \quad \mathbf{x}_4 = (1.5, 1.5), \quad \mathbf{x}_5 = (1.0, 2.0),$$
$$\mathbf{x}_6 = (1.0, -2.0), \quad \mathbf{x}_7 = (1.0, -3.0), \quad \mathbf{x}_8 = (1.0, -2.5).$$
We consider three prototypes ($M = 3$)
$$\mathbf{w}_0 = (0.0, 0.0), \quad \mathbf{w}_1 = (-0.5, 0.0), \quad \mathbf{w}_2 = (1.0, 0.0).$$
If we select $\mathbf{x}_4$, then the winner is $\mathbf{w}_2 = (1.0, 1.0)$, where we used the Euclidean norm. We set $\eta = 0.1$. Then
$$\mathbf{w}_2(1) = \mathbf{w}_2(0) + \eta(\mathbf{x}_4 - \mathbf{w}_2).$$

Thus we find
$$\mathbf{w}_2(1) = (1.05, 1.05).$$

In the following Java program the algorithm is implemented.

```
// Neuron.java

import java.util.*;
import java.io.*;

class Neuron
{
  private double eta = 0.1;  // learning rate
  private double factor = 0.98;
  private final int steps = 400;
  private int clusterSize = 0;
  private int pointsSize = 0;

  private double[][] cluster = null;
  private double[][] points = null;

  private Random random = new Random();

  public Neuron()
  {
  initCluster();
  initPoints();

  System.out.println("Initial points:");
  System.out.println("1:"+points[0][0]+","+points[0][1]+"\t"+
                     "2:"+points[1][0]+","+points[1][1]+"\t"+
                     "3:"+points[2][0]+","+points[2][1]+"\t");

  for(int i=0;i<steps;i++) { step(); }

  System.out.println("Result after " + steps + " steps");
  System.out.println("1:"+points[0][0]+","+points[0][1]+"\n"+
                     "2:"+points[1][0]+","+points[1][1]+"\n"+
                     "3:"+points[2][0]+","+points[2][1]+"\n");

  } // end default constructor

  private void step()
  {
  int clusterIndex = random.nextInt()%clusterSize;
```

```
if(clusterIndex < 0) clusterIndex = -clusterIndex;
double[] clusterPoint = cluster[clusterIndex];

int nearestPointIndex = 0;
double[] nearestPoint = points[0];

for(int i=0;i<pointsSize;i++)
{
double[] point = points[i];

if(squareDist(point,clusterPoint)
               < squareDist(nearestPoint,clusterPoint))
{
nearestPointIndex = i;
nearestPoint = point;
}
}

nearestPoint[0] =
  nearestPoint[0]+eta*(clusterPoint[0]-nearestPoint[0]);
nearestPoint[1] =
  nearestPoint[1]+eta*(clusterPoint[1]-nearestPoint[1]);
eta *= factor;
points[nearestPointIndex] = nearestPoint;
}

private double
  squareDist(double[] point,double[] clusterPoint)
{
return Math.pow(point[0]-clusterPoint[0],2)
       + Math.pow(point[1]-clusterPoint[1],2);
}

private void initCluster()
{
double[][] x = {{ -1.5, -1.5 }, { 2.0, 2.0 },
                { -2.0, -2.0 }, { 1.0, 1.0 },
                { 1.5, 1.5 }, { 1.0, 2.0 },
                { 1.0, -2.0 }, { 1.0, -3.0 },
                { 1.0, -2.5 }};
clusterSize = x.length;
cluster = x;
}
```

```
private void initPoints()
{
double[][] w = {{ 0.0, 0.0 },{ -0.5, 0.0 },{ 1.0, 0.0 }};
pointsSize = w.length;
points = w;
}

public static void main(String args[])
{
new Neuron();
}
}
```

11.3   Multilayer Perceptrons

11.3.1   Introduction

In a practical application of the back-propagation algorithm, learning results from the many presentations of a prescribed set of training examples to the multilayer perceptron. One complete presentation of the entire training set during the learning process is called an *epoch*. The learning process is maintained on an epoch-by-epoch basis until the synaptic weights and threshold levels of the network stabilise and the average squared error over the entire training set converges to some minimum value. Randomising the order of presentation of training examples from one epoch to the next may improve the learning rate. This randomisation tends to make the search in weight space stochastic over the learning cycles, thus avoiding the possibility of limit cycles in the evolution of the synaptic weight vectors. We follow in our notation closely Hassoun [27]. For a given training set, back-propagation learning may thus proceed in one of two basic ways.

Let

$$\{ \mathbf{x}_k, \ \mathbf{d}_k \}$$

be the training data, where $k = 0, 1, \ldots, m - 1$. Here m is the number of training examples (patterns). The sets $\mathbf{x}_k$ $(k = 0, 1, \ldots, m - 1)$ are the input pattern and the sets $\mathbf{d}_k$ are the corresponding (desired) output pattern. One complete presentation of the entire training set during the learning process is called an epoch.

1. *Pattern Mode.* In the *pattern mode* of back-propagation learning, weight updating is performed after the presentation of each training example; this is the mode of operation for which the derivation of the back-propagation algorithm presented here applies. To be specific, consider an epoch consisting of m training examples (patterns) arranged in the order

$$\mathbf{x}_0, \mathbf{d}_0, \quad \mathbf{x}_1, \mathbf{d}_1, \quad \ldots, \quad \mathbf{x}_{m-1}, \mathbf{d}_{m-1}.$$

The first example $\mathbf{x}_0$, $\mathbf{d}_0$ in the epoch is presented to the network, and the sequence of forward and backward computations described below is performed, resulting in certain adjustments to the synaptic weights and threshold levels of the network. Then, the second example $\mathbf{x}_1$, $\mathbf{d}_1$ in the epoch is presented, and the sequence of forward and backward computations is repeated, resulting in further adjustments to the synaptic weights and threshold levels. This process is continued until the last training pattern $\mathbf{x}_{m-1}$, $\mathbf{d}_{m-1}$ is taken into account.

2. *Batch Mode.* In the *batch mode* of back-propagation learning, weight updating is performed after the presentation of all the training examples that constitute an epoch.

11.3.2 Cybenko's Theorem

Single-hidden-layer neural networks are universal approximators. A rigorous mathematical proof for the universality of feedforward layered neural networks employing continuous sigmoid type activation functions, as well as other more general activation units, was given by Cybenko [16]. Cybenko's proof is based on the Hahn-Banach theorem. The following is the statement of Cybenko's theorem.

Theorem. Let f be any continuous sigmoid-type function, for example

$$f(s) = 1/(1 + \exp(-\lambda s)), \qquad \lambda \geq 1.$$

Then, given any continuous real-valued function g on $[0,1]^n$ (or any other compact subset of $\mathbf{R}^n$) and $\epsilon > 0$, there exists vectors $\mathbf{w}_1, \mathbf{w}_2, \ldots, \mathbf{w}_N$, $\boldsymbol{\alpha}$, and $\boldsymbol{\theta}$ and a parameterised function

$$G(\cdot, \mathbf{w}, \boldsymbol{\alpha}, \boldsymbol{\theta}) : [0,1]^n \to \mathbf{R}$$

such that

$$|G(\mathbf{x}, \mathbf{w}, \boldsymbol{\alpha}, \boldsymbol{\theta}) - g(\mathbf{x})| < \epsilon \qquad \text{for all} \quad \mathbf{x} \in [0,1]^n$$

where

$$G(\mathbf{x}, \mathbf{w}, \boldsymbol{\alpha}, \boldsymbol{\theta}) = \sum_{j=1}^{N} \alpha_j f(\mathbf{w}_j^T \mathbf{x} + \theta_j)$$

and

$$\mathbf{w}_j \in \mathbf{R}^n, \quad \theta_j \in \mathbf{R}, \quad \mathbf{w} = (\mathbf{w}_1, \mathbf{w}_2, \ldots, \mathbf{w}_N)$$

$$\boldsymbol{\alpha} = (\alpha_1, \alpha_2, \dots, \alpha_N), \quad \boldsymbol{\theta} = (\theta_1, \theta_2, \dots, \theta_N).$$

For the proof we refer to the paper by Cybenko [16].

Thus a one hidden layer feedforward neural network is capable of approximating uniformly any continuous multivariate function to any desired degree of accuracy. This implies that any failure of a function mapping by a multilayer network must arise from inadequate choice of parameters, i.e., poor choices for $\mathbf{w}_1, \mathbf{w}_2, \dots, \mathbf{w}_N$, $\boldsymbol{\alpha}$, and $\boldsymbol{\theta}$ or an insufficient number of hidden nodes.

Hornik et al.[30] employing the Stone-Weierstrass theorem and Funahashi [22] proved similar theorems stating that a one-hidden-layer feedforward neural network is capable of approximating uniformly any continuous multivariate function to any desired degree of accuracy.

11.3.3   Back-Propagation Algorithm

We consider one hidden layer. The notations we use follow closely Hassoun [27]. Thus we consider a two-layer feedforward architecture. This network receives a set of scalar signals

$$x_0, \ x_1, \ x_2, \dots, x_{n-1}$$

where x_0 is a bias signal set to 1. This set of signals constitutes an input vector $\mathbf{x}_k \in \mathbf{R}^n$. The layer receiving this input signal is called the hidden layer. The hidden layer has J units. The output of the hidden layer is a J dimensional real-valued vector $\mathbf{z}_k = (z_0, z_1, \dots, z_{J-1})$, where we set $z_0 = 1$ (bias signal). The vector $\mathbf{z}_k$ supplies the input for the output layer of L units. The output layer generates an L-dimensional vector $\mathbf{y}_k$ in response to the input vector $\mathbf{x}_k$ which, when the network is fully trained, should be identical (or very close) to the desired output vector $\mathbf{d}_k$ associated with $\mathbf{x}_k$.

The two activation functions f_h (input layer to hidden layer) and f_o (hidden layer to output layer) are assumed to be differentiable functions. We use the logistic functions

$$f_h(s) := \frac{1}{1 + \exp(-\lambda_h s)}, \qquad f_o(s) := \frac{1}{1 + \exp(-\lambda_o s)}$$

where $\lambda_h, \lambda_o \geq 1$. The *logistic function*

$$f(s) = \frac{1}{1 + \exp(-\lambda s)}$$

satisfies the nonlinear differential equation

$$\frac{df}{ds} = \lambda f(1 - f).$$

The components of the desired output vector $\mathbf{d}_k$ must be chosen within the range of f_o. We denote by w_{ji} the weight of the jth hidden unit associated with the input signal x_i. Thus the index i runs from 0 to $n-1$, where $x_0 = 1$ and j runs from 1 to $J-1$. We set $w_{0i} = 0$. Now we have m input/output pairs of vectors

$$\{ \mathbf{x}_k, \mathbf{d}_k \}$$

where the index k runs from 0 to $m-1$. The aim of the algorithm is to adaptively adjust the $(J-1)n + LJ$ weights of the network such that the underlying function/mapping represented by the training set is approximated or learned. We can define an *error function* since the learning is supervised, i.e. the target outputs are available. We denote by w_{lj} the weight of the lth output unit associated with the input signal z_j from the hidden layer. We derive a supervised learning rule for adjusting the weights w_{ji} and w_{lj} such that the error function

$$E(\mathbf{w}) = \frac{1}{2} \sum_{l=0}^{L-1} (d_l - y_l)^2$$

is minimised (in a local sense) over the training set. Here $\mathbf{w}$ represents the set of all weights in the network.

Since the targets for the output units are given, we can use the delta rule directly for updating the w_{lj} weights. We define

$$\Delta w_{lj} := w_{lj}^{new} - w_{lj}^c .$$

Since

$$\Delta w_{lj} = -\eta_o \frac{\partial E}{\partial w_{lj}}$$

we find using the chain rule

$$\Delta w_{lj} = \eta_o (d_l - y_l) f_o'(net_l) z_j$$

where $l = 0, 1, \ldots, L-1$ and $j = 0, 1, \ldots, J-1$. Here

$$net_l := \sum_{j=0}^{J-1} w_{lj} z_j$$

is the weighted sum for the lth output unit, f_o' is the derivative of f_o with respect to net_l, and w_{lj}^{new} and w_{lj}^c are the updated (new) and current weight values, respectively. The z_j values are calculated by propagating the input vector $\mathbf{x}$ through the hidden layer according to

$$z_j = f_h \left(\sum_{i=0}^{n-1} w_{ji} x_i \right) = f_h(net_j)$$

where $j = 1, 2, \ldots, J - 1$ and $z_0 = 1$ (bias signal). For the hidden-layer weights w_{ji} we do not have a set of target values (desired outputs) for hidden units. However, we can derive the learning rule for hidden units by attempting to minimise the output-layer error. This amounts to propagating the output errors $(d_l - y_l)$ back through the output layer toward the hidden units in an attempt to estimate dynamic targets for these units. Thus a gradient descent is performed on the criterion function

$$E(\mathbf{w}) = \frac{1}{2} \sum_{l=0}^{L-1} (d_l - y_l)^2$$

where $\mathbf{w}$ represents the set of all weights in the network. The gradient is calculated with respect to the hidden weights

$$\Delta w_{ji} = -\eta_h \frac{\partial E}{\partial w_{ji}}, \qquad j = 1, 2, \ldots, J - 1, \qquad i = 0, 1, \ldots, n - 1$$

where the partial derivative is to be evaluated at the current weight values. Using the chain rule we find

$$\frac{\partial E}{\partial w_{ji}} = \frac{\partial E}{\partial z_j} \frac{\partial z_j}{\partial net_j} \frac{\partial net_j}{\partial w_{ji}}$$

where

$$\frac{\partial net_j}{\partial w_{ji}} = x_i, \qquad \frac{\partial z_j}{\partial net_j} = f_h'(net_j).$$

Since

$$\frac{\partial E}{\partial z_j} = -\sum_{l=0}^{L-1} (d_l - y_l) f_o'(net_l) w_{lj}$$

we obtain

$$\Delta w_{ji} = \eta_h \left(\sum_{l=0}^{L-1} (d_l - y_l) f_o'(net_l) w_{lj} \right) f_h'(net_j) x_i.$$

Now we can define an estimated target d_j for the jth hidden unit implicitly in terms of the backpropagated error signal as follows

$$d_j - z_j := \sum_{l=0}^{L-1} (d_l - y_l) f_o'(net_l) w_{lj}.$$

The complete approach for updating weights in a feedforward neural net utilising these rules can be summarised as follows. We do a pattern-by-pattern updating of the weights.

1. *Initialisation.* Initialise all weights to small random values and refer to them as current weights w_{lj}^c and w_{ji}^c.

2. *Learning rate.* Set the learning rates η_o and η_h to small positive values.

3. *Presentation of training example.* Select an input pattern $\mathbf{x}_k$ from the training set (preferably at random) propagate it through the network, thus generating hidden- and output-unit activities based on the current weight settings. Thus find z_j and y_l.

4. *Forward computation.* Use the desired target vector $\mathbf{d}_k$ associated with $\mathbf{x}_k$, and employ

$$\Delta w_{lj} = \eta_o(d_l - y_l)f'(net_l)z_j = \eta_o(d_l - y_l)\lambda_o f(net_l)(1 - f(net_l))z_j$$

to compute the output layer weight changes Δw_{lj}.

5. *Backward computation.* Use

$$\Delta w_{ji} = \eta_h \left(\sum_{l=0}^{L-1}(d_l - y_l)f_o'(net_l)w_{lj} \right) f_h'(net_j)x_i$$

or replacing the derivatives

$$\Delta w_{ji} =$$

$$\eta_h \left(\sum_{l=0}^{L-1}(d_l - y_l)\lambda_o f_o(net_l)(1 - f_o(net_l))w_{lj} \right) \lambda_h f_h(net_j)(1 - f_h(net_j))x_i$$

to compute the hidden layer weight changes. The current weights are used in these computations. In general, enhanced error correction may be achieved if one employs the updated output-layer weights

$$w_{lj}^{new} = w_{lj}^c + \Delta w_{lj}.$$

However, this comes at the added cost of recomputing y_l and $f'(net_l)$.

6. *Update weights.* Update all weights according to

$$w_{ji}^{new} := w_{ji}^c + \Delta w_{ji}$$

and

$$w_{lj}^{new} := w_{lj}^c + \Delta w_{lj}$$

for the output and for the hidden layers, respectively.

7. *Test for convergence.* This is done by checking the output error function to see if its magnitude is below some given threshold. Iterate the computation by presenting new epochs of training examples to the network until the free parameters of the network stabilise their values. The order of presentation of training examples should be randomised from epoch to epoch. The learning rate parameter is typically adjusted (and usually decreased) as the number of training iterations increases.

An example of the back-propagation algorithm applied to the XOR problem is given in [55]. In the C++ program we apply the back-propagation algorithm to the parity function, where $m = 16$ is the number of input vectors each of length 5 (includes the bias input). The training set is given in Table 11.1. The number of hidden layer units is 5 which includes the bias input $z_0 = 1$. The neural network must calculate the parity bit such that the parity is even. By modifying m, n, J and L the program can easily be adapted to other problems. The arrays x[i] are the input values. The value x[i][0] is always 1 for the threshold. The arrays d[i] are the desired outputs for each input x[i]. In this case d[i] is the odd-parity bit calculated from x[i][1]-x[i][4]. In the program the value y[0], after each calculation, gives the neural network approximation of the parity calculation.

The following table gives the training set for the odd parity function over four bits. The equation is

$$P = \overline{A_3 \oplus A_2 \oplus A_1 \oplus A_0}$$

where P is the *odd parity function*, $\oplus$ denotes the XOR-operation and A_0, A_1, A_2 and A_3 are the inputs.

```
// backpropagation.cpp

#include <iostream>
#include <cmath>        // for exp
using namespace std;

// activation function (input layer -> hidden layer)
double fh(double net)
{
   double lambdah = 10.0;
   return 1.0/(1.0 + exp(-lambdah*net));
}

// activation function (hidden layer -> output layer)
```

Inputs				Parity
0	0	0	0	1
0	0	0	1	0
0	0	1	0	0
0	0	1	1	1
0	1	0	0	0
0	1	0	1	1
0	1	1	0	1
0	1	1	1	0
1	0	0	0	0
1	0	0	1	1
1	0	1	0	1
1	0	1	1	0
1	1	0	0	1
1	1	0	1	0
1	1	1	0	0
1	1	1	1	1

Table 11.1: Training Set for Parity Function

```
double fo(double net)
{
  double lambdao = 10.0;
  return 1.0/(1.0 + exp(-lambdao*net));
}

double scalar(double* a1,double* a2,int length)
{
  double result = 0.0;
  for(int i=0;i<length;i++)
  { result += a1[i]*a2[i]; }
  return result;
}

int main(void)
{
  int k, i, j, l, t;  // summation index
  // k runs over all input pattern k = 0, 1, .. , m-1
  // l runs over all output units l = 0, 1, .. , L-1
  // j runs over all hidden layer units j = 0, 1, .. , J-1
  // i runs over the length of input vector i = 0, 1, .. , n-1
```

```
// learning rates
double etao = 0.05;
double etah = 0.05;

double lambdao = 10.0;
double lambdah = 10.0;

int m = 16; // number of input vectors for parity
int n = 5;  // length of each input vector for parity
// input vectors memory allocation
double** x = new double* [m];
for(k=0;k<m;k++) x[k] = new double[n];

x[0][0] = 1.0; x[0][1] = 0.0; x[0][2] = 0.0; x[0][3] = 0.0;
x[0][4] = 0.0;
x[1][0] = 1.0; x[1][1] = 0.0; x[1][2] = 0.0; x[1][3] = 0.0;
x[1][4] = 1.0;
x[2][0] = 1.0; x[2][1] = 0.0; x[2][2] = 0.0; x[2][3] = 1.0;
x[2][4] = 0.0;
x[3][0] = 1.0; x[3][1] = 0.0; x[3][2] = 0.0; x[3][3] = 1.0;
x[3][4] = 1.0;
x[4][0] = 1.0; x[4][1] = 0.0; x[4][2] = 1.0; x[4][3] = 0.0;
x[4][4] = 0.0;
x[5][0] = 1.0; x[5][1] = 0.0; x[5][2] = 1.0; x[5][3] = 0.0;
x[5][4] = 1.0;
x[6][0] = 1.0; x[6][1] = 0.0; x[6][2] = 1.0; x[6][3] = 1.0;
x[6][4] = 0.0;
x[7][0] = 1.0; x[7][1] = 0.0; x[7][2] = 1.0; x[7][3] = 1.0;
x[7][4] = 1.0;
x[8][0] = 1.0; x[8][1] = 1.0; x[8][2] = 0.0; x[8][3] = 0.0;
x[8][4] = 0.0;
x[9][0] = 1.0; x[9][1] = 1.0; x[9][2] = 0.0; x[9][3] = 0.0;
x[9][4] = 1.0;
x[10][0]= 1.0; x[10][1]= 1.0; x[10][2]= 0.0; x[10][3]= 1.0;
x[10][4]= 0.0;
x[11][0]= 1.0; x[11][1]= 1.0; x[11][2]= 0.0; x[11][3]= 1.0;
x[11][4]= 1.0;
x[12][0]= 1.0; x[12][1]= 1.0; x[12][2]= 1.0; x[12][3]= 0.0;
x[12][4]= 0.0;
x[13][0]= 1.0; x[13][1]= 1.0; x[13][2]= 1.0; x[13][3]= 0.0;
x[13][4]= 1.0;
x[14][0]= 1.0; x[14][1]= 1.0; x[14][2]= 1.0; x[14][3]= 1.0;
x[14][4]= 0.0;
x[15][0]= 1.0; x[15][1]= 1.0; x[15][2]= 1.0; x[15][3]= 1.0;
```

```
x[15][4]= 1.0;

// desired output vectors
// corresponding to set of input vectors x
// number of outputs for parity problem
int L = 1;
double** d = new double* [m];
for(k=0;k<m;k++) d[k] = new double[L];
d[0][0] = 1.0; d[1][0] = 0.0; d[2][0] = 0.0; d[3][0] = 1.0;
d[4][0] = 0.0; d[5][0] = 1.0; d[6][0] = 1.0; d[7][0] = 0.0;
d[8][0] = 0.0; d[9][0] = 1.0; d[10][0]= 1.0; d[11][0]= 0.0;
d[12][0]= 1.0; d[13][0]= 0.0; d[14][0]= 0.0; d[15][0]= 1.0;

// error function for each input vector
double* E = new double[m];
double totalE = 0.0; // sum of E[k] k = 0, 1, .. , m

// weight matrix (input layer -> hidden layer);
// number of hidden layers includes 0
// current
int J = 5;
double** Wc = new double* [J];
for(j=0;j<J;j++) Wc[j] = new double [n];

Wc[0][0]= 0.0;   Wc[0][1]= 0.0;   Wc[0][2]= 0.0;
Wc[0][3]= 0.1;   Wc[0][4]= -0.2;
Wc[1][0]= -0.2;  Wc[1][1]= 0.5;   Wc[1][2]= -0.5;
Wc[1][3]= 0.3;   Wc[1][4]= 0.1;
Wc[2][0]= -0.3;  Wc[2][1]= -0.3;  Wc[2][2]= 0.7;
Wc[2][3]= 0.1;   Wc[2][4]= -0.2;
Wc[3][0]= 0.2;   Wc[3][1]= 0.1;   Wc[3][2]= 0.5;
Wc[3][3]= -0.3;  Wc[3][4]= -0.1;
Wc[4][0]= -0.3;  Wc[4][1]= -0.1;  Wc[4][2]= 0.1;
Wc[4][3]= 0.3;   Wc[4][4]= 0.2;

// new
double** Wnew = new double* [J];
for(j=0;j<J;j++) Wnew[j] = new double [n];

// weight matrix (hidden layer -> output layer)
// current
double** Whc = new double* [L];
for(l=0;l<L;l++) Whc[l] = new double [J];
Whc[0][0] = -0.2; Whc[0][1] = 0.3; Whc[0][2] = 0.5;
```

```
// new
double** Whnew = new double* [L];
for(l=0;l<L;l++) Whnew[l] = new double [J];

// vector in hidden layer
double* z = new double [J];
z[0] = 1.0;

// vector output layer (output layer units)
// for the parity problem the output layer has one element
double* y = new double [L];

// increment matrix (input layer -> hidden layer)
double** delW = new double* [J];
for(j=0;j<J;j++) delW[j] = new double [n];

// increment matrix (hidden layer -> output layer)
double** delWh = new double* [L];
for(l=0;l<L;l++) delWh[l] = new double [J];

// net vector (input layer -> hidden layer)
double* netj = new double [J];
netj[0] = 0.0;

// net vector (hidden layer -> output layer)
double* netl = new double [L];

// training session
int T = 10000; // number of iterations
for(t=0;t<T;t++)
{
// for loop over all input pattern
for(k=0;k<m;k++)
{
for(j=1;j<J;j++)
{ netj[j] = scalar(x[k],Wc[j],n); z[j] = fh(netj[j]); }

for(l=0;l<L;l++)
{
netl[l] = scalar(z,Whc[l],J); y[l] = fo(netl[l]);
}

for(l=0;l<L;l++)
```

```
for(j=0;j<J;j++)
delWh[l][j] =
etao*(d[k][l]-y[l])*lambdao*fo(netl[l])*(1.0-fo(netl[l]))*z[j];

double* temp = new double [J];
for(j=0;j<J;j++)
temp[j] = 0.0;

for(j=0;j<J;j++)
for(l=0;l<L;l++)
temp[j] +=
 (d[k][l]-y[l])*fo(netl[l])*(1.0-fo(netl[l]))*Whc[l][j];

for(j=0;j<J;j++)
for(i=0;i<n;i++)
delW[j][i] =
 etah*temp[j]*lambdah*fh(netj[j])*(1.0-fh(netj[j]))*x[k][i];

for(i=0;i<n;i++)
 delW[0][i] = 0.0;

// updating the weight matrices
for(j=0;j<J;j++)
for(i=0;i<n;i++)
 Wnew[j][i] = Wc[j][i] + delW[j][i];

for(l=0;l<L;l++)
for(j=0;j<J;j++)
 Whnew[l][j] = Whc[l][j] + delWh[l][j];

// setting new to current
for(j=0;j<J;j++)
for(i=0;i<n;i++)
 Wc[j][i] = Wnew[j][i];

for(l=0;l<L;l++)
for(j=0;j<J;j++)
 Whc[l][j] = Whnew[l][j];

E[k] = 0.0;
double sum = 0.0;
for(l=0;l<L;l++)
 sum += (d[k][l]-y[l])*(d[k][l]-y[l]);
```

```
E[k] = sum/2.0;
totalE += E[k];
}  // end for loop over all input pattern
if(totalE < 0.0005) goto L;
 else totalE = 0.0;
}  // end training session

L:
cout << "number of iterations = " << t << endl;

// output after training
for(j=0;j<J;j++)
for(i=0;i<n;i++)
cout << "Wc[" << j << "][" << i << "] = "
    << Wc[j][i] << endl;
cout << endl;

for(l=0;l<L;l++)
for(j=0;j<J;j++)
cout << "Whc[" << l << "][" << j << "] = "
    << Whc[l][j] << endl;

// testing the Parity function
// input (1,0,0,0,0)
for(j=1;j<J;j++)
{ netj[j] = scalar(x[0],Wc[j],n); z[j] = fh(netj[j]); }

for(l=0;l<L;l++)
{
netl[l] = scalar(z,Whc[l],J); y[l] = fo(netl[l]);
cout << "y[" << l << "] = " << y[l] << endl;
}

// input (1,0,0,0,1)
for(j=1;j<J;j++)
{ netj[j] = scalar(x[1],Wc[j],n); z[j] = fh(netj[j]); }

for(l=0;l<L;l++)
{
netl[l] = scalar(z,Whc[l],J); y[l] = fo(netl[l]);
cout << "y[" << l << "] = " << y[l] << endl;
}

// input (1,0,0,1,0)
```

```
for(j=1;j<J;j++)
{ netj[j] = scalar(x[2],Wc[j],n); z[j] = fh(netj[j]); }

for(l=0;l<L;l++)
{
netl[l] = scalar(z,Whc[l],J); y[l] = fo(netl[l]);
cout << "y[" << l << "] = " << y[l] << endl;
}

// input (1,0,0,1,1)
for(j=1;j<J;j++)
{ netj[j] = scalar(x[3],Wc[j],n); z[j] = fh(netj[j]); }
for(l=0;l<L;l++)
{
netl[l] = scalar(z,Whc[l],J); y[l] = fo(netl[l]);
cout << "y[" << l << "] = " << y[l] << endl;
}

// input (1,0,1,0,0)
for(j=1;j<J;j++)
{ netj[j] = scalar(x[4],Wc[j],n); z[j] = fh(netj[j]); }
for(l=0;l<L;l++)
{
netl[l] = scalar(z,Whc[l],J); y[l] = fo(netl[l]);
cout << "y[" << l << "] = " << y[l] << endl;
}

// input (1,0,1,0,1)
for(j=1;j<J;j++)
{ netj[j] = scalar(x[5],Wc[j],n); z[j] = fh(netj[j]); }
for(l=0;l<L;l++)
{
netl[l] = scalar(z,Whc[l],J); y[l] = fo(netl[l]);
cout << "y[" << l << "] = " << y[l] << endl;
}

// input (1,0,1,1,0)
for(j=1;j<J;j++)
{ netj[j] = scalar(x[6],Wc[j],n); z[j] = fh(netj[j]); }
for(l=0;l<L;l++)
{
netl[l] = scalar(z,Whc[l],J); y[l] = fo(netl[l]);
cout << "y[" << l << "] = " << y[l] << endl;
}
```

```
// input (1,0,1,1,1)
for(j=1;j<J;j++)
{ netj[j] = scalar(x[7],Wc[j],n); z[j] = fh(netj[j]); }
for(l=0;l<L;l++)
{
netl[l] = scalar(z,Whc[l],J); y[l] = fo(netl[l]);
cout << "y[" << l << "] = " << y[l] << endl;
}

// input (1,1,0,0,0)
for(j=1;j<J;j++)
{ netj[j] = scalar(x[8],Wc[j],n); z[j] = fh(netj[j]); }
for(l=0;l<L;l++)
{
netl[l] = scalar(z,Whc[l],J); y[l] = fo(netl[l]);
cout << "y[" << l << "] = " << y[l] << endl;
}

// input (1,1,0,0,1)
for(j=1;j<J;j++)
{ netj[j] = scalar(x[9],Wc[j],n); z[j] = fh(netj[j]); }
for(l=0;l<L;l++)
{
netl[l] = scalar(z,Whc[l],J); y[l] = fo(netl[l]);
cout << "y[" << l << "] = " << y[l] << endl;
}

// input (1,1,0,1,0)
for(j=1;j<J;j++)
{ netj[j] = scalar(x[10],Wc[j],n); z[j] = fh(netj[j]); }
for(l=0;l<L;l++)
{
netl[l] = scalar(z,Whc[l],J); y[l] = fo(netl[l]);
cout << "y[" << l << "] = " << y[l] << endl;
}

// input (1,1,0,1,1)
for(j=1;j<J;j++)
{ netj[j] = scalar(x[11],Wc[j],n); z[j] = fh(netj[j]); }
for(l=0;l<L;l++)
{
netl[l] = scalar(z,Whc[l],J); y[l] = fo(netl[l]);
cout << "y[" << l << "] = " << y[l] << endl;
```

```
    }

    // input (1,1,1,0,0)
    for(j=1;j<J;j++)
    { netj[j] = scalar(x[12],Wc[j],n); z[j] = fh(netj[j]); }
    for(l=0;l<L;l++)
    {
    netl[l] = scalar(z,Whc[l],J); y[l] = fo(netl[l]);
    cout << "y[" << l << "] = " << y[l] << endl;
    }

    // input (1,1,1,0,1)
    for(j=1;j<J;j++)
    { netj[j] = scalar(x[13],Wc[j],n); z[j] = fh(netj[j]); }
    for(l=0;l<L;l++)
    {
    netl[l] = scalar(z,Whc[l],J); y[l] = fo(netl[l]);
    cout << "y[" << l << "] = " << y[l] << endl;
    }

    // input (1,1,1,1,0)
    for(j=1;j<J;j++)
    { netj[j] = scalar(x[14],Wc[j],n); z[j] = fh(netj[j]); }
    for(l=0;l<L;l++)
    {
    netl[l] = scalar(z,Whc[l],J); y[l] = fo(netl[l]);
    cout << "y[" << l << "] = " << y[l] << endl;
    }

    // input (1,1,1,1,1)
    for(j=1;j<J;j++)
    { netj[j] = scalar(x[15],Wc[j],n); z[j] = fh(netj[j]); }
    for(l=0;l<L;l++)
    {
    netl[l] = scalar(z,Whc[l],J); y[l] = fo(netl[l]);
    cout << "y[" << l << "] = " << y[l] << endl;
    }
    return 0;
}
```

The output is

```
number of iterations = 10000
Wc[0][0] = 0
Wc[0][1] = 0
```

```
Wc[0][2] = 0
Wc[0][3] = 0.1
Wc[0][4] = -0.2
Wc[1][0] = -0.890614
Wc[1][1] = 0.199476
Wc[1][2] = -0.592286
Wc[1][3] = 0.605594
Wc[1][4] = 0.604114
Wc[2][0] = -0.379614
Wc[2][1] = -0.777377
Wc[2][2] = 0.777529
Wc[2][3] = 0.758172
Wc[2][4] = 0.760994
Wc[3][0] = 0.538437
Wc[3][1] = 0.372678
Wc[3][2] = 0.512117
Wc[3][3] = -0.656055
Wc[3][4] = -0.65043
Wc[4][0] = -0.0856427
Wc[4][1] = -0.165472
Wc[4][2] = 0.161642
Wc[4][3] = 0.151453
Wc[4][4] = 0.151421

Whc[0][0] = -2.05814
Whc[0][1] = 1.47181
Whc[0][2] = -2.45669
Whc[0][3] = 1.37033
Whc[0][4] = 3.96504
y[0] = 0.987144
y[0] = 5.96064e-07
y[0] = 5.32896e-07
y[0] = 0.989954
y[0] = 0.0183719
y[0] = 0.986117
y[0] = 0.98594
y[0] = 0.0110786
y[0] = 0.0200707
y[0] = 0.998834
y[0] = 0.998846
y[0] = 0.00840843
y[0] = 0.983464
```

```
y[0] = 0.00589264
y[0] = 0.00599696
y[0] = 0.996012
```

The values y[0] approximate the parity function.

Chapter 12

X-ray Tomography

12.1   Introduction

Tomography refers to the cross-sectional imaging of an object from either transmission or reflection data collected by illuminating the object from many different directions. Fundamentally, tomographic imaging deals with reconstructing an image from its projections. In the strict sense of the word, a projection at a given angle is the integral of the image in the direction specified by that angle. Thus tomography is a technique for solving a specific class of inverse problems. Radon [49] showed how a reconstruction was possible. Cormack [15] introduced Fourier transforms into the reconstruction algorithms.

Suppose that we shine a beam of photons (for example x-rays or microwaves) down the length of a long rod. Suppose that the electromagnetic wave passes through an infinitesimal hunk of rod it loses a fraction of its intensity that is proportional to the mass of the hunk. If we denote by $I(x)$ the intensity of the electromagnetic wave at x and by $\rho(x)$ the mass density of the rod at x, then

$$\frac{I(x + dx) - I(x)}{I(x)} = -\gamma \rho(x) dx$$

where γ is the positive constant of proportionality. Dividing across by dx and taking the limit as $dx \to 0$ we obtain

$$\frac{d}{dx} \ln I(x) = -\gamma \rho(x).$$

Integrating this expression from $-\infty$ to $+\infty$ we find

$$\ln \frac{I(\infty)}{I(-\infty)} = -\gamma \int_{-\infty}^{\infty} \rho(x) dx.$$

In X-ray tomography, we shine thin beams through different parts of the body and want to recover the density $\rho(x)$ of the body from the various values of

$$\int_{\text{beam path}} \rho(x)dx$$

measured. The mathematical tool to do this is the *Radon transform*.

12.2 Radon Transform

We formulate the problem in $\mathbf{R}^n$ and then consider the special cases. Let $\mathbf{P}^n$ be the set of all *hyperplanes* in $\mathbf{R}^n$. For example in $\mathbf{R}^2$ the hyperplanes would be lines. By definition, all hyperplanes in $\mathbf{R}^n$ are $(n-1)$-dimensional. The vectors in $\mathbf{R}^n$ are considered as column vectors. Each hyperplane ξ can be written as

$$\xi := \{\, \mathbf{x} \in \mathbf{R}^n \,:\, \hat{\omega}^T \mathbf{x} = p \,\}$$

where $\hat{\omega}$ is a (column) unit vector in $\mathbf{R}^n$, $p \in \mathbf{R}$ and ^{T} denotes transpose. Thus $\hat{\omega}^T$ is a row vector and therefore $\omega^T \mathbf{x}$ is the scalar product. If the vector $\hat{\omega}$ is normal to a hyperplane, so is $-\hat{\omega}$.

Example. In $\mathbf{R}^2$ we can write

$$x_1 \cos\theta + x_2 \sin\theta = p$$

where p is the shortest distance between the straight line and the positive x_1-direction and θ is the angle between the distance vector and the positive x_1-direction.

We have the properties
1) $(\hat{\omega}, p)$ and $(\hat{\omega}', p')$ give the same hyperplane if and only if

$$(\hat{\omega}, p) = \pm(\hat{\omega}', p')\,.$$

2) Let

$$S^n := \{\, (x_1, x_2, \ldots, x_{n+1}) \,:\, x_1^2 + x_2^2 + \cdots + x_{n+1}^2 = 1 \,\}\,.$$

The map

$$(\hat{\omega}, p) \in S^{n-1} \times \mathbf{R} \to \xi$$

is a double cover of $\mathbf{P}^n$ and can be used to define coordinate patches on $\mathbf{P}^n$, turning it into a manifold.
3) A function φ on $\mathbf{P}^n$ can be identified with a function on $S^{n-1} \times \mathbf{R}$ obeying $\varphi(\hat{\omega}, p) = \varphi(-\hat{\omega}, -p)$. We typically use the same symbol (for example,

φ) to denote both the function on $\mathbf{P}^n$ and the corresponding function on $S^{n-1} \times \mathbf{R}$.

Definition. The *Radon transform* associates to each function $f : \mathbf{R}^n \to \mathbf{R}$ the function $\hat{f} : \mathbf{P}^n \to \mathbf{R}$ is defined by

$$\hat{f}(\xi) := \int_\xi f(\mathbf{x}) dm(\mathbf{x})$$

where $dm(\mathbf{x})$ is the standard Euclidean measure on ξ.

Helgason [29] describes the requirement on the regularity on the function f and the resulting regularity on the function $\hat{f}$. We assume that the function f is an element of the Hilbert space $L_2(\mathbf{R}^n)$.

Example. As a special case a projection of a two-dimensional function $f(x_1, x_2)$ is a line integral in a certain direction. The line integral of f in the vertical direction is the projection of f onto the x_1-axis. The line integral in the horizontal direction is the projection of f onto the x_2-axis. Projections can be computed along any angle θ. The Radon transform of f is the line integral of f parallel to the x_2' axis

$$R_\theta(x_1') = \int_{-\infty}^{\infty} f(x_1' \cos\theta - x_2' \sin\theta, x_1' \sin\theta + x_2' \cos\theta) dx_2'$$

where

$$\begin{pmatrix} x_1' \\ x_2' \end{pmatrix} = \begin{pmatrix} \cos\theta & \sin\theta \\ -\sin\theta & \cos\theta \end{pmatrix} \begin{pmatrix} x_1 \\ x_2 \end{pmatrix}.$$

Let us assume that $\hat{f}$ is given. Then there are two algorithms to find f. Note that once we know how to determine f from its integrals over linear spaces of codimenion one, we also know how to determine f from its integrals over linear spaces of higher codimension. For example, the algorithms with $n = 2$ allow us to recover a function defined on a planar region from its integrals over lines. As any three dimensional body is a union of planar regions, we can also recover a function on a three dimensional body from its integral over lines, just by treating planar slices of the body individually.

The first algorithm is based on the following Lemma. It shows how to compute the conventional Fourier transform $\widetilde{f}$ of f from its Radon transform $\hat{f}$. Once $\widetilde{f}$ is known, we find f be applying the inverse Fourier transform to $\widetilde{f}$.

Lemma. For all $s \in \mathbf{R}$ and $\hat{\boldsymbol{\omega}} \in S^{n-1}$ we have

$$\widetilde{f}(s\hat{\boldsymbol{\omega}}) = \int_{-\infty}^{\infty} \hat{f}(\hat{\boldsymbol{\omega}}, r) e^{-isr} dr.$$

Proof. By definition

$$\tilde{f}(s\hat{\omega}) = \int_{\mathbf{R}^n} f(\mathbf{x})e^{-is\hat{\omega}^T\mathbf{x}}d^n\mathbf{x}$$

$$= \int_{-\infty}^{\infty} dr \int_{\hat{\omega}^T\mathbf{x}=r} dm(\mathbf{x})f(\mathbf{x})e^{-is\hat{\omega}^T\mathbf{x}}$$

$$= \int_{-\infty}^{\infty} dr e^{-isr} \int_{\hat{\omega}^T\mathbf{x}=r} dm(\mathbf{x})f(\mathbf{x})$$

$$= \int_{-\infty}^{\infty} e^{-isr}\hat{f}(\hat{\omega}, r)dr .$$

Example. If $n = 3$ and $\hat{\omega} = \hat{\mathbf{k}}$, then $dr = dz$ and $dm(\mathbf{x}) = dxdy$.

To introduce the second algorithm we define the dual transform.

Definition. The *dual Radon transform* associates to each function $\varphi :$ $\mathbf{P}^n \to \mathbf{R}$ the function $\check{\varphi} : \mathbf{R}^n \to \mathbf{R}$ defined by

$$\check{\varphi}(\mathbf{x}) = \int_{\mathbf{x}\in\xi} \varphi(\xi)d\mu(\xi)$$

where $d\mu(\xi)$ is the unique measure on $\{\xi \in \mathbf{P}^n : \mathbf{x} \in \xi\}$ which is invariant under rotations around $\mathbf{x}$ and has mass one.

Consider now the measure $d\mu(\xi)$. By translating, it suffices to consider $\mathbf{x} = \mathbf{0}$. Then

$$\{\xi \in \mathbf{P}^n : \mathbf{0} \in \xi\}$$

is just the sphere S^{n-1} with antipodal points identified and a function ψ on $\{\xi \in \mathbf{P}^n : \mathbf{0} \in \xi\}$ is identified with an even function $\psi(\hat{\omega})$ on S^{n-1}. Let Ω_n be the surface area of a unit sphere in $\mathbf{R}^n$. Then

$$\int_{\mathbf{0}\in\xi} \psi(\xi)d\mu(\xi) = \frac{1}{\Omega_n} \int_{S^{n-1}} \psi(\hat{\omega})d\hat{\omega} \qquad (1)$$

or

$$\int_{\mathbf{0}\in\xi} \psi(\xi)d\mu(\xi) = \int_{SO(n)} \psi(R\hat{\omega}_0)dR \qquad (2)$$

where $d\hat{\omega}$ is the standard Euclidean measure on S^{n-1}, $SO(n)$ is the compact Lie group of rotations in $\mathbf{R}^n$, $\hat{\omega}_0$ is any fixed unit vector in $\mathbf{R}^n$ and dR is the Haar measure on $SO(n)$. The compact Lie group $SO(n)$ is defined by all $n \times n$ matrices over $\mathbf{R}$ such that

$$SO(n) := \{ A : A^T A = I_n , \det A = 0 \} .$$

The dimension of the Lie group is $\frac{1}{2}n(n-1)$. Thus if $n = 2$ we have dimension 1.

Example. When $n = 2$ we have the Lie group $SO(2)$. The element of the Lie group $SO(2)$ are matrices of the form

$$R = \begin{pmatrix} \cos\theta & -\sin\theta \\ \sin\theta & \cos\theta \end{pmatrix}$$

with $0 \le \theta < 2\pi$ and may be labelled by the angle of rotation θ with $0 \le \theta < 2\pi$. S^1 is the unit circle in $\mathbf{R}^2$ centred on the origin and $d\hat{\omega} = d\theta$ with the volume $\Omega_2 = 2\pi$. We have

$$dR = d\begin{pmatrix} \cos\theta & -\sin\theta \\ \sin\theta & \cos\theta \end{pmatrix} = \begin{pmatrix} -\sin\theta d\theta & -\cos\theta d\theta \\ \cos\theta d\theta & -\sin\theta d\theta \end{pmatrix}.$$

Thus

$$R^{-1}dR = dRR^{-1} = \begin{pmatrix} 0 & 1 \\ -1 & 0 \end{pmatrix} d\theta$$

and the Haar measure $dR = d\theta/(2\pi)$.

To prove that the two right hand sides of (1) and (2) are equal, it suffices to observe that both of the maps

$$\psi \rightarrow \frac{1}{\Omega_n} \int_{S^{n-1}} \psi(\hat{\omega}) d\hat{\omega}$$

and

$$\psi \rightarrow \int_{SO(n)} \psi(R\hat{\omega}_0) dR$$

are rotation invariant, mass one linear functionals on the space, $C(S^{n-1})$, of continuous functions on S^{n-1}. To rotate a function $f(\mathbf{x})$, replace its argument $\mathbf{x}$ (column vector) by $R^{-1}\mathbf{x}$, i.e. $f(R^{-1}\mathbf{x})$ for some $R \in SO(n)$. There exists only one such linear functional.

Lemma. We have

$$(\hat{f})^{\vee}(\mathbf{x}) = \frac{\Omega_{n-1}}{\Omega_n} \int_{\mathbf{R}^n} \frac{f(\mathbf{y})}{|\mathbf{x} - \mathbf{y}|} d\mathbf{y}.$$

Proof. Using the definitions of the Radon transform and the dual transform and then translating and applying (2) yields

$$(\hat{f})^{\vee}(\mathbf{x}) = \int_{\mathbf{x} \in \xi} \hat{f}(\xi) d\mu(\xi)$$

$$= \int_{\mathbf{x} \in \xi} \left(\int_{\xi} f(\mathbf{y}) dm(\mathbf{y}) \right) d\mu(\xi)$$

$$= \int_{\mathbf{0} \in \xi} \left(\int_{\xi} f(\mathbf{x} + \mathbf{y}) dm(\mathbf{y}) \right) d\mu(\xi)$$

$$= \int_{SO(n)} \left(\int_{\xi_0} f(\mathbf{x} + R\mathbf{y}) dm(\mathbf{y}) \right) dR$$

where ξ_0 is any fixed hyperplane through the origin. As R runs over $SO(n)$, $\mathbf{x} + R\mathbf{y}$ runs over the surface of the sphere of radius $|\mathbf{y}|$ centered on $\mathbf{x}$. The equality of the right-hand side of (1) and (2) tells us that the integral

$$\int_{SO(n)} \psi(R\hat{\boldsymbol{\omega}}_0) dR$$

is the average value of ψ over the sphere S^{n-1}. Therefore

$$(\hat{f})^{\check{}}(\mathbf{x}) = \int_{\xi_0} \left(\int_{SO(n)} f(\mathbf{x} + R\mathbf{y}) dR \right) dm(\mathbf{y})$$

$$= \int_{\xi_0} \left(\frac{1}{\Omega_n} \int_{S^{n-1}} f(\mathbf{x} + |\mathbf{y}|\hat{\boldsymbol{\omega}}) d\hat{\boldsymbol{\omega}} \right) dm(\mathbf{y}) .$$

Choose ξ_0 to be the hyperplane in $\mathbf{R}^n$ containing all points whose last coordinate is zero. This can be identified with $\mathbf{R}^{n-1}$. Using spherical coordinates on $\mathbf{R}^{n-1}$ and observing that

$$\int_{S^{n-1}} f(\mathbf{x} + |\mathbf{y}|\hat{\boldsymbol{\omega}}) d\hat{\boldsymbol{\omega}}$$

is a function only of the length of $\mathbf{y}$ we find

$$(\hat{f})^{\check{}}(\mathbf{x}) = \int_{\mathbf{R}^{n-1}} \left(\frac{1}{\Omega_n} \int_{S^{n-1}} f(\mathbf{x} + |\mathbf{y}|\hat{\boldsymbol{\omega}}) d\hat{\boldsymbol{\omega}} \right) d\mathbf{y}$$

$$= \int_0^\infty dr \, r^{n-2} \Omega_{n-1} \left(\frac{1}{\Omega_n} \int_{S^{n-1}} f(\mathbf{x} + r\hat{\boldsymbol{\omega}}) d\hat{\boldsymbol{\omega}} \right)$$

$$= \frac{\Omega_{n-1}}{\Omega_n} \int_0^\infty dr \int_{S^{n-1}} d\hat{\boldsymbol{\omega}} r^{n-2} f(\mathbf{x} + r\hat{\boldsymbol{\omega}})$$

$$= \frac{\Omega_{n-1}}{\Omega_n} \int_0^\infty dr \int_{S^{n-1}} d\hat{\boldsymbol{\omega}} r^{n-1} \frac{1}{r} f(\mathbf{x} + r\hat{\boldsymbol{\omega}})$$

$$= \frac{\Omega_{n-1}}{\Omega_n} \int_{\mathbf{R}^n} \frac{1}{|\mathbf{y}|} f(\mathbf{x} + \mathbf{y}) d\mathbf{y}$$

$$= \frac{\Omega_{n-1}}{\Omega_n} \int_{\mathbf{R}^n} \frac{f(\mathbf{y})}{\|\mathbf{x} - \mathbf{y}\|} d\mathbf{y}$$

where we used the change of the variables $\mathbf{y} \to \mathbf{y} - \mathbf{x}$.

12.3   Discretisation

Only for a small number of functions the Radon transform can be calculated analytically. A discrete approximation to the Radon transform would be useful in particular for digital images. For this purpose we consider the Radon transform in the following form. The Radon transform $\check{f}(p, \tau)$ of a continuous two-dimensional function $f(x, y)$ is found be stacking or integrating values of f along slanted lines. The location of the line is determined from the line parameters, namely slope p and the line offset τ, i.e. we set $y = px + \tau$. Thus

$$\check{f}(p, \tau) = \int_{-\infty}^{\infty} f(x, px + \tau) dx \,.$$

In seismics this linear Radon transform is also known as *slant stacking* or the $\tau - p$ transform. There are many definitions for the discrete Radon transform derived from the continuous one. The simplest way is to sample the four variables x, y, p, τ linearly and only use a limited set of samples, i.e.

$$x \to x_m = x_{min} + m\Delta x, \quad m = 0, 1, \ldots, M - 1$$
$$y \to y_n = y_{min} + n\Delta y, \quad n = 0, 1, \ldots, N - 1$$
$$p \to p_k = p_{min} + k\Delta p, \quad k = 0, 1, \ldots, K - 1$$
$$\tau \to \tau_h = \tau_{min} + h\Delta \tau, \quad h = 0, 1, \ldots, H - 1$$

Here the x_{min} is the position of the first sample, Δx the sampling distance of x, and m is a discrete index set used to number the M samples of x. Analogously, for the independent variables y, p, τ we have same sampling, but the sampling distance and the number of samples could be different. Thus we have the following approximation for the Radon transform

$$\check{f}(p_k, \tau_h) = \int_{-\infty}^{\infty} f(x, p_k x + \tau_h) dx \approx \Delta x \sum_{m=0}^{M-1} f(x_m, p_k x_m + \tau_h) \,.$$

Sampling of the function $f(x, y)$ gives a digital image $f(x_m, y_n) = f(m, n)$. A new symbol should be assigned to the digital image, however from the indices it is clear whether the continuous or the discrete version is used. Likewise will the discrete Radon transform be written as

$$\check{f}(k, h) = \check{f}(p_k, \tau_h) \,.$$

Hence, the discrete Radon transform can be represented as a digital image. However, given the digitally sampled image $f(m, n)$ we have the following problem. The approximation given above requires samples not found in the digital image, since linear sampling of all variables implies that $p_k x_m + \tau_h$

in general never coincides with the samples y_n. The problem can be solved using, for example, a nearest neighbour approximation in the y-direction. Thus the Radon transform can be approximated by the discrete Radon transform

$$\check{f}(k, h) = \Delta x \sum_{m=0}^{M-1} f(m, n(m; k, h))$$

with

$$n(m; k, h) = \left[\frac{p_k x_m + \tau_h - y_{min}}{\Delta y} \right]$$

where $[\cdot]$ means rounding the argument to the nearest integer. Another problem is that the discrete point $(m, n(m; k, h))$ need not lie within the finite image. If the point lies outside the image the value needed could be set to zero, i.e., the point gives no contribution to the discrete Radon transform. The Δx term is only needed so that the discrete Radon transform quantitatively approximate the continuous Radon transform. The discrete Radon transform is a linear function as in the continuous case.

For a C++ implementation of this transform we set

$$n = [n^*], \qquad n^* = \frac{p_k x_m + \tau_h - y_{min}}{\Delta y} = \alpha m + \beta$$

where

$$\alpha := \frac{p_k \Delta x}{\Delta y}, \qquad \beta := \frac{p_k x_{min} + \tau_h - y_{min}}{\Delta y} .$$

The C++ code fragment to do this transformation is given by

```
for(int k=0;k<K;k++)
{
for(int h=0;h<H;h++)
{
double alpha = p[k]*Delta_x/Delta_y;
double beta = (p[k]*x_min + tau[h] - y_min)/Delta_y;
double sum = 0.0;
for(int m=0;m<M;m++)
{
int n = (int) (alpha*m + beta + 0.5);
if((n >= 0) && (n < N) sum += g[m][n];
}
f_radon[k][h] = Delta_x*sum;
}
}
```

Chapter 13

Data Compression

13.1 Introduction

Under data compression ([6], [42], [51], [52]) we understand increasing the amount of data that can be stored in a given domain, such as space, time, or frequency, or contained in a given message length. We also understand under data compression reducing the amount of storage space required to store a given amount of data, or reducing the length of a message required to transfer a given amount of information. Data compression may be accomplished by simply squeezing a given amount of data into a smaller space, for example, by increasing packing density or by transferring data on punched cards onto a magnetic tape or CD ROM. Data compression does not reduce the amount of data used to represent a given amount of information, where data compaction does. Both data compression and data compaction result in the use of fewer data elements for a given amount of information.

Data compression is particularly useful in communications because it enables devices to transmit the same amount of data in fewer bits. There are a variety of data compression techniques, but only a few have been standardised. For example, the CCITT has defined a standard data compression technique for transmitting faxes and a compression standard for data communications through modems. In addition, there are file compression formats, such as ARC and ZIP. Data compression is also widely used in backup utilities, spreadsheet applications, and a database management systems. Certain types of data, such as bit-mapped graphics, can be compressed to a small fraction of their normal size.

Data compression operates in general by taking "symbols" from an input "text", processing them, and writing "codes" to a compressed file. Symbols are usually bytes, but they could also be pixels, 80 bit floating point num-

206

bers, or EBCDIC characters. To be effective, a data compression scheme needs to be able to transform the compressed file back into an identical copy of the input text. The compressed file should be smaller than the input text.

Dictionary based compression systems operate by replacing groups of symbols in the input text with fixed length codes. A well-known example of a dictionary technique is LZW data compression. LZW operates by replacing strings of essentially unlimited length with codes that usually range in size from 9 to 16 bits. Statistical methods of data compression take a completely different approach. They operate by encoding symbols one at a time. The symbols are encoded into variable length output codes. The length of the output code varies based on the probability or frequency of the symbol. Low probability symbols are encoded using many bits, and high probability symbols are encoded using fewer bits. An example is arithmetic encoding. In practice, the dividing line between statistical and dictionary methods is not always so distinct. Some schemes cannot be clearly put in one camp or the other, and there are always hybrids which use features from both techniques. In the world of small systems, dictionary based data compression techniques seem to be more popular at this time. However, by combing arithmetic coding with powerful modelling techniques, statistical methods for data compression can actually achieve better performance.

Lossy compression refers to data compression techniques in which some amount of data is lost. Lossy compression technologies attempts to eliminate redundant or unnecessary information. Most video compression technologies, such as MPEG, use a lossy techniques. For example wavelet compression is a lossy compression of an image. Images compressed using wavelets are smaller than JPEG images and can be transferred and downloaded at quicker speeds. Wavelet technology can compress colour images from 20:1 to 300:1, grayscale images from 10:1 to 50:1. MPEG-4 uses wavelets for compression. MPEG-4 was standardised in October 1998 in the ISO/IEC document 14496.

Lossless compression refers to data compression techniques in which no data is lost. The PKZIP compression technology is an example of lossless compression. For most types of data, lossless compression techniques can reduce the space needed by only about 50%. For greater compression, one must use a lossy compression technique. Note, however, that only certain types of data – graphics, audio, and video – can tolerate lossy compression. We must use lossless compression techniques when compressing data and programs.

Most of the data compression methods in common use today fall into one of two camps: dictionary based schemes and statistical methods. Dictionary based compression systems operate by replacing groups of symbols in the input text with fixed length codes. An example of a dictionary based scheme is LZW compression.

Data compression can be achieved by assigning short codes to the most frequently encountered source characters and necessarily longer codes to the others. The *Morse code* is such a variable length code which is reasonably efficient for both English and German text. The most frequently encountered letter, 'E', has the shortest Morse code ("·") while the less frequently used letters (e.g. 'Q') have longer codes (e.g. "– – · –").

The Morse code is a punctuated code in that after each letter there is a letter space of 3 time units and after each word there is a word space of 6 time units. This introduces a significant deterioration of efficiency.

One requirement for a code to be generally useful is that it should be uniquely decodable. A code is said to be uniquely decodable if, for each code-word sequence of finite length, the resulting string of letters of the code alphabet is different from any other codeword sequence.

13.2   LZW Compression

13.2.1   Introduction

In 1984, Terry Welch proposed the LZW algorithm [62]. The algorithm is used to reduce the size of files, e.g. for archiving or transmission. The LZW algorithm is based on the LZ77 algorithm, which was proposed by A. Lempel and J. Ziv in 1977 [65]. LZ77 is a universal algorithm in that it assumes no information about the file before compression. This method uses a sliding window method while compressing. The data that is within the range of the window is what is active in the algorithm. LZSS was implemented by Storer and Szymanski. It addressed the problem of inefficient use of space in the token, as well as how comparisons are done. The LZ78 method drops all of the things that made the previous methods slow and cumbersome. Mainly, instead of having file buffers, which require several file pointers inside the file, LZ78 simply breaks input into phases to be processed. In this way it moves sequentially through the file. Like LZ77 and LZ78, LZW is a dictionary (also called codebook or string table) based compression algorithm and does not perform any analysis of the input text. The addition of T. Welch in 1984 is an initialisation of the dictionary to the standard 256 ASCII characters, represented by the codes $0 - 255$. By having this pre-established starting point, even the smaller files were able to be compressed, as more of the code was able to be represented by the dictionary entries. Larger files would have slight gain in the efficiency of their encoding.

LZW is widely known for its application in GIF and in the V.42 communication standard. The idea behind the LZW algorithm is simple but there are implementation details that one needs to take care of. The Lempel, Ziv and Welch compression relies on reoccurrence of bytes sequences (strings) in its input. It maintains a table mapping input strings to their associated output codes. The table initially contains mappings for all possible strings of length one. Input is taken one byte at a time to find the longest initial string present in the table. The code for that string is output and then the string is extended with one more input byte, b. A new entry is added to the table mapping the extended string to the next unused code (obtained by incrementing a counter). The process repeats starting from byte b. The number of bits in an output code, and hence the maximum number of entries in the table is usually fixed and once this limit is reached, no more entries are added.

There are a number of methods for optimisation such as dictionary freezing, dictionary pruning, and deconstruction of the dictionary.

13.2.2 Compression Procedure

The first thing we do in LZW compression is initialise our codebook (also called string table or dictionary). To do so, we need to choose a code size and know how many values our characters can possibly take. If, for example, our code size is 12 bits we can store 2^{12}, or 4096 entries in our code table. Assume we have 32 possible different characters. This corresponds to, say, a picture in which there are 32 different colours possible for each pixel. To initialise the table, we set code #0 to character #0, code #1 to character #1, and so on, until for our example code #31 to character #31. We are specifying that each code from 0 to 31 maps to a root. There will be no more entries in the codebook that have this property. Now we start compressing our data. First we need the current prefix (the existing string) which we denote by w. It is the prefix where we store strings and compare to other strings. Initially, the current prefix is empty,

```
w = " "
```

Next we define a string wK which is the current prefix concatenated with the next character from the charstream (input text), i.e.

```
wK = w + K
```

where + stands for concatenation. The `string` class in C++ also uses + for concatenating strings. Next we take the zeroth character from the charstream we call c. We form wK. Since w is empty at this moment in time we have

```
w = "c"
```

Obviously "c" is in our codebook. Take now the next character from the charstream we call d. Then

```
wK = w + K = "cd"
```

The string "cd" is not in the codebook with the next number after the root. Then we write w which is c to the codestream (output) and set w = K. Thus w = "d". Taking the next character from the charstream we continue with this algorithm till no characters are left. We output the code for w to the end of R.

Thus the algorithm for the compression can be summarised as follows.

```
[1] Initialise codebook (dictionary, string table)
[2] w -> empty string
[3] K -> next character in charstream (input text)
[4] Is wK in codebook?
    (yes: w -> wK
          goto [3]
    )
    (no: add wK to the codebook
         append the code for w to the codestream (output)
         w -> K
         goto [3]
    )
[5] Algorithm ends if no character left in the charstream
```

When we get to step [3] and there are not any more characters left, we output the code for w and throw the table away.

13.2.3   Examples

Example 1. We consider the text string

```
T = "xxxyyxyyxyxxyx"
```

Obviously we initialise our codebook with the letters x and y. The length of the codebook is for this simple example not important. Thus we have a codebook

```
0 -> x
1 -> y
```

We initialise w to the empty string, i.e. w = "". The output string is also set to the empty string R = "". Next we take the zeroth character from the string T which is a K = "x". Then wK = "x". This we compare with our codebook and see that code 0 is a "x". Now we set w = "x". Now we read the first character from the input text which is also an K = "x". Then wK = "xx". However "xx" is not in the codebook yet. Thus we set 2 -> xx and we insert the 0 in our output string

R = "0".

We now set w = "x". Now we read the next character from T which is again an K = "x". Then wK = "xx". The string "xx" is in the codebook. Thus we set w = "xx". The next character is an "y". Thus we have wK = "xxy". This string is not in the codebook. Thus we add it to the codebook 3 -> xxy. Then we append the code for "xx" to the output string

R = "02"

and set w = "y". The next character is an "y". Thus wK = "yy". This string is not in the codebook. Thus 4 -> yy

R = "021"

and w = "y". The next character is an x. Thus wK = "yx". This string is not in the codebook. Thus 5 -> yx

R = "0211"

and w = "x". The next character is a "y". Thus wK = "xy". This string is not in the codebook. Thus 6 -> xy

R = "02110"

and w = "y". The next character is a "y". Thus wK = "yy". This string is in the codebook. Thus w = "yy". The next character is an "x". Thus wK = "yyx". This string is not in the codebook. Thus 7 -> yyx

R = "021104"

and w = "x". The next character is a "y". Thus wK = "xy". This string is in the codebook. Thus w = "xy". The next character is an "x". Thus wK = "xyx". This string is not in the codebook. Thus 8 -> xyx

```
R = "0211046"
```

and w = "x". The next character is an "x". Thus wK = "xx". This string is in the codebook. Thus w = "xx". The next character is a "y". Thus wK = "xxy". This string is in the codebook. Thus w = "xxy". The last character is an "x". Thus wK = "xxyx". This string is not in the codebook. Thus

```
9 -> xxyx
```

```
R = "02110463"
```

and w = "x". Thus we concatenate a 0 to R yielding

```
R = "021104630"
```

Thus the encoding is done. The codebook is

```
0 -> x
1 -> y
2 -> xx
3 -> xxy
4 -> yy
5 -> yx
6 -> xy
7 -> yyx
8 -> xyx
9 -> xxyx
```

and

```
R = "02110463"
```

Thus the original string T contained 14 characters, the compressed string contains 8 characters.

The following C++ program implements the LZW algorithm for this example. We use the string class of C++.

```
// LZW1.cpp
```

```cpp
#include <iostream>
#include <string>
using namespace std;

int main(void)
```

```
{
  string T = "xxxyyxyyxyxxyx"; // input text (charstream)
  string R = "";              // output text

  // initialise w, K, wK to empty string
  string w = "";
  string K = "";
  string wK = "";
  char c;

  // codebook
  int size = 10;
  string* value = new string[size];
  value[0] = "x";   value[1] = "y";

  int counter = 1;
  counter++;
  int len = T.length();

  for(int i=0;i<len;i++)
  {
  char c = T[i];
  K = c;
  string wK = w + K; // + concatenate strings
  int flag = 0;
  int j;

  for(j=0;j<counter;j++)
  {
  if(wK == value[j])
  {
  flag = 1;
  goto L1;
  }
  }

  L1:
  if(flag == 1)   { w = wK; }
  if(flag == 0)
  {
  value[counter] = wK;
  int pos;
  for(j=0;j<counter;j++)
  {
```

```
if(w == value[j])
{
pos = j;
goto L2;
}
}
L2:
c = pos + 48; // ASCII table '0' <-> 48
R += c;
w = K;
counter++;
}
} // end outer for loop

// concatenating the last character to output
c = T[len-1];
string s = "";
s += c;
int temp;

for(int k=0;k<2;k++)
{
if(s == value[k])
{
temp = k;
goto L3;
}
}
L3:
char ch = temp + 48;
R += ch;
// display output string
cout << R << endl;
// display codebook
for(int j=0;j<size;j++)
cout << value[j] << endl;

return 0;
}
```

Example 2. We have a four character alphabet:

A   B   C   D

The input string (charstream) is

T = "ABACABA"

First we initialise our codebook to

#0 -> A, #1 -> B, #2 -> C, #3 -> D

The zeroth character in T is A which is in the codebook. Thus w = "A". Next we get the character B. Thus wK = "AB". This string is not in the codebook. Thus

#4 -> AB

R = "#0"

and w = "B". The next character is an A. Thus wK = "BA". This string is not in the codebook. Thus

#5 -> BA

R = "#0#1"

and w = "A". The next character is a C. Thus wK = "AC". This string is not in the codebook. Thus

#6 -> AC

R = "#0#1#0"

and w = "C". The next character is an A. Thus wK = "CA". This string is not in the table. Thus

#7 -> CA

R = "#0#1#0#2"

and w = A. The next character is a B. Thus wK = "AB". This string is in the codebook. Thus w = "AB". The last character is an A. Thus wK = "ABA". This string is not in the codebook. Thus

#8 -> ABA

R = "#0#1#0#2#4"

and w = "A". There are no more characters. Thus we output #0 for the code for A. Thus

R = "#0#1#0#2#4#0"

This is the codestream.

13.2.4   Decompression Procedure

The decompression algorithm is as follows:

```
[1] Initialise codebook (dictionary, string table);
[2] get first code: <code>
[3] output the string for code to the charstream;
[4] <old> = <code>
[5] <code> <- next code in codestream;
[6] does <code> exit in the codebook?
    (yes: output the string for <code> to the charstream T;
          w <- translation for old;
          K <- first character of translation for <code>;
          add wK to the codebook;
          <old> <- <code>;
    )
    (no: w <- translation for <old>;
         K <- first character of w;
         output string wK to charstream T and add it to codebook;
         <old> <- <code>
    )
[7] goto [5];
[8] Algorithm ends if no code is left in the codestream;
```

Example. Consider the codestream from our first example

```
R = "021104630"
```

and

```
0 = x
1 = y
```

We set

```
T = ""
```

First we find 0 in R. Thus we add x to our output text. Thus T = "x".
Now we have only one character, so we can not make any codes. Thus we
continue in the string R. The next character is a 2. We do not have this
2. We take the previous text inserted, and add the last character from the
last used code. This gives us xx (just inserted x, and we used code x). This
new code we insert in the codebook

```
0 = x
1 = y
2 = xx
```

Now we add it to the charstream, i.e. T = "xxx". The next character in R is 1. 1 exists in the code with y. Thus T = "xxxy". We add 3 = xxy to the code book. Thus

```
0 = x
1 = y
2 = xx
3 = xxy
```

The next character in R is a 1 again. 1 exists in the codebook. Thus T = "xxxyy" and we add 4 = yy to the codebook

```
0 = x
1 = y
2 = xx
3 = xxy
4 = yy
```

The next character in R is 0. 0 exists in the codebook. Thus T = "xxxyyx" and we add yx = 5 to the codebook

```
0 = x
1 = y
2 = xx
3 = xxy
4 = yy
5 = yx
```

The next character is 4. 4 is in the codebook. Thus T = "xxxyyxyy" and we add xy = 6 to the codebook. Thus

```
0 = x
1 = y
2 = xx
3 = xxy
4 = yy
5 = yx
6 = xy
```

Repeating this procedure we find T given above and the codebook given above.

13.3 Entropy Encoding

Given a source of symbols, drawn from a known alphabet. We have the task of writing down the symbols as the source produces them. Let us assume that our alphabet consists of the 8 symbols

```
A B C D E F G H
```

Each time we get a symbol from the source, then, there are 8 possibilities. A bit is a unit of information. A bit can be either 0 or 1. Writing a bit, therefore, conveys exactly enough information to distinguish between two possibilities. This is not enough information to uniquely identify every symbol in our alphabet. Thus we will be required to write more than one bit for each symbol of input.

Given an arbitrary symbol x we may adopt the following algorithm:

```
if x=A or x=B, write 0,
    then:
    if x=A write 0
    if x=B write 1

    if x=C or D or E or F or G or H, write 1,
        then:
            if x=C or D, write 0,
            then:
            if x=C, write 0
            if x=D, write 1

            if x=E or F or G or H write 1,
            then:
                if x=E or F, write 0,
                then:
                    if x=E, write 0
                    if x=F, write 1

                if x=G or H, write 1,
                    then:
                        if x=G, write 0
                        if x=H, write 1
```

Since a bit provides exactly enough information to distinguish between two possibilities, we can use each bit we write to distinguish between two different groups of symbols. If the group we identify contains more than one symbol, we must divide it into two smaller groups and write another bit, etc., until a single symbol is identified. The sequence of bits we write for each symbol is that symbol's code.

```
Symbol  Code  Code Length
======  ====  ===========
A       00    2
```

B	01	2
C	100	3
D	101	3
E	1100	4
F	1101	4
G	1110	4
H	1111	4

Before we ask how efficient this method of encoding is, relative to the other possibilities, we have to find out how much freedom we have in choosing encodings. By changing the way we divide the symbols into groups, we can change how many bits we write for each symbol. It is required that each symbol can be uniquely identified in the end. Given an N symbol alphabet, with symbols from

$$x_0, x_1, \ldots, x_{N-1}$$

$$\sum_{i=0}^{N-1} 2^{-L_i} = 1$$

where L_i is the code length of symbol x_i. For the given example we have

$$2 \cdot 1/2^2 + 2 \cdot 1/2^3 + 4 \cdot 1/2^4 = 1/2 + 1/4 + 1/4 = 1.$$

How efficient is this encoding? It depends on how common each of the symbols is. If all symbols are equally likely, then our average code length is

$$(4 \cdot 4 + 2 \cdot 3 + 2 \cdot 2)/8 = 26/8 = 3.25 \text{bits}.$$

If each symbol is equally likely, then, our encoding is certainly not the best we can do, because an encoding exists that uses only 3 bits per symbol $(8 * 1/8 = 1)$. What if A's and B's are more common than the other symbols? Our encoding uses 2 bits to encode A or B, but spends 4 bits to encode E, F, G, or H. If a symbol is more likely to be A or B than it is to be E, F, G, or H, however, then we write two bits for a symbol more often than we write 4, and our average code length will be less than 3 bits per symbol. Thus the efficiency of a particular encoding depends on the symbol probabilities. It is possible to create an optimal encoding from the probabilities themselves, and the mapping is trivial.

If we assign each symbol x_i a probability p_i, then the optimal encoding has

$$2^{-L_i} = p_i$$

for every symbol. Since every symbol must be one of the symbols from our alphabet, the sum of all the symbol probabilities must be 1, and so the optimal encoding satisfies the constraint on the code lengths.

For our example, we see that our encoding is optimal when the probabilities of A,B,C,D,E,F,G,H are

$$\frac{1}{4}, \frac{1}{4}, \frac{1}{8}, \frac{1}{8}, \frac{1}{16}, \frac{1}{16}, \frac{1}{16}, \frac{1}{16}.$$

If we assume these probabilities and calculate our average code length (properly, weighting a symbol's length by its probability of occurring), we find that the average code length is

$$\frac{1}{2} * 2 + \frac{1}{4} * 3 + \frac{1}{4} * 4 = 1 + \frac{3}{4} + 1 = 2.75$$

bits per symbol – better than 3. Given the above distribution of symbol probabilities, 2.75 bits per symbol (on average) is the best we can do. In Shannon's information theory, 2.75 bits/symbol is the entropy of the source, and so the method of encoding that assigns optimal code lengths according to symbol probabilities is referred to as entropy encoding.

We also need a coding method that effectively takes advantage of that knowledge. The best known coding method based on probability statistics is Huffman coding. D. A. Huffman published a paper in 1952 ([31]) describing a method of creating a code table for a set of symbols given their probabilities. The Huffman code table was guaranteed to produce the lowest possible output bit count possible for the input stream of symbols, when using fixed length codes. Huffman called these "minimum redundancy codes", but the scheme is now universally called Huffman coding. Other fixed length coding systems, such as Shannon-Fano codes, were shown by Huffman to be non-optimal.

13.4   Huffman Code

Huffman coding assigns an output code to each symbol, with the output codes being as short as 1 bit, or considerably longer than the input symbols, strictly depending on their probabilities. The optimal number of bits to be used for each symbol is the log base 2 of $(1/p)$, where p is the probability of a given character. Thus, if the probability of a character is $1/256$, such as would be found in a random byte stream, the optimal number of bits per character is log base 2 of 256, or 8. If the probability goes up to $1/2$, the optimum number of bits needed to code the character would go down to 1. The problem with this scheme lies in the fact that Huffman codes have to be an integral number of bits long. For example, if the probability of a character is $1/3$, the optimum number of bits to code that character is around 1.6. The Huffman coding scheme has to assign either 1 or 2 bits to the code, and either choice leads to a longer compressed message than is theoretically possible. This non-optimal coding becomes a noticeable problem when the probability of a character becomes very high. If a statistical method can be developed that can assign a 90given character, the optimal code size would be 0.15 bits. The Huffman coding system would probably assign a 1 bit code to the symbol, which is 6 times longer than is necessary.

A second problem with Huffman coding comes about when trying to do adaptive data compression. When doing non-adaptive data compression, the compression program makes a single pass over the data to collect statistics. The data is then encoded using the statistics, which are unchanging throughout the encoding process. For the decoder to decode the compressed data stream, it first needs a copy of the statistics. The encoder will typically prepend a statistics table to the compressed message, so the decoder can read it in before starting. This adds a certain amount of excess baggage to the message. When using simple statistical models to compress the data, the encoding table tends to be rather small. For example, a simple frequency count of each character could be stored in as little as 256 bytes with fairly high accuracy. This would not add significant length to any except the very smallest messages. However, in order to get better compression ratios, the statistical models by necessity have to grow in size. If the statistics for the message become too large, any improvement in compression ratios will be wiped out by the added length needed to prepend them to the encoded message. In order to bypass this problem, adaptive data compression is called for. In adaptive data compression, both the encoder and decoder start with their statistical model in the same state. Each of them process a single character at a time, and update their models after the character is read in. This is very similar to the way most dictionary based schemes such as LZW coding work. A slight amount of efficiency is lost by beginning the message with a non-optimal model, but it is usually more than made up for by not having to pass any statistics with the message. The problem with combining adaptive modelling with Huffman coding is that rebuilding the Huffman tree is a very expensive process. For an adaptive scheme to be efficient, it is necessary to adjust the Huffman tree after every character. Algorithms to perform adaptive Huffman coding were not published until over 20 years after Huffman coding was first developed. Even now, the best adaptive Huffman coding algorithms are still relatively time and memory consuming.

Example. Consider a code defined on a binary alphabet $\mathcal{C} = \{0, 1\}$. A code C with codewords

$$c \in \{0, 1, 00, 01, 10, 11\}$$

is for example not uniquely decodable since the string "01" could be decoded as either the concatenation of 2 codewords [0]+[1] or as the single code word

[01]. On the other hand, a code with codewords

$$c \in \{\, 0, 10, 11 \,\}$$

is uniquely decodable. Try and form a string with these codewords which is not uniquely decodable.

A class of very useful codes are the prefix or instantaneous codes. A code is called a prefix code if no code-word is a prefix of any other code-word. Prefix codes are uniquely decodable. Hence, from the *Kraft inequality* we know that the expected code length is greater or equal to the entropy of the source.

Example. Consider for example a source (e.g. the text file to be compressed) of four possible output symbols

$$x \in \mathcal{X} = \{\, A,\, B,\, C,\, D \,\}\,.$$

Assume the probabilities for the four symbols are

$$\{\, p_m \,\} = \left\{ \frac{1}{2},\ \frac{1}{4},\ \frac{1}{8},\ \frac{1}{8} \right\}\,.$$

We can construct a prefix code C with $M = 4$ codewords. We construct a binary Huffman code for this source. We first combine the two least probable symbols C and D pushing the binary letters 0 and 1 into the code-word strings. The joint probability is $\frac{1}{4}$. This process is repeated by combining repetitively the two least probable symbols. We find

$$c \in C = \{\, 0, 10, 110, 111 \,\}\,.$$

Note that this code is uniquely decodable and furthermore, there is no need to add punctuating symbols between the code-words. Prefix codes are self-punctuating. The average length for this code is

$$L(C) = \sum_{m=1}^{4} p_m l_m = \frac{1}{2} \cdot 1 + \frac{1}{4} \cdot 2 + 2 \cdot \frac{1}{8} \cdot 3 = 1\frac{3}{4}\,.$$

A prefix code based on an alphabet of size s_A can be represented graphically by an s-ary tree for a binary tree where each node has s_A branches.

Each node of the tree for this code has two branches since the code is based on a binary alphabet. The code-words are represented by the leaves of the tree. Since no code-word is a prefix of any other code-word, each code-word eliminates its descendants (nodes which are not a leaf).

Huffman codes are optimal in the sense that their expected length is equal or shorter than the expected length of any other uniquely prefix code. Huffman codes are constructed by combining at each step the s least probable source symbols into a new source symbol with the combined probability and inserting into each code-word string one of the s letters of the alphabet.

The following C++ program reads in the number of different source symbols (e.g. the ASCII symbols in the case of a text file) and produces a binary Huffman code for this source.

```cpp
// Huffman.cpp

#include <cstdlib>
#include <iostream>
using namespace std;

int main(void)
{
  // maximum number of symbols in source alphabet
  const int maxsymbols = 50;

  // array for probability distribution of source
  double pm[maxsymbols+1];

  int M; // no of source symbols
  cout << "M = "; // read in number of source symbols and
  cin  >> M;      // make sure that M > 2 and M < maxsymbols

  if((M < 2) || (M > maxsymbols))
  {
  cout << "*** ERROR ***: invalid no of symbols for source";
  exit(0);
  }
  double sumpm = 0.0;   // used to check that sum_m p_m = 1

  int m;
  for(m=1;m<=M;++m)
  {
  cout << "p_" << m << " = ";         // and check that
  cin  >> pm[m];                       // 0 <= pm <= 1
  if((pm[m] < 0.0) || (pm[m] > 1.0))
  {
  cout << "*** ERROR ***: invalid p_m" << endl;
  exit(1);
```

```
    }
    sumpm += pm[m];
    }

    double eps = 0.001;  // check that sum_m p_m = 1
    if((sumpm < 1.0-eps) || (sumpm > 1+eps))
    {
    cout << "*** ERROR ***: probabilities dont add up to 1.0";
    exit(2);
    }

    struct node
    {
    double prob;
    char   digit;
    node* next;
    };

// tree always stores the lowest level of node in the tree,
// treep moves level for level up the tree
    node *tree[maxsymbols+1], *treep[maxsymbols+1];

    for(m=1;m<=M;++m)
    {
    tree[m] = new node;
    tree[m] -> prob  = pm[m];
    tree[m] -> digit = '-';
    tree[m] -> next  = 0;
    treep[m] = tree[m];
    }

    int Mp = M;
    double min1, min2;
    int mmin1, mmin2;

    while(Mp >= 2)
    {                       // find 2 lowest probabilities
    min1 = min2 = 1.0;      // in current level of tree
    int m;
    for(m=Mp;m>=1;--m)
    {
    if(treep[m]->prob < min1) {
    mmin1 = m;
    min1  = treep[m]->prob;
```

```
}
}
for(m=Mp;m>=1;--m)
{
if((treep[m]->prob<min2) && (treep[m]->prob>=min1)
                        && (m!=mmin1))
{
mmin2 = m;
min2  = treep[m] -> prob;
}
}

// now create a new node in the tree for the combined
// symbol of the two least probable source symbols
node* dumnode = new node;
dumnode -> prob = treep[mmin1] -> prob+treep[mmin2] -> prob;
dumnode -> digit = ' ';
dumnode -> next = 0;

if(mmin1<mmin2)
{                       // for consistency in codes make
int idum = mmin2;  // certain that mmin1 is always
mmin2 = mmin1;     // the larger index
mmin1 = idum;
}

treep[mmin2] -> digit = '0';     // set the digit for the 2
treep[mmin2] -> next  = dumnode; // symbols which have been
treep[mmin1] -> digit = '1';     // combined into a single
treep[mmin1] -> next  = dumnode; // artificial symbol

// Now build the next level of tree
int mpp;
if(mmin1 < mmin2) mpp = mmin1;
else mpp = mmin2;

treep[mpp] = dumnode;
int mp=1;
for(m=1;m<=Mp;++m)
{
if((m != mmin1) && (m != mmin2))
{
if(mp == mpp) ++mp;
treep[mp] = treep[m];
```

```
  ++mp;
  }
  }
  --Mp;
  }

// now the full tree is constructed and we only have to
// read of the code-word strings in reverse order.
char codeword[maxsymbols+1];

node* nd;

cout << endl;
cout << "  m  |           p_m         |   code-word" << endl;
cout << "========================================="
     << endl;

  for(m=1;m<=M;++m)
  {
  nd = tree[m];
  cout.width(3);
  cout << m << "  |   ";
  cout.width(15);
  cout << pm[m] << "  |   ";
  codeword[1] = nd->digit;
  int mp = 1;

  while(nd->next != 0)
  {
  ++mp;
  nd = nd -> next;
  codeword[mp] = nd -> digit;
  }
  int mpp;
  for(mpp=mp;mpp>=1;--mpp)
  cout << codeword[mpp];
  cout << endl;
  }

  return 0;
} // end main
```

13.5 Arithmetic Coding

Arithmetic coding ([64],[63],[51],[52]) is a method of encoding data using a variable number of bits. The number of bits used to encode each symbol varies according to the probability assigned to that symbol. Low probability symbols use many bits, high probability symbols use fewer bits.

If we want to encode symbols from a source optimally, we assign each symbol x_i a code with length

$$L_i = -\log_2 p_i$$

where p_i is the probability of the symbol's occurrence. This only works if p_i is a negative power of 2. Otherwise $-\log_2 p_i$ will not be an integer, so the optimal code length L_i will not be an integer. An optimal encoding would then have to write a non-integral number of bits. It seems impossible to write, say 3.35 bits to encode a particular symbol. However, we can actually do it if we have infinite many symbols to write.

The approach to do this is as follows: Rather than writing bits for each symbol, we write a single number, in the interval [0,1) that encodes the entire source. Then we write this number as a sequence of bits. Thus, if we write it in binary with a decimal point, a number in the interval $[0, 1)$ will be of the form

`0.##########....`

where each # is either a 0 or a 1. We encode our number by writing out the bits to the right of the decimal point. To encode a symbol, rather than writing bits, we simply make a decision that reduces the range of numbers we might finally write.

We have seen all the symbols in the source, and made all of these decisions that reduce the range of numbers we might write. We will be left having to write a number in some interval

$$[x, x + R)$$

where

$$0 \le x < x + R \le 1.$$

R is the final size of this range.

How many bits do we have to write before we get a number in this range? The answer is always less than

$$-\log_2 R + 2$$

bits. Since a smaller final range means writing more bits, each of the range-reducing decision we must make increases the number of bits we must write. If we begin with a range $[x, x + R)$ and encode a symbol by deciding that we will finally write a number in the range

$$[x + lR, x + (l + P)R)$$

where $0 \leq l < l + P < 1$. Thus

$$x \leq x + lR < x + (l + P)R \leq x + R.$$

Then we increase the number of bits we must write from $-\log_2 R + 2$ to $-\log_2 PR + 2$. The difference is

$$(-\log_2(PR) + 2) - (-\log_2 R + 2) = \log_2 R - \log_2(PR) = -\log_2 P$$

bits. If we have an alphabet of N symbols, with probabilities p_i, and we have a current interval $[x, x + R)$, we can divide the interval into N disjoint sub-intervals, one for each possible symbol x_i, and we can set the size of each symbol's sub-interval to $p_i R$. To encode a symbol, then, we simply decide that we will finally write a number in that symbol's sub-interval. We replace the current interval with the sub-interval corresponding to the appropriate symbol x_i, which will result, in the end, in writing an optimal $-\log_2 p_i$ bits for that symbol – even if $-\log_2 p_i$ is not an integer. Since the sub-intervals for possible symbols are disjoint, the program that will finally read the number we write can tell which symbol we encoded.

Implementations of arithmetic encoding do not do mathematics using very long binary numbers. Instead, numbers x and R that form the current interval $[x, x + R)$ are stored as integers, scaled up by some power of 2 that keeps the interval size, R, in a workable range. Probabilities are stored as integers of slightly smaller size. When the interval size decreases past its lower bound, the scaling power increases, and the integers x and R are doubled, until R returns to an appropriate size. x, the lower bound on the interval, does not decrease as R does, and so repeated doubling would cause the integer to overflow. To prevent this, implementations write out the more significant bits of x as it increases. No matter how big x become before we write out its higher order bits, the possibility exists that the bits we do write out might need to change due to carry propagation. For example, assume our interval is

$$[0.5 - 2^{-1000}, 0.5 + 2^{-1000}]$$

it is still possible to finally write $0.5 + 2^{-1001}$. This causes 1000 bits of x to change. Various implementations have different ways of dealing with this. The arithmetic encoder does not output 1 bits, or the most recent 0 bit, immediately. Instead, it simply counts the number of 1's (say M) produced after the last zero. Upon producing another 0 bit, then, it will output a 0 followed by M ones. Upon receiving a 2 bit (i.e., a carry propagation), it will output a 1 followed by M zeros.

Arithmetic encoding works when we write an endless stream of symbols from some source to some sink. In real systems is often not the case. We are typically compressing an input file of finite length, and we expect to be able to decompress this to recreate the same file. To make this possible, we need to tell the decompressor how many symbols we write. There are two approaches to this:

The first is simply to write out the length at the beginning of the compressed stream. This needs about $O(\log(N))$ bits, where $\log(N)$ is the length in symbols. The second is to reserve a special EOF symbol that does not occur in the input. When we are finished encoding symbols from our source, we write the EOF symbol at the end, which tells the decoder to stop. Since we must assign a probability to this symbol whenever we might stop encoding, however, this makes the encoding of all other symbols slightly less efficient, and wastes $O(N)$ bits altogether. Obviously, the EOF symbol is given a very small probability.

Both of these methods are only slightly wasteful when the input is of any significant size. We present a better way. Recall that when we are finished encoding, we have to write a number in some interval $[x, x + R)$, and we know that we have to write about $-\log_2 R + 2$ bits to do this. Exactly how many bits it takes, however, depends on the bits we do not write. Arithmetic encoders will accept an input of finite length and write out a number with finite precision. By specifying $-\log_2 R + 2$ bits, the encoder can make sure that the number it writes is in the required range no matter what the decoder thinks about the bits that follow – if the encoder were to continue writing any number of 1's and zeros, the number would still be in the proper range. We can do better if we assume that unwritten bits are zero. An arithmetic encoder that adopts this approach will accept an input of finite length and write out a number of infinite precision that is finitely odd. Finitely odd means that the right-most 1 bit is finitely far from the beginning of the output or, equivalently, that the number it writes is divisible by some negative power of 2. In the binary decimal representation that an arithmetic encoder writes, a finitely odd number is either:

an infinite string of 0s; or a finite number of 0s and 1s, followed by the last 1, followed by an infinite string of zeros.

When the arithmetic encoder writes a finitely odd number, it simply omits the infinite zero tail, and the decoder assumes that unwritten bits are all zero.

When we are finished encoding, then, and we must write a number in $[x, x + R)$, we write some finitely odd number in that range, but we write it with infinite precision. There are an infinite number of such numbers in any range, and we could encode any one of them. We can achieve better end handling by using the number we do write to tell the decoder where the end of file is. The procedure is as follows:

During our encoding, we eventually arrive at the first place that the input might end, and we know that whether it ends or not, we will write a number in the range $[x_0, x_0 + R]$. We simply decide that if the input does end here, we write out the most even number in that range, resulting in the shortest possible output that identifies that range. We call this number E_0. On the other hand, if the input does not end here, we simply continue encoding normally. Eventually, we arrive at the second place that the input might end, and we know that whether it ends or not, we must write a number in $[x_1, x_1 + R]$. Now we decide that if the input does end here, we write out the most even number in the range that is not E_0. We can not write E_0, of course, since that would mean the file ends at the previous possible position. This number will be E_1. Otherwise we continue. Finally, the input will end, and we write out the most even number in the final range that does not indicate a previous end.

Thus arithmetic coding completely bypasses the idea of replacing an input symbol with a specific code. Instead, it takes a stream of input symbols and replaces it with a single floating point output number. The longer (and more complex) the message, the more bits are needed in the output number. Practical methods were found to implement this on computers with fixed sized registers. The output from an arithmetic coding process is a single number less than 1 and greater than or equal to 0. This single number can be uniquely decoded to create the exact stream of symbols that went into its construction. In order to construct the output number, the symbols being encoded have to have a set of probabilities assigned to them. For example, we encode the string `"WILLISTEEB"` with the alphabet

```
X := { 'B', 'E', 'I', 'L', 'S', 'T', 'W' }
```

Thus we would have a probability distribution that looks like this:

Character	Probability
B	1/10
E	2/10

I	2/10
L	2/10
S	1/10
T	1/10
W	1/10

Once the character probabilities are known, the individual symbols need to be assigned a range along a "probability line", which is 0 to 1. It does not matter which characters are assigned which segment of the range, as long as it is done in the same manner by both the encoder and the decoder. For the seven characters we set the range

Character	Probability	Range
B	1/10	0.00 - 0.10
E	2/10	0.10 - 0.30
I	2/10	0.30 - 0.50
L	2/10	0.50 - 0.70
S	1/10	0.70 - 0.80
T	1/10	0.80 - 0.90
W	1/10	0.90 - 1.00

Each character is assigned an interval length of the 0-1 range that corresponds to its probability of appearance. The character owns everything up to, but not including the higher number. So the character 'W' has the range 0.90 - 0.9999.... The most significant portion of an arithmetic coded message belongs to the first symbol to be encoded. When encoding the string "WILLISTEEB", the first symbol is 'W'. In order for the first character to be decoded properly, the final coded message has to be a number greater than or equal to 0.90 and less than 1.0. What we do to encode this number is keep track of the range that this number could fall in. Thus after the first character is encoded, the low end for this range is 0.90 and the high end of the range is 1.0. After the first character is encoded, we know that our range for our output number is now bounded by the low number and the high number. Each new symbol to be encoded will further restrict the possible range of the output number. The next character to be encoded, 'I', is in the range 0.30 through 0.50. If it was the first number in our message, we would set our low and high range values directly to those values. However 'I' is the second character. Thus 'I' owns the range that corresponds to 0.30-0.50 in the new subrange of 0.9 - 1.0. Applying this logic will further restrict our number to the range 0.93 to 0.95. The algorithm to accomplish this for a message of any length is as follows:

```
low = 0.0
high = 1.0
```

```
while there are still input symbols do
    get an input symbol
    code_range = high - low.
    high = low + code_range*high_range(symbol)
    low = low + code_range*low_range(symbol)
end of while
output low
```

Applying this algorithm to the string WILLISTEEB we have

New Character	Low value	High Value
	0.0	1.0
W	0.9	1.0
I	0.93	0.95
L	0.940	0.944
L	0.9420	0.9428
I	0.94224	0.9424
S	0.942352	0.942368
T	....	....
E	....	....
E	....	....
B	0.942364992	0.9423649984

The final low value, 0.942364992 uniquely encodes the message "WILLISTEEB" using our present encoding scheme.

Given this encoding scheme, it is easy to see how the decoding process will operate. We find the first symbol in the message by seeing which symbol owns the code space that our encoded message falls in. Since the number 0.942364992 falls between 0.9 and 1.0, we know that the first character must be 'W'. We then need to remove the 'W' from the encoded number. Since we know the low and high ranges of 'W', we can remove their effects by reversing the process that put them in. First, we subtract the low value of 'W' from the number, giving 0.042364992. Then we divide by the range of 'W', which is 0.1. This gives a value of 0.42364992. We can then calculate where that lands, which is in the range of the next letter, 'I'. The algorithm for decoding the incoming number is:

```
get encoded number
do
    find symbol whose range straddles the encoded number
    output the symbol
    range = lowvalue(symbol) - highvalue(symbol)
    subtract lowvalue(symbol) from encoded number
```

```
      divide encoded number by range
until no more symbols
```

We have conveniently ignored the problem of how to decide when there are no more symbols left to decode. This can be handled by either encoding a special EOF symbol, or carrying the stream length along with the encoded message. The decoding algorithm for the string "WILLISTEEB" is as follows:

Encoded Number	Output Symbol	Low	High	Range
0.942364992	W	0.9	1.0	0.1
0.42364992	I	0.3	0.5	0.2
0.6182496	L	0.5	0.7	0.2
0.591248	L	0.5	0.7	0.2
0.45624	I	0.3	0.5	0.2
0.7812	S	0.7	0.8	0.1
0.812	T	0.8	0.9	0.1
0.12	E	0.1	0.3	0.2
0.1	E	0.1	0.3	0.1
0.0	B	0.0	0.1	0.1

In summary, the encoding process is one of narrowing the range of possible numbers with every new symbol. The new range is proportional to the predefined probability attached to that symbol. Decoding is the inverse procedure, where the range is expanded in proportion to the probability of each symbol as it is extracted.

The basic idea for encoding is implemented in the following clumsy Java program using the class BigDecimal. It is left as an exercise to write the code for decoding. Of course in real life one would not implement it this way.

```java
// Arithmetic.java

import java.math.BigDecimal;

public class Arithmetic
{
  public static void main(String[] args)
  {
  BigDecimal low = new BigDecimal("0.0");
  BigDecimal high = new BigDecimal("1.0");

  BigDecimal Blow = new BigDecimal("0.0");
  BigDecimal Bhigh = new BigDecimal("0.1");
```

```
BigDecimal Elow = new BigDecimal("0.1");
BigDecimal Ehigh = new BigDecimal("0.3");
BigDecimal Ilow = new BigDecimal("0.3");
BigDecimal Ihigh = new BigDecimal("0.5");
BigDecimal Llow = new BigDecimal("0.5");
BigDecimal Lhigh = new BigDecimal("0.7");
BigDecimal Slow = new BigDecimal("0.7");
BigDecimal Shigh = new BigDecimal("0.8");
BigDecimal Tlow = new BigDecimal("0.8");
BigDecimal Thigh = new BigDecimal("0.9");
BigDecimal Wlow = new BigDecimal("0.9");
BigDecimal Whigh = new BigDecimal("1.0");

String input = new String("WILLISTEEB");
int length = input.length();

for(int i=0;i<length;i++)
{
BigDecimal code_range = high.subtract(low);
char c = input.charAt(i);

switch(c)
{
case 'B':
high = low.add(code_range.multiply(Bhigh));
low = low.add(code_range.multiply(Blow));
break;

case 'E':
high = low.add(code_range.multiply(Ehigh));
low = low.add(code_range.multiply(Elow));
break;

case 'I':
high = low.add(code_range.multiply(Ihigh));
low = low.add(code_range.multiply(Ilow));
break;

case 'L':
high = low.add(code_range.multiply(Lhigh));
low = low.add(code_range.multiply(Llow));
break;

case 'S':
```

```
high = low.add(code_range.multiply(Shigh));
low = low.add(code_range.multiply(Slow));
break;

case 'T':
high = low.add(code_range.multiply(Thigh));
low = low.add(code_range.multiply(Tlow));
break;

case 'W':
high = low.add(code_range.multiply(Whigh));
low = low.add(code_range.multiply(Wlow));
break;
} // end switch
} // end for

System.out.println("low = " + low);
System.out.println("high = " + high);

}
}
```

The output is

```
low  = 0.94236499200
high = 0.94236499840
```

The process of encoding and decoding a stream of symbols using arithmetic coding is not complicated. However it seems impractical. Most computers support floating point numbers of 32-bits, 64-bits and 80-bits. Does this mean we have to start over every time we finish encoding 10 or 15 symbols? Do we need a floating point processor? Arithmetic coding is best accomplished using standard 16-bit and 32-bit integer mathematics. No floating point mathematics is required. What is used instead is an incremental transmission scheme, where fixed size integer state variables receive new bits in at the low end and shift them out the high end, forming a single number that can be as many bits long as are available on the computer's storage medium.

We showed how the algorithm works by keeping track of a high and low number that bracket the range of the possible output number. When the algorithm first starts up, the low number is set to 0.0, and the high number is set to 1.0. The first simplification made to work with integer mathematics is to change the 1.0 to 0.999...., or .111... in binary. In order to store these numbers in integer registers, we first justify them so the implied decimal point is on the left hand side of the word. Then we load as much of the initial high and low values as will fit into the word size we are working with.

If we imagine our "WILLISTEEB" example in a 5 digit register, the decimal equivalent of our setup would look like this:

```
high = 99999
low  = 00000
```

To find our new range numbers, we need to apply the encoding algorithm described above. We first had to calculate the range between the low value and the high value. The difference between the two registers will be 100000, not 99999. This is because we assume the high register has an infinite number of 9's added on to it, so we need to increment the calculated difference. We then compute the new high value using the formula given above

```
high = low + high_range(symbol)
```

In this case the high range was 1.0, which gives a new value for high of 100000. Before storing the new value of high, we need to decrement it, once again because of the implied digits appended to the integer value. So the new value of high is 99999. The calculation of low follows the same path, with a resulting new value of 20000. Thus

```
high =  99999   (999...)
low  =  90000   (000...)
```

At this point, the most significant digits of high and low match. Owing to the nature of our algorithm, high and low can continue to grow closer to one another without quite ever matching. This means that once they match in the most significant digit, that digit will never change. So we can now output that digit as the first digit of our encoded number. This is done by shifting both high and low left by one digit, and shifting in a 9 in the least significant digit of high. As this process continues, high and low are continually growing closer together, then shifting digits out into the coded word. The process for our string "WILLISTEEB" looks like this:

	high	low	range	cumulative output
initial state	99999	00000	100000	
encode W (0.9-1.0)	99999	90000	10000	
shift out 9	99999	00000	100000	.9
encode I (0.3-0.5)	49999	30000	20000	.9
encode L (0.5-0.7)	43999	40000	4000	.9
shift out 4	39999	00000	40000	.94
encode L (0.5-0.7)	27999	20000	8000	.94

```
shift out 2                79999  00000    80000   .942
encode I (0.3-0.5)         39999  24000    16000   .942
encode S (0.7-0.8)         36799  35200     1600   .942
shift out 3                67999  52000    16000   .9423
.........                  .....  ....      ....    ....
```

After all the letters have been accounted for, two extra digits need to be shifted out of either the high or low value to finish up the output word.

This scheme works well for incrementally encoding a message. There is enough accuracy retained during the double precision integer calculations to ensure that the message is accurately encoded. However, there is potential for a loss of precision under certain circumstances. In the event that the encoded word has a string of 0s or 9s in it, the high and low values will slowly converge on a value, but may not see their most significant digits match immediately. At this point, the values are permanently stuck. The range between high and low has become so small that any calculation will always return the same values. However, since the most significant digits of both words are not equal, the algorithm cannot output the digit and shift. The way to rectify this underflow problem is to prevent this. From the algorithm we know: "if the most significant digit of high and low match, shift it out".

If the two digits do not match, but are now on adjacent numbers, a second test needs to be applied. If **high** and **low** are one apart, we then test to see if the 2nd most significant digit in high is a 0, and the 2nd digit in low is a 9. This means we will find underflow. When underflow occurs, we head it off with a slightly different shift operation. Instead of shifting the most significant digit out of the word, we delete the 2nd digits from high and low, and shift the rest of the digits left to fill up the space. The most significant digit stays in place. We then have to set an underflow counter to remember that we threw away a digit, and we are not quite sure whether it was going to end up as a 0 or a 9. After every recalculation operation, if the most significant digits do not match up, we can check for underflow digits again. If they are present, we shift them out and increment the counter. When the most significant digits do finally converge to a single value, we first output that value. Then, we output all of the underflow digits that were previously discarded. The underflow digits will be all 9s or 0s, depending on whether **high** and **low** converged to the higher or lower value.

In the ideal decoding process, we had the entire input number to work with. Thus the algorithm has to divide the encoded number by the symbol probability. In practice, we can not perform an operation like that on a number that could be billions of bytes long. Like the encoding process, the

decoder can operate using 16 and 32 bit integers for calculations. Instead
of maintaining two numbers, high and low, the decoder has to maintain
three integers. The first two, high and low, correspond exactly to the
high and low values maintained by the encoder. The third number, code,
contains the current bits being read in from the input bit stream. The
code value will always lie in between the high and low values. As they
come closer and closer to it, new shift operations will take place, and high
and low will move back away from code. The high and low values in the
decoder correspond to the high and low that the encoder was using. They
will be updated after every symbol just as they were in the encoder, and
should have the same values. By performing the same comparison test
on the upper digit of high and low, the decoder knows when it is time to
shift a new digit into the incoming code. The same underflow tests are
performed as well, in lockstep with the encoder. In the ideal algorithm,
it was possible to determine what the current encoded symbols was just
by finding the symbol whose probabilities enclosed the present value of the
code. In the integer algorithm, the probability scale is determined by the
difference between high and low. Thus instead of the range being between
0.0 and 1.0, the range will be between two positive 16-bit integer counts.
The current probability is determined by where the present code value falls
along that range. If we divide (value-low) by (high-low+1), we obtain the
actual probability for the present symbol. In Java the integer data type
long is 64-bits and the integer data type int is 32-bits.

```java
// ArithmeticC.java
//
// Arithmetic Compression
// I. H. Witten, R. M. Neal, J. G. Cleary
// Arithmetic Coding for Data Compression
// Communications of the ACM, 1987, pp. 520--540

import java.io.*; // for FileInputStream, FileOutputStream

public class ArithmeticC
{
  final static int no_of_chars = 256;
  final static int no_of_symbols = no_of_chars;
  static int[] char_to_index = new int[no_of_chars];
  static char[] index_to_char = new char[no_of_symbols+1];
  static long[] freq = new long[no_of_symbols+1];
  static long[] cum_freq = new long[no_of_symbols+1];

  final static int code_bits = 62;
```

```
static int buffer;
static int bits_to_go;
static int zbuffer;
static int lobuffer;

static FileOutputStream out = null;

static void start_outputing_bits()
{
buffer = 0;
bits_to_go = 8;
zbuffer = 0;
lobuffer = 0;
}

static void output_bit(int bit) throws IOException
{
buffer >>= 1;                      // shift operation
if(bit != 0) buffer |= 0x80; // bitwise OR
bits_to_go -= 1;
if(bits_to_go == 0) {
if(buffer != 0) {
if(lobuffer != 0) out.write((byte) 0x40);
if(zbuffer > 0 && buffer == 0x40) lobuffer = 1;
if(buffer != 0x40) lobuffer = 0;
for(;zbuffer>0;zbuffer--) out.write((byte) 0);
 if(lobuffer != 1) out.write((byte) buffer);
 }
 else zbuffer++; // increment
 bits_to_go = 8;
 buffer = 0;
 }
 }

static void done_outputing_bits() throws IOException
{
if(buffer != 0)  {
if(bits_to_go != 0) buffer >>= bits_to_go;
if(lobuffer != 0) out.write((byte) 0x40);
if(zbuffer > 0 && buffer == 0x40) lobuffer = 1;
if(buffer != 0x40) lobuffer = 0;
for(;zbuffer>0;zbuffer--) out.write((byte) 0);
 if(lobuffer != 1) out.write((byte) buffer);
 }
```

```
}

static long low, high, temp;
static long bits_to_follow;

static void bit_plus_follow(int bit) throws IOException
{
output_bit(bit);
while(bits_to_follow > 0) {
  output_bit((bit == 0) ? 1 : 0);
  bits_to_follow -= 1;
 }
 }

static void start_encoding()
{
low = 0;
high = (((long) 1 << code_bits)-1);
bits_to_follow = 0;
}

static long dss(long r,long top,long bot) throws IOException
{
long t1, t2;
if(bot == 0) System.out.println(" not possible \n");
t1 = r/bot;
t2 = r-(t1*bot);
t1 = t1*top; t2 = t2*top;
t2 = t2/bot;
return t1 + t2;
}

static void encode_symbol(int symbol,long cum_freq[])
      throws IOException
{
long range;
range = (long)(high-low)+1;
high = low + dss(range,cum_freq[symbol-1],cum_freq[0])-1;
low = low + dss(range,cum_freq[symbol],cum_freq[0]);

low ^= (((long) 1 << code_bits)-1);  // shift and XOR
high ^= (((long) 1 << code_bits)-1); // shift and XOR
temp = low; low = high; high = temp;
```

```
for(;;) {
if(high < (2*((((long) 1 << code_bits)-1)/4+1)))
{
bit_plus_follow(0);
}
else if(low >= (2*((((long) 1 << code_bits)-1)/4+1))) {
bit_plus_follow(1);
low -= (2*((((long) 1 << code_bits)-1)/4+1));
high -= (2*((((long) 1 << code_bits)-1)/4+1));
}
else if(low >= ((((long) 1 << code_bits)-1)/4+1)
        && high < (3*((((long) 1 << code_bits)-1)/4+1)))
{
bits_to_follow += 1;
low -= ((((long) 1 << code_bits)-1)/4+1);
high -= ((((long) 1 << code_bits)-1)/4+1);
}
else break;
low = 2*low;
high = 2*high+1;
}
low ^= (((long) 1 << code_bits)-1);
high ^= (((long) 1 << code_bits)-1);
temp = low; low = high; high = temp;
}

static void done_encoding() throws IOException {
 if(bits_to_follow > 0) { bit_plus_follow(1); }
 else
 {
 if(high!=(((long) 1 << code_bits)-1)) bit_plus_follow(1);
 }
 }

static void start_model()
{
int i;
for(i=0;i<no_of_chars;i++) {
  char_to_index[i] = i+1;
  index_to_char[i+1] =(char) i;
  }

 for(i=0;i<=no_of_symbols;i++)
 {
```

```
freq[i] = 1;
cum_freq[i] = no_of_symbols-i;
}
freq[0] = 0;
}

static void update_model(int symbol) throws IOException
{
int i;
for(i=symbol;freq[i]==freq[i-1];i--);
  if(i < symbol) {
     int ch_i, ch_symbol;
     ch_i = index_to_char[i];
     ch_symbol = index_to_char[symbol];
     index_to_char[i] =(char) ch_symbol;
     index_to_char[symbol] =(char) ch_i;
     char_to_index[ch_i] = symbol;
     char_to_index[ch_symbol] = i;
     }
     freq[i]++;
     while(i>0) { i -= 1; cum_freq[i]++; }
  }

public static void compress(String ifile,String ofile)
       throws IOException
{
int zerf = 0, onef = 0;

FileInputStream in = null;
  try {
    in = new FileInputStream(ifile);
    out = new FileOutputStream(ofile);
    byte[] array = new byte[1];

    int rb;
    start_model();
    start_outputing_bits();
    start_encoding();
    for(;;) {
     int ch;
     int symbol;
     if((rb = in.read(array,0,1)) == -1) {
        break;
     }
  }
```

```
      ch = array[0] & 0xff; // bitwise AND with 255

      symbol = char_to_index[ch];
      if(symbol == 1) zerf = 1;
      if(zerf == 1 && symbol == 2) onef = 1;
      if(symbol > 1) zerf = 0;
      if(symbol > 2) onef = 0;
      encode_symbol(symbol,cum_freq);
      update_model(symbol);
      }

      if((zerf + onef) > 0) {
          encode_symbol(2,cum_freq);
          update_model( 2);
      }

      done_encoding();
      done_outputing_bits();

      in.close();
      out.close();
      }
      catch(Exception e) {
      System.out.println("Error:");
      e.printStackTrace();
      }
  }

public static void main(String[] args) throws IOException
{
String ifile = null, ofile = null;

System.out.println("Arithmetic coding: ");

if(args.length > 0) {
ifile = args[0];
System.out.println(args[0]);
}
else {
System.out.println("Error: No input file provided");
System.exit(0);
}
System.out.println(" to ");
```

```
if(args.length > 1) {
ofile = args[1];
System.out.println(args[1]);
}
else {
System.out.println("Error: No output file provided");
System.exit(0);
}
System.out.println("\n");

compress(ifile,ofile);
} // end main
}   // end class ArithmeticC
```

13.6   Burrows-Wheeler Transform

The data compression with the *Burrows-Wheeler transform* is based on permutations and sorting the input string. The Burrows-Wheeler transform
[10], or BWT, transforms a block of data into a format that is extremely
well suited for compression. The BWT is reversible since it relies on permutations. We show how a block of data transformed by the BWT can be compressed using standard techniques. Michael Burrows and David Wheeler
released a research report in 1994 discussing work they had been doing at
the Digital Systems Research Center in Palo Alto, California. Their paper,
"A Block-sorting Lossless Data Compression Algorithm" presented a data
compression algorithm based on a previously unpublished transformation
discovered by Wheeler in 1983. The paper discusses a complete set of algorithms for compression and decompression.

The BWT is an algorithm that takes a block of data and rearranges it using
a sorting algorithm. The resulting output block contains exactly the same
data elements that it started with, differing only in their ordering. The
transformation is reversible, meaning the original ordering of the data elements can be restored with no loss of fidelity. The BWT is performed on an
entire block of data at once. Most of today's familiar lossless compression
algorithms operate in streaming mode, reading a single byte or a few bytes
at a time. With this new transform, we want to operate on the largest
chunks of data possible. Since the BWT operates on data in memory, we
may encounter files too big to process in one fell swoop. In these cases, the
file must be split up and processed a block at a time. Often one works with
block sizes of 50Kbytes up to 250 Kbytes.

As an example we consider the string S of N = 5 characters

```
S = "WILLI"
```

with the alphabet

```
X := { 'I', 'L', 'W' }
```

This string contains five bytes of data. A string is just a collection of bytes. We treat the buffer as if the last character wraps around back to the first. Next we shift the string and thus obtain four more strings, namely

```
WILLI
ILLIW
LLIWI
LIWIL
IWILL
```

The next step in the BWT is to perform a lexicographical sort on the set of these strings. That is, we want to order the strings using a fixed comparison function. After sorting, the set of strings is

```
F   L    row
ILLIW    0
IWILL    1
LIWIL    2
LLIWI    3
WILLI    4
```

with the columns F and L. Thus we do 5 special permutations (including the identity) of the original string. At least one of the rows contains the original string. In our example exactly one row. Let I be the index of the first such row, numbering from 0. For the given example we have I = 4. We know that the string 0, the original unsorted string, has now moved down to row 4 in the array. Second, we have tagged the first and last columns in the matrix with the special designations F and L, for the first and last columns of the array. The five strings can be considered as a 5×5 matrix M with the characters as entries. Thus

```
M[0][0] = 'I',   M[0][1] = 'L',   .... , M[4][4] = 'I'
```

Thus the string L is the last column of the matrix M. Thus

```
L = "WLLII"
```

Thus

```
L[0] = 'W',   L[1] = 'L',   L[2] = 'L',   L[3] = 'I',   L[4] = 'I'
```

Column F contains all the characters in the original string in sorted order. Thus our original string "WILLI" is represented in F as "IILLW". The characters in column L do not appear to be in any particular order, but they have an interesting property. Each of the characters in L is the prefix character to the string that starts in the same row in column F.

Next we describe how to reconstruct S from the knowledge of L and I. First we calculate the first column of the matrix M. This is obviously done by sorting the characters of L. Thus F = "IILLW". Both L and F are permutations of S, and therefore of one another. Since the rows of M are sorted, and F is the first column of M, the characters in F are also sorted. Next we define an $N \times N$ ($N = 5$) matrix M' by

```
M'[i][j] = M[i][(j-1) mod N]
```

Thus for our example we have

```
row    M        M'
 0    ILLIW    WILLI
 1    IWILL    LIWIL
 2    LIWIL    LLIWI
 3    LLIWI    ILLIW
 4    WILLI    IWILL
```

Using F and L, the first column of M and M' respectively, we calculate a vector T that indicates the correspondence between the rows of the two matrices, in the sense that for each $j = 0, 1, \ldots, N - 1$, row j of M' corresponds to row T[j] of M. If L[j] is the kth instance of ch in L, then T[j] = i, where F[i] is the kth instance of the ch in F. T represents a one-to-one correspondence between elements of F and elements of L. We have F[T[j]] = L[j].

Row $j = 0$ in M' contains WILLI. Row 4 in M contains WILLI. Thus $T[0] = 4$.

Row $j = 1$ in M' contains LIWIL. Row 2 in M contains LIWIL. Thus $T[1] = 2$.

Row $j = 2$ in M' contains LLIWI. Row 3 in M contains LLIWI. Thus $T[2] = 3$.

Row $j = 3$ in M' contains ILLIW. Row 0 in M contains ILLIW. Thus $T[3] = 0$.

Row $j = 4$ in M' contains IWILL. Row 1 in M contains IWILL. Thus $T[4] = 1$.

Thus the transformation vector can be calculated to be

```
{ 4, 2, 3, 0, 1 }.
```

It provides the key to restoring L to its original order. Given L and the primary index, we can restore the original string S = "WILLI". The following Java code does the job:

```java
// RestoreString.java

public class RestoreString
{
  public static void decode(String L,int[] T,int I,int N)
  {
  int index = I;
  char[] S = new char[N];
  for(int i=0;i<N;i++)
  {
  S[N-i-1] = L.charAt(index);
  index = T[index];
  } // end for
  for(int i=0;i<N;i++)
  {
  System.out.println("S[" + i + "] = " + S[i]);
  }
  } // end decode

  public static void main(String args[])
  {
  String L = new String("WLLII");
  int N = L.length();
  int I = 4;
  int[] T = new int[N];
  T[0] = 4; T[1] = 2; T[2] = 3; T[3] = 0; T[4] = 1;
  decode(L,T,I,N);
  }
}
```

It is left as an exercise to write the code to find T.

Now L can be compressed with a simple locally-adaptive compression algorithm. Thus could take the output of the BWT and just apply a conventional compressor to it, but Burrows and Wheeler suggest an improved approach. They recommend using a Move to Front scheme, followed by an entropy encoder. A Move to Front (or MTF) encoder is a fairly trivial piece of work. It simply keeps all 256 possible codes in a list. Each time a character is to be output, we send its position in the list, then move it to the front.

13.7   Wavelet Data Compression

Wavelet compression is used mainly in lossy image compression. For this kind of compression we are given an image and we are interested in removing some of the information in the original image, without degrading the quality of the picture to much. In this way we obtain a compressed image, which can be stored using less storage and which also can be transmitted more quickly, or using less bandwidth, over a communication channel. The compressed image is thus an approximation of the original. Here we consider compression based on wavelet transform and wavelet decompositions.

Consider the function $\psi \in L_2(\mathbf{R}^d)$. We define

$$\psi_I(\mathbf{x}) = 2^{\nu d/2}\psi(2^\nu \mathbf{x} - \mathbf{k})$$

for each dyadic cube

$$I = I_{\nu \mathbf{k}} := \{\ \mathbf{x} \in \mathbf{R}^d\ :\ 2^{-\nu}k_i \le x_i < 2^{-\nu}(k_i + 1),\ i = 1, \ldots, d\ \}$$

where $\nu \in \mathbf{Z}$, $\mathbf{k} \in \mathbf{Z}^d$. For a general function f in the Hilbert space $L_2(\mathbf{R}^d)$ the expansion

$$f = \sum_{I\ dyadic} a_I \psi_I$$

is called the *wavelet decomposition* of f. It is well-known that under appropriate conditions on the function ψ it is possible to obtain such decompositions. We consider orthonormal wavelets when the functions ψ_I are orthonormal on $L_2(\mathbf{R})$ (or, more generally, when a finite collection of functions $\psi^{(i)}$, $i = 1, \ldots, N$, together with their dyadic translates and dilates, yields an orthonormal basis

$$\{\ \psi_I^{(i)}\ \}_{i=1}^N,\, I\ dyadic$$

on the Hilbert space $L_2(\mathbf{R}^d)$ and form a basis for the space $\mathcal{F}$ under consideration. The scalar product in the Hilbert space $L_2(\mathbf{R}^d)$ is denoted by $\langle\,,\,\rangle$. In the orthonormal case, the coefficients a_I are given by

$$a_I = \langle f, \psi_I \rangle\,.$$

The transformation

$$f \to \{\ \langle f, \psi_I \rangle\ \}_{I\ dyadic}$$

is called the *wavelet transform*. We approximate the original function f by functions with only finitely many nonzero wavelet coefficients. Let $\{\psi_I\}_{I\ dyadic}$ be an orthonormal wavelet basis in some distribution space $\mathcal{F}$, and let

$$\sigma_N(f)_{\mathcal{F}} := \inf_{\#\Gamma \le N} \|f - \sum_{I \in \Gamma} b_I \psi_I\|_{\mathcal{F}}, \qquad N \ge 1\,.$$

We are thus interested in the following nonlinear approximation problem: how shall we pick N coefficients b_I in order to minimise the error $\sigma_n(f)_{\mathcal{F}}$ when $\mathcal{F}$ is one of the standard distribution spaces? We can prove that there are N coefficients $\{\langle f, \psi_I \rangle\}_{I \in \Gamma}$, $\#\Gamma = N$, such that

$$\sigma_N(f)_{\mathcal{F}} \approx \|f - \sum_{I \in \Gamma} \langle f, \psi_I \rangle \psi_I\|_{\mathcal{F}}$$

and the algorithm for choosing $\{\langle f, \psi_I \rangle\}_{I \ dyadic}$ among all $\langle f, \psi_I \rangle$ is based on the size of the coefficients. For example, using the Haar basis we find that the Hilbert space L_2 is isomorphic to the Hilbert space l_2 of sequences.

For example consider the Haar system on the line $\{h_I\}_{I \ dyadic}$. The functions h_I are obtained from the single function

$$h(x) := \begin{cases} 1 & \text{if} & 0 \le x < 1/2 \\ -1 & \text{if} & 1/2 < x < 1 \\ 0 & \text{otherwise} \end{cases}$$

by translation and dilation

$$h_I(x) := 2^{\nu/2} h(2^\nu x - k)$$

when

$$I = I_{\nu k} = [2^{-\nu} k, 2^{-\nu}(k+1))$$

for some integers ν and k. The Haar system is an orthonormal basis on $L_2(\mathbf{R})$. It follows that we have the expansion

$$f(x) = \sum_{I \ dyadic} \langle f, h_I \rangle h_I(x)$$

and

$$\|f\|_{L_2} = \left(\sum_{I \ dyadic} |\langle f, h_I \rangle|^2 \right)^{1/2}.$$

The mapping

$$S_h : f \to \{\langle f, h_I \rangle\}_{I \ dyadic}$$

is thus an isometry between the Hilbert space L_2 and the Hilbert space l_2.

Two-dimensional wavelets have been discussed in chapter 7.

13.8   Fractal Data Compression

The idea of fractal image compression grew out of the theory of *iterated function systems* (IFSs) ([3], [4]). While the practical application of fractal techniques to compression of real-world images has not lived up to the promise of tremendous compression ratios originally touted for IFS images, the technique has shown that it can be a viable competitor with conventional compression methods. The fractal image encoding technique represents images in terms of the relationships of subimages to one another. The basic idea behind fractal image compression is to express the image as an iterated function system. This means the method is based on a measure of deviation between a given image and its approximation by an IFS code. The Collage theorem states that there is a convergent process to minimise this deviation. The problem is how to efficiently generate the IFS from the image. Classification of subimages can speed up the encoding process and neural networks (Kohonen self-organising neural network) are a natural candidate for improving this classification. Problems are that even if we have an IFS for object A and an IFS for object B, there is no way to combine these IFSs to obtain an IFS for object A union B or object A intersect B.

There are several approaches for computing the fractal dimension of data and images based on different definitions of the dimension and specific assumptions about the data to analyse. Some of them are the capacity, Minkowski-Bouligand's, packing, correlation, k-th nearest neighbour dimension. The most common numerical techniques are box-counting, Sarkar's method, Peleg's method, Higuchi's method, methods based on spectral and fuzzy theory, morphological covers, Gabor filtering.

Since Barnsley introduced IFS theory in 1988 [3] as a new technique for still image compression, major contributions have been brought to shift fractal encoding to a computationally realistic level. However, the encoding process still remains expensive in CPU time, due to a costly full search through the image. The algorithms are based on PIFS, HIFS, LIFS, RIFS, IFSZ, IFSM, IFSP. Attempts have been made to improve both ration and quality (generalised square isometries, conformal, mappings, postprocessing, etc.) as well as encoding time (Saupe's approach, constrained search, etc.). Besides the IFS image compression there is the so-called fractal transform which is a variant of vector quantisation, where we use the image itself, sampled at a higher scale, as the VQ codebook. The fractal transform can be analysed using local IFSs. Jacquin [32] was the first to propose a block-based fractal coding scheme for grey level images. The coding performance can be greatly improved by applying an aliasing free codebook design, an enhanced luminance transformation combined with a vector quantisation, and an adaptive geometrical search scheme [5].

Multifractals are a generalisation of fractal concepts to more complex objects. Among other applications, they provide a good basis for the problem of performing image segmentation, that is the problem of finding a compact description of an image in terms of edges or regions, which is a key problem in low level image processing.

Definition. A (hyperbolic) iterated function system consists of a complete metric space $(\mathbf{X}, d)$ together with a finite set of contraction mappings w_n: $\mathbf{X} \to \mathbf{X}$, with respective contractivity factors s_n, for $n = 1, 2, \ldots, N$. The notation for the iterated function system is

$$\{ \mathbf{X} : \ w_n, \ n = 1, 2, \ldots, N \}$$

and its contractivity factor is $s = \max\{s_n : n = 1, 2, \ldots, N\}$. Let $(\mathbf{X}, d)$ be a complete metric space and let $(\mathcal{H}(\mathbf{X}, h(d))$ denote the corresponding space of nonempty compact subsets, with the Hausdorff metric $h(d)$.

We put the word "hyperbolic" in parentheses in this definition because it is sometimes dropped in practice.

Definition. Let $(\mathbf{X}, d)$ be a complete metric space, $x \in \mathbf{X}$, and $B \in \mathcal{H}(\mathbf{X}, h(d))$. We define

$$d(x, B) := \min\{ d(x, y) : y \in B \}.$$

Definition. Let $(\mathbf{X}, d)$ be a complete metric space. Let $A, B \in \mathcal{H}(\mathbf{X}, h(d))$. We define

$$d(A, B) := \max\{ d(x, B) : x \in A \}.$$

$d(A, B)$ is called the distance from set $A \in \mathcal{H}(\mathbf{X}, h(d))$ to the set $B \in \mathcal{H}(\mathbf{X}, h(d))$.

Definition. Let $(\mathbf{X}, d)$ be a complete metric space. Then the Hausdorff distance between points A and B in $\mathcal{H}(\mathbf{X}, h(d))$ is defined by

$$h(A, B) := d(A, B) \vee d(B, A).$$

The following theorem summarises the main facts about a hyperbolic IFS.

Theorem 1. Let $\{ \mathbf{X} : \ w_n, \ n = 1, 2, \ldots, N\}$ be a hyperbolic iterated function system with contractivity factor s. Then the transformation $W : \mathcal{H}(\mathbf{X}) \to \mathcal{H}(\mathbf{X})$ defined by

$$W(B) := \bigcup_{n=1}^{N} w_n(B)$$

for all $B \in \mathcal{H}(\mathbf{X})$, is a contraction mapping on the complete metric space $(\mathcal{H}(\mathbf{X}), h(d))$ with contractivity factor s. That is

$$h(W(B), W(C)) \leq s \cdot h(B, C)$$

for all $B, C \in \mathcal{H}(\mathbf{X})$. Its unique fixed point, $A \in \mathcal{H}(\mathbf{X})$, obeys

$$A = W(A) = \bigcup_{n=1}^{N} w_n(A)$$

and is given by

$$A = \lim_{n \to \infty} W^{\circ n}(B)$$

for any $B \in \mathcal{H}(\mathbf{X})$. The fixed point $A \in \mathcal{H}(\mathbf{X})$ is called the attractor of the iterated function system.

Definition. The fixed point $A \in \mathcal{H}(\mathbf{X})$ described in the theorem is called the deterministic fractal (attractor) of the IFS.

Sometimes we will use the name "attractor" in connection with an IFS which is simply a finite set of maps acting on a complete metric space $\mathbf{X}$. By this we mean that one can make an assertion which is analogous to the last sentence of the Theorem.

Example. Consider the IFS $\{\mathbf{R} : w_1, w_2\}$ where

$$w_1(x) = \frac{1}{3}x, \qquad w_2(x) = \frac{1}{3}x + \frac{2}{3}$$

with the metric space ($\mathbf{R}$,Euclidean) and $(\mathcal{H}(\mathbf{R}), h(\text{Euclidean}))$. This is indeed an IFS with contractivity factor $s = \frac{1}{3}$. Let $B_0 = [0, 1]$. Then $B_n := W^{(n)}(B_0), n = 1, 2, 3, \ldots$ We have

$$w_1([0, 1]) = [0, 1/3], \qquad w_2([0, 1]) = [2/3, 1]$$

etc. Thus we find that $A = \lim_{n \to \infty} B_n$ is the classical Cantor set. We can verify that

$$A = \frac{1}{3}A \cup \left\{ \frac{1}{3}A = \frac{2}{3} \right\}.$$

Here we use the following notation: for a subset A of $\mathbf{R}$

$$xA := \{xy : y \in A\}$$

and

$$A + x := \{y + x : y \in A\}.$$

Example. We consider the *Sierpinski triangle* [55] which is an hyperbolic IFS of the form $\{ \mathbf{R}^2 : w_n \}$ with $n = 1, 2, 3$. We have

$$w_1 \begin{pmatrix} x_1 \\ x_2 \end{pmatrix} = \begin{pmatrix} 0.5 & 0 \\ 0 & 0.5 \end{pmatrix} \begin{pmatrix} x_1 \\ x_2 \end{pmatrix} + \begin{pmatrix} 1 \\ 1 \end{pmatrix}$$

$$w_2 \begin{pmatrix} x_1 \\ x_2 \end{pmatrix} = \begin{pmatrix} 0.5 & 0 \\ 0 & 0.5 \end{pmatrix} \begin{pmatrix} x_1 \\ x_2 \end{pmatrix} + \begin{pmatrix} 1 \\ 50 \end{pmatrix}$$

$$w_3 \begin{pmatrix} x_1 \\ x_2 \end{pmatrix} = \begin{pmatrix} 0.5 & 0 \\ 0 & 0.5 \end{pmatrix} \begin{pmatrix} x_1 \\ x_2 \end{pmatrix} + \begin{pmatrix} 25 \\ 50 \end{pmatrix}$$

```java
// IFS1.java

import java.awt.Graphics;
import java.awt.Rectangle;
import java.awt.Event;
import java.applet.Applet;

public class IFS1 extends Applet implements Runnable
{
  public final static int maxLines = 10;
  public int lines = 0;
  public double w[] [];
  Thread drawThread = null;
  int h, z;
  long dots = 20000;
  double t = 1.0, b = -1.0, l = -1.0, r = 1.0;

  public void init()
  {
  Sierpinski();
  }

  public void stop()
  {
  drawThread = null;
  gcont = null;
  }

  void Sierpinski()
  {
  w = new double[3] [7];
  lines = 3;
  w[0] [0] =  0.5;   w[1] [0] =  0.5;   w[2] [0] =  0.5;
```

```
w[0][1] =  0.0;   w[1][1] =  0.0;   w[2][1] =  0.0;
w[0][2] =  0.0;   w[1][2] =  0.0;   w[2][2] =  0.0;
w[0][3] =  0.5;   w[1][3] =  0.5;   w[2][3] =  0.5;
w[0][4] = -0.5;   w[1][4] = -0.5;   w[2][4] =  0.5;
w[0][5] =  0.5;   w[1][5] = -0.5;   w[2][5] = -0.5;
w[0][6] =  0.333; w[1][6] =  0.333; w[2][6] =  0.334;
}

public boolean action(Event e)
{
switch(e.id)
{ case Event.WINDOW_DESTROY: System.exit(0); return true;
  default: return false;
}
}

int transX(double x)
{ return (int)((double)(x-1)/(r-1)*z); }

int transY(double y)
{ return (int)((double)(y-t)/(b-t)*h); }

Graphics gcont;

public void paint(Graphics g)
{
gcont = g.create();
drawThread = new Thread(this);
drawThread.start();
}

public void run()
{
Rectangle r = getBounds();
long i;
int x = r.width/2; int y = r.height/2;

double u = 0.0, v = 0.0, newu, newv, sum = 0.0, rnd;
int l = 0;
h = r.height; z = r.width;
for(i=1;i<=dots;i++)
{
rnd = Math.random();
l = 0; sum = w[l][6];
```

```
    while((rnd > sum) && (l < lines))
    { l++;   sum += w[l][6]; }
    if(l < lines)
    {
    newu = w[l][0]*u + w[l][1]*v;
    newv = w[l][2]*u + w[l][3]*v;
    u = newu + w[l][4]; v = newv + w[l][5];
    }
    gcont.drawLine(transX(u),transY(v),transX(u),transY(v));
    if(i%5 == 0) drawThread.yield();
    }
    gcont = null;
    }
}

<HTML>
<BODY>
<APPLET CODE="IFS1.class" width=200 height=200>
</APPLET>
</BODY>
</HTML>
```

Chapter 14

Digital Signal Processors

14.1 Introduction

A digital signal processor (DSP) ([8], [12], [24], [40], [50], [59]) is a fast and powerful microprocessor that can handle signals in real time. For example, stereo equipment handles sound signals of up to 20 kilohertz (20 000 cycles per second), requiring a digital signal processor to perform hundreds of millions of operations per second. Thus a digital signal processor is a special purpose CPU (central processing unit) that provides ultra-fast instruction sequences, such as shift and add, and multiply and add, which are commonly used in math-intensive signal processing applications. Digital signal processing chips are also used as MPEG codecs, MP3 decoders, Wi-Fi or Bluetooth baseband chips, DVD decoders, digital camera JPEG encoders, DSL modems. cable modems, AC-3 audio codecs, disk read channels and gigabit LAN chips. They are almost never programmable by the user. Since different applications have varying ranges of frequencies, different digital signal processors are required.

Conventional microprocessors use the *von Neumann architecture*: program and data are all in a single memory. Address and data buses are shared between instruction and data fetches. Von Neumann architecture is inexpensive, simple and effective, but there are performance problems. First the von Neumann bottleneck: fetch for next instruction collides with data fetch/store. Secondly buses may be idle during instruction decode. Thirdly digital signal processor algorithms often have multiply-accumulate requirements (scalar product) `coefficient[n]*data[n]`, where two operands must be fetched. Most digital signal processor chips use *Harvard architecture*: separate memory spaces for program and data. Examples are the DSP56301 24-bit digital signal processor of Freescale and the ADSP-2106x-SHARC.

DSPs belong to two basic classes: fixed point, typically a 16-bit architecture based on 16-bit integer data types, and floating point, usually with a 32-bit architecture, based on a data type that has both mantissa and exponent. Digital signal processors are also classified by their dynamic range, the spread of numbers that must be processed in the course of an application. This number is a function of the processor's data width (the number of bits it manipulates) and the type of arithmetic it performs (fixed or floating point). For example, a 32 bit processor has a wider dynamic range than a 24-bit processor, which has a wider range than 16-bit processor. Floating point chips have wider ranges than fixed point devices.

For example, the Freescale DSP56000 processor [21] has two 24-bit data registers in each path (**x0**, **x1**, **y0**, **y1**). Register **x** is the concatenation of **x1** and **x0** and thus can store 48 bits of an accumulator. Likewise for register **y**. There are 8 address registers. There are two 56-bit accumulators **a** and **b** with 8-bit extension register (**a2** or **b2**), 24-bit most significant word result (**a1** or **b1**) and 24-bit least significant word result (**a0** or **b0**). The DSP56000 fixed point DSP uses 24-bit program words.

The arithmetic logic unit (ALU) is centered around the multiply-accumulate function. Sometimes, the computational unit is divided into ALU, MAC (multiply and accumulate), and shifter.

The Harvard architecture of the Freescale DSP5630/DSP56600 cores includes two data memory spaces: x and y. An efficient structure of the application's data segment can improve the code performance by being able to use instructions that support this architecture. Consider

```
move    x:(r0),x0
move    x:(r4),y0
```

Here we put two data arrays into the same memory space, while the code had to access an item from each array one after another. Instead, if one of the arrays can be put into the other data memory space (y in this example) then the two items can be accessed on the same instruction

```
move    x:(r0),x0  y:(r4),y0
```

The Freescale DSP56300/DSP56600 provides the `tfr` instruction which is unique by giving the ability to combine two move operations into a single instruction in a way that is not supported by the usual parallel opcodes. For example

```
move    x0,a
move    r1,r2
```

This can be optimised by combing the two move instruction into a single tfr instruction

```
tfr   x0,a   r1,r2
```

The Freescale DSP56301 also provides nested hardware DO loops.

14.2 Instruction Sets

The arithmetic-logic unit (ALU) is typically centered around multiply-accumulate structures with a large accumulator. For example, digital filters and convolution require accumulated sum-of-products. One also has multiple address generators to handle separate memory spaces. Address units handle modulo buffer arithmetic.

Instruction sets of DSP can be partioned into groups of functionally similar instructions as follows.

Arithmetic instructions

```
add, subtract, multiply, increment, decrement, compare,
negation, absolute value, multiply and accumulate
```

For some DSPs we have these instructions for floating numbers and integer numbers. For example, for the TMS320C6000 the instruction for integer multiplication is

```
MPY .M1 A1,A2,A3
```

The integers of A1 and A2 are multiplied and stored in A3. The unit used is M1. Some DSP's have a multiply and accumulate instruction (mac). For example, for the DSP563000 of Freescale semiconductors we have

Operation	Assembler syntax
$D \pm S1*S2 \rightarrow D$ (parallel move)	mac $(\pm)$S1,S2,D (parallel move)
$D \pm S1*S2 \rightarrow D$ (parallel move)	mac $(\pm)$S2,S1,D (parallel move)
$D \pm (S1*2^{-n}) \rightarrow D$ (no parallel move)	mac $(\pm)$S,#n,D (no parallel move)

where D is the destination accumulator, S1 and S2 are the source registers, and #n is an immediate operand.

As an example the integer compare for equality instruction for the processor TMS320C62x/64x/67x is given by

```
cmpeq .L1X A1,B1,A2
```

where A1 and B1 are the source and A2 is the destination. After the instruction A2 contains either 0000 0000h for false or 0000 0001h for true. The unit is L1.

Bitwise instructions

and, or, xor, not (one complement), two complement, clear bitfield, set bitfield, shift left, shift right, rotate left, rotate right, zero

For example, for the bitwise XOR operation of the TMS320C6000 we have the instruction

XOR .L1 A1,A2,A3

The bitwise XOR of the bitstrings in A1 and A2 is calculated and the resulting bitstring is stored in A3. The zero operation is used to fill the destination register with 0s by subtracting the destination from itself and placing the result in the destination register. For the TI C64x, the operation performed is MVK 0, dst. In the case where dst is an slong, the TI C64x will use the sub operation like the TI C62x/C67x.

Transfer, Control, and Skip

jump (labels), conditional branch, call, conditional call, return, conditional return, return from interrupt (RTI), return from subroutine (RTS), idle

Input/Output

input, output

Data transfer

load, move, store, exchange, stack control, pop, push

For example, the TI C62x instructions to load a register with a constant are MVK, MVKL, MVKH. Each of these instructions can load a 16-bit constant to a register. Contents of one register can be copied to another register by using the MV instruction. Since the TI C62x processor has the so-called load/store architecture, we must first load the content of memory to a register to be able to manipulate it. The basic assembly instructions we can use for loading are LDB, LDH, and LDW for loading up 8-, 16-, and 32-bit data from memory. There are some variations to these instructions for different handling of the signs of the loaded values. For the Intel 8051 the PUSH instruction increments the stack pointer by one, then transfers the contents

of a single byte variable (specified by direct addressing) into the internal
RAM location. For the Intel 8051 the POP instruction copies the contents
of the internal RAM addressed by the stack pointer to the byte variable
indicated, then decrements the stack pointer by one.

Interrupt and Miscellaneous

```
enable interrupt, disable interrupt, nop (no operation}
```

For the TI C6x processor the instruction fetch consists of four phases; generate fetch address (F1), send address to memory (F2), wait for data (F3),
and read opcode from memory (F4). Decoding consists of two phases; dis-
patching to functional units (D1) and decoding (D2). The execution step
may consist of up to six phases (E1 to E6) depending on the instructions.
For example, the multiply (MPY) instruction has one delay resulting in two
execution phases. Similarly, load (LDx) and branch (B) instructions have
four and five delays, respectively. When the outcome of an instruction is
used by the next instruction, an appropriate number of NOPs (no operation
or delay) must be added. After multiply one NOP must be added. After load
(LDx) four NOPs must be added. After branch (B) five NOPs must be added
in order to allows the pipeline to operate properly. Otherwise, before the
outcome of the current instruction is available (which is used by the next
instruction), the next instructions are executed by the pipeline, generating
undesired results. The following code is an example of pipelined code with
NOPs inserted:

```
       MVK   40,A2
loop:  LDH   *A5++,A0
       LDH   *A6++,A1
       NOP   4
       MPY   A0,A1,A3
       NOP
       ADD   A3,A4,A4
       SUB   A2,1,A2
[A2]   B     loop
       NOP   5
       STH   A4,*A7
```

In line 4, we need four NOPs since the register A1 is loaded by the LDH
instruction in line 3 with four delays. After four delays, the value of A1 is
available to be used in the MPY A0,A1,A3 instruction in line 5. Similarly,
we need five delays after the [A2] B loop instruction in line 9 to prevent
the execution of STH A4,*A7 before branching occurs.

14.3 IEEE Floating Point Format

IEEE 754-1990 standard for binary floating point arithmetic defines what is commonly referred to as *IEEE floating point*. The 32-bit IEEE floating point format is:

$$V = 1.M * 2^{(E-127)}$$

where V is the value of the number, E the exponent (range) and M the mantissa (precision). In 32-bit IEEE format, 1 bit is allocated as the sign bit, the next 8 bits are allocated as the exponent field, and the last 23 bits are the fractional parts (mantissa) of the normalised number. Thus

```
    sign exponent fraction
       0 00000000   00000000000000000000000
bit   31 [30-- 23] [22   --                 0]
```

A sign bit of 0 indicates a positive number, and a 1 is a negative number. The exponent is represented by excess 127 notation. The 23 fraction bits actually represents 24 bits of precision, as a leading 1 in front of the decimal is implied. Special cases are:

1) $E = 255$ -> 11111111b, $M = 0$ (all 23 bits are zero).
With the sign bit $S = 1$ => negative infinity
2) $E = 255$ -> 11111111b, $M = 0$ (all 23 bits are zero).
With the sign bit $S = 0$ => positive infinity
3) $E = 0$ -> 00000000b, $M = 0$ (all 23 bits are zero).
With the sign bit $S = 1$ => negative zero
4) $E = 0$ -> 00000000b, $M = 0$ (all 23 bits are zero).
With the sign bit $S = 0$ => positive zero
5) $E = 255$ -> 11111111b, $M \neq 0$.
Not a number (NaN). Overflow, error.
6) $E = 0$, $M \neq 0$. Denormalised, tiny number, smaller than smallest allowed.

With exponent field 00000000 and 11111111 now reserved, the range is restricted to 2^{-126} to 2^{127}.

Example. Consider the number $9 + 97/128 = 9.7578125$.
1) First we convert the number to base 2, i.e. 1001.1100001.
2) Next we shift the binary representation to the format $1.xxxxxxxx * 2^E$. Thus we obtain $1.0011100001 * 2^3$.
3) Now we add 127 (excess 127 code) to the exponent field, which is $E = 3$ and convert it back to binary. Thus $3 + 127 = 130$. Now 130 in binary is 10000010b.

4) Next we determine the sign bit. If a negative number, set to 1. Otherwise to 0. In our case S = 0 (positive number).

5) Finally we put the binary representation together, using only the fractional part of the number represented by step 2) (i.e. remove the 1. preceding the fractional part). Thus we obtain

```
S Exponent Mantissa
0 10000010 00111000010000000000000
```

In hex notation we have 411C2000.

For double precision (64-bit) floating point numbers, 1 bit determines the sign $\pm$, 11 bits determine the exponent (bias 1023), and the remaining bits (52) determine the mantissa (or fraction) with implicit leading 1 before the fractional part. The conversion is similar to the 32-bit case, but more bits are used for the exponent and mantissa for greater range and precision.

14.4 Data Representation

In many digital signal processors the data representations are numerical values represented as binary fractions in the range: $-1.0 \le$ value < 1.0. For example the accumulator of the Freescale DSP5600 processor represent fixed-point numbers between -1 and 0.9999998 inclusive. The extension register offers protection against overflow: it can accurately represent numbers of higher precision and sets the overflow status bit when the other 48 bits are 01111...111. Why do we use fractional representation? Firstly the product of two fractional numbers is also a fractional number. Secondly normalised representation is convenient. Thirdly coefficients from digital filter designs are typically already in fractional form.

The accumulator register holds intermediate results. An n-bit number $\times$ n-bit number yields an $2n - 1$ bit number. Accumulators typically have extra guard bits or extension registers for overflow. For example the Freescale DSP56000 processor has two 56-bit accumulators (48 bit result with 8 guard bits).

14.5 Addressing Modes

Addressing modes form part of the instruction set architecture for DSPs. Some machine language will need to refer to (addresses of) operands in memory. An addressing mode specifies how to calculate the effective memory address of an operand by using information held in registers and/or constants contained within a machine instruction. Instructions can be classified according to how the operand address portion of the instruction is specified. Addressing modes are the ways one can compute an effective address where the effective address is the address of operand used by the instruction. Most DSPs have several different address modes. Addressing modes can be considered either from a functional point of view (i.e. an assembler language point of view) or an implementation point of view (a machine language point of view). Most DSPs allow the following addressing modes:

immediate addressing, direct addressing, extended addressing, index addressing, indirect addressing

Immediate addressing mode: In this addressing mode the operand immediately follows the op-code and is stored in the next one. For example, for the Motorola DSP56300/DSP56600

```
move #5,r0
```

We move (op-code move) the number 5 into the register r0, where the # is used to indicate immediate addressing. For example, for the Intel 80 × 86 architecture

```
mov ah, 09h
```

moves the hex number 09h into the register ah. Note that the destination register ah is after the op-code for the Intel 80×86. For the TI TMS320C54x we have as an example

```
ld   #0,A   ; load instruction sets A=0
cmpm AR1,#1 ; sets flag TC=1 if AR1==1 else TC=0
```

Register addressing: Operand is contained in the register. As an example, for the Intel 80 × 86 architecture

```
add ax, bx
```

which adds the contents in register bx (source) to the contents of register ax (destination).

Direct addressing: Operand field of instruction contains effective address (called displacement mode by Stallings). For example, for the Intel 80 × 86 architecture

```
add ax, a
```

Register indirect addressing: In the register indirect addressing mode, the contents of the register is an effective address (called base by Stalling). For example, for the Intel 80 × 86 architecture

```
mov bx, offset Table
add ax, [bx]
```

Only the base register **bx**, **bp** and the index register **si**, **di** can be used for register indirect addressing. It is the square bracket that indicates that the memory location is pointed to by **bx**, rather than **bx** itself, is the source operand. For the TI TMS320C54x we have as an example

```
ld    10,A ; sets A = (contents of memory location)
add   6,B  ; sets B = B + (contents of memory location DP+6)
```

The ADSP-21000 SHARC DSPs support absolute and relative-direct addressing, premodify and postmodify registering, immediate-value-indirect addressing, and modulo and bit-reverse addressing. Two addressing modes are supported for memory fetches. Direct addressing uses immediate address values; indirect addressing uses the I register of the two data address generators (DAGs). The dual-ported memory allows independent data transfer from the core and the I/O. Three on-chip buses allow two data transfers from the core and one from I/O in one cycle.

The DSP 56000 has the addressing of a conventional DSP processor except bit-reversed addressing. The DSP 56000 has conditional moves to reduce branching. For example, a logical inverter can be implemented as

```
; invert input
    clr   b    input,a   ; b=0, a=input
    tst   a    #$01,y1    ; test a, set y1=1
    teq   y1,b            ; if a=0, then b=y1=1
    move  b,output        ; output=b
```

The DSP56300/56600 allows peripheral addressing. The on-chip peripherals have special addressing modes. Moving data to/from an on-chip peripheral can be done by a **movep** instruction, where the address of the peripheral is defined by very few address bits as part of the opcode. The use of **movep** usually does not save execution time, but makes it possible to put two **movep** instructions in an interrupt vector, instead of only one if a long absolute addressing mode is used.

The **ld** instruction for the TI TMS320C54x illustrates the many possible addressing modes which can be selected:

```
ld  #7,A         ; immediate data: sets A = 7
ld  0,A          ; DP-referenced direct:
                 ; sets A = (contents of the address DP + 0)
ld  mydata,A     ; DP-referenced direct:
                 ; sets A = (contents of the address DP
                 ; + lower seven bits of mydata
ld  #mydata,A    ; immediate data:
                 ; sets A = 16 bit address mydata
ld  *(mydata),A  ; *(lk) direct: sets A = (contents of the
                 ; 16 bit address mydata)
ld  B,A          ; accumulators: sets A = B
ld  *AR1+,A      ; indirect:
                 ; sets A = (contents of address pointed to
                 ; by AR1), and then increments AR1 by one
ldm AR2,A        ; memory-mapped register: sets A = AR2
```

Some DSPs have a `load effective address` (LEA) instruction. This performs any address calculation, and then places the resulting effective address in a register. This may be useful when passing the address of an array element to a subroutine.

14.6 Applications: Sum-of-Product

One of the main applications is for linear digital filters (see chapter 3). A simple FIR filter is given by

$$y[n] = \sum_{j=0}^{N-1} b[j] \cdot x[n-j] \,.$$

Thus the current output is a sum of products of coefficients and past input values. A typical procedure would be:

Clear accumulator,
fetch coefficient and data,
multiply accumulate,
repeat fetch and multiply
accumulate until done.

There is a need to fetch next coefficient and next stored value at each step in the filter. Many digital signal processors support a parallel move or fetch operation while multiply accumulate is computed. This design avoids an idle arithmetic-logic unit and data buses.

Thus one of the fundamental building blocks in any digital signal processor algorithm be it convolution, filtering or fast Fourier transforms is the sum of products equation (scalar product of the two arrays **a** and **b**)

$$y = \sum_{j=0}^{n-1} a(j) \cdot b(j)$$

with given $a(j)$ and $b(j)$. For example, the TMS320C64X processors of Texas Instruments provide the `DOTP2` instruction. This instruction returns the dot-product between two pairs of signed, packed 16-bit values. The values in `scr1` (source 1) and `scr2` are treated as signed, packed 16-bit quantities. The signed result is written either to a single 32 bit register, or sign-extended into a 64-bit register pair. For example, let

$$a_{hi} = 6A32 \text{ (hex)}, \quad a_{low} = 1193 \text{ (hex)}.$$

Thus in base 10 we have $a_{hi} = 27186$ and $a_{low} = 4499$. For the b-register we have

$$b_{hi} = B174 \text{ (hex)}, \quad b_{low} = 6CA4 \text{ (hex)}.$$

Since B in binary is 1011 (most significant bit is 1) we have a negative integer number which we find using *two's complement*. B174 in binary is 1011 0001 0111 0100. Thus the one complement is 0100 1110 1000 1011 and therefore the two complement is 0100 1110 1000 1100. In base 16 we have 4E8C and in base 10 we have 20108. Thus B174 represents the negative integer -20108. The instruction `DOTP2` now calculates

`a_hi*b_hi + a_low*b_low`

The command

`DOTP2   .M1   A5,A6,A8`

stores a_{high} and a_{low} in the 32 bit register A5 and b_{high} and b_{low} in the 32 bit register A6. The result is E6DF F6D4 (hex). Since E in binary is 1110, the most significant bit is 1 and thus the integer number is negative. In base 10 we have -421529900. The result is stored in the 32 bit register A8.

As an example consider the inner loop of a *finite response filter* (FIR), given as

$$y[n] = \sum_{j=0}^{Ntap-1} x[n-j] \cdot h[j]$$

where $x[n-j]$ is a sample value, $h[j]$ is a coefficient, $y[n]$ is the filter output, and $Ntap$ is the number of coefficients.

A Freescale DSP5685x family processor would implement the inner loop of an FIR filter via a sequence of instructions such as:

```
MOVEU.W X:DLYPTR,R0  ; load data address into R0 pointer
MOVEU.W #COEFADDR,R3 ; load coefficient address into
                     ; R3 pointer
REP     #NTAP        ; repeat the next instruction Ntap times
MAC     X0,Y1,B  X:(R0)+,Y1   X:(R3)+,X0
                     ; multiply and accumulate a sample and
                     ; coefficient
```

Since the DSP5685x features dedicated looping hardware, dual address generators, an enhanced Harvard memory architecture, and specialised signal processing instructions, the processor can carry out the inner loop by executing Ntap multiply-accumulate (MAC) instructions. During each instruction cycle the DSP5685x multiplies a sample by its corresponding coefficient, loads the next sample and coefficient, and updates the address pointers - all via a single instruction.

For the Freescale DSP56300/DSP56600 the for-loop of the C-code

```
for(i=0;i<100;i++) { a += data[i]; }
```

could be implement as

```
    move #MEMORY_AREA,r0
    clr  a        #100,b
    move x:(r0)+,x0
_LOOP_TOP
    add  x0,a    x:(r0)+,x0
    sub  #1,b
    tst  b
    jne  _LOOP_TOP
```

On the TMS320C62x family, the FIR filter's inner loop would be implemented via a sequence of instructions such as

```
loop:
    ADD.L1      A0,A3,A0  ; A0 = A0+A3
    ADD.L2      B1,B7,B1  ; B1 = B1+B7
    MPYHL.M1X   A2,B2,A3  ; A3 = A2(hi)*B2(lo)
    MPYLH.M2X   A2,B2,B7  ; B7 = A2(lo)*B2(hi)
    LDW.D2      *B4++,B2  ; load into B2
    LDW.D1      *A7--,A2  ; load into A2
    ADD.S2      -1,B0,B0  ; decrement counter
    [B0]        B.S1 loop ; branch if B0 nonzero
```

where .L1, .L2, .S1, .S2, .M1, .M2 .D1 and .D2 are the eight functional units. The TMS320C62x employs a very long instruction word architecture that allows it to execute the eight instructions in parallel. Its dual multi-pliers and dual adders allow the MAC operation to be performed for two taps at once, so the eight instructions above must be executed only $Ntap/2$ times each. However, the TMS320C62x requires separate instructions for loop control and memory loads, while the DSP5685x can perform these operations as part of its MAC instruction.

The SHARC DSP 2106x and 2116x also allows looping constructs. An example is

```
.segment/dm data;
.var x[5] = 1, 2, 3, 4, 5;

.segment/pm text;
top:
    i0=x;
    i1=x;
    m0=1;
    r0=1;
    lcntr=5 do bottom until lc;
        r1=dm(i0,m0);
        r1=r1+r0;
bottom:
        dm(i1,m0)=r1;
    nop;
    nop;
    nop;
    nop;
    nop;
    jump top;
```

The code contains two segments. The first is called **data** and the second is called **text**. The data segment contains an initialised variable (an array counting from 0) with 5 elements. The code segment contains a loop that runs over the data and adds one to each element. To print the values in the array we would use p *(x..+4), where * is the indirection operator. To print the address of x we would use p x and to print all addresses we use p x..+4.

The following program for the Intel 8051 processor reads numbers from a terminal and writes them to a terminal and also shows how looping (the for-loop and while-loop) is used.

```
; looping.asm
```

```
.equ Cout,0x0030      ; send Acc to serial port
.equ Cin,0x0032       ; get Acc fron serial port
.equ pHex,0x0034      ; print Hex value of Acc
.equ pHex16,0x0036    ; print Hex value of DPTR
.equ pString,0x0038   ; print string pointed to by DPTR,
                      ; must be terminated by 0
                      ; or a high bit set
                      ; pressing ESC stops printing
.equ gHex,0x003A      ; get Hex input into Acc
                      ; carry set if ESC has been pressed
.equ gHex16,0x003C    ; get Hex input into DPTR
                      ; carry set if ESC has been pressed
.equ ESC,0x003E       ; check for ESC key
                      ; carry set if ESC has been pressed
.equ Upper,0x0040     ; convert Acc to uppercase
                      ; non-ASCII values are unchanged
.equ Init,0x0042      ; initialise serial port
.equ Newline,0x0046   ; print a '\r'
.equ Menu,0x0044      ; return to this point after
                      ; executing the program

.org 0x8000           ; place the program in SRAM

.equ x,10h            ; RAM location for variable x
.equ y,11h            ; RAM location for variable y
.equ i,12h            ; RAM location for variable i

START:

If: MOV    DPTR,#IfMsg1
    LCALL  pString ; long call
    ACALL  GetVal  ; use GetVal subroutine to read x & y
    MOV    A,x       ; load x into Acc
    CJNE   A,y,not_equal ; compare x and y
equal:
    MOV    DPTR,#IfMsg2 ; "then code"
    LCALL  pString      ; long call
    AJMP   While        ; absolute jump
not_equal:
    MOV    DPTR,#IfMsg3 ; "else code"
    LCALL pString       ; long call
    AJMP While          ; absolute jump

IfMsg1: .DB "If construct:\r",0
```

```
IfMsg2: .DB "\rx is equal to y\r",0
IfMsg3: .DB "\rx is not equal to y\r",0

While:  MOV   DPTR,#While1 ; DPTR data pointer register
        LCALL pString
again:  ACALL GetVal       ; use GetVal subroutine to read x & y
        MOV   A,x          ; load x into Acc
        CJNE  A,y,again    ; compare x and y goto again
                           ; while x != y
        AJMP  For          ; absolute jump

While1: .DB "While loop: \r",0

For:    MOV   DPTR,#ForMsg1 ; for loop
        LCALL pString
        MOV   i,#0          ; i starts at 0
for1:   MOV   A,i           ; load i into A
        CJNE  A,#10,for2    ; is i==10? yes: goto Done
                            ; no: goto for2
        AJMP  Done          ; absolute jump
for2:   MOV   A,i           ; print value of i
        LCALL pHex
        LCALL Newline
        INC   i             ; increment i (i++)
        AJMP  for1          ; absolute jump
ForMsg1:   .DB  "for loop\r",0

Done:   LJMP  Menu  ; return to monitor

GetVal: MOV DPTR,#GetMsg ; subroutine GetVal
        LCALL pString    ; long call
        LCALL gHex       ; read a 8 bit number in hex
                         ; from the terminal
        MOV x,A          ; store value in x
        LCALL Newline
        LCALL gHex       ; read a 8 bit number in hex
                         ; from the terminal
        MOV   y,A        ; store value in y
        RET              ; the RETurn instruction pops
                         ; the high/low bytes of the
                         ; saved PC (program counter)
                         ; from the stack, then decrements
                         ; the stack pointer by two
```

```
GetMsg: .DB  "\rEnter values for x and y (in hex)\r",0

      .end
```

14.7 Survey of Microprocessors

Here we give a summary of microprocessors used in applications.

The ADSP-2106x-SHARC - super Harvard architecture computer - is a high performance 32-bit digital signal processor [1]. The ADSP-2106x has the following architectural features:

1) 32-bit IEEE floating-point computation units - multiplier, ALU, Shifter. The ADSP-21000 family processors handle 32-bit IEEE floating-point format, 32-bit integer and fraction formats (two's complement and unsigned), and extended-precision 40-bit IEEE floating format.
2) Data Register File. The ADSP-2106x has an enhanced Harvard architecture combined with a 10-port data register file. In every cycle:
a) two operands can be read or written to or from the registers file
b) two operands can be supplied to the ALU
c) two operands can be supplied to the multiplier
d) two results can be received from the ALU and the multiplier
3) Data Address Generators (DAG1, DAG2)
4) Program sequencer with Instruction Cache
5) Interval Timer
6) Dual-Ported SRAM
7) Off-chip memory (4 Gigabyte address, 32-bit address)
8) 48-bit bus for program and data memory
9) DMA controller (10 DMA channels)
10) External Port for Interfacing to Off-Chip Memory and Peripherals
11) Host Port and Multiprocessor Interface
12) Serial Ports with 3- to 32-bit data word width and μ-law/A-law hardware companding. There are two 40 MBit/s synchronous serial ports.
13) Link Ports
14) Joint Test Action Group (JTAG) Test Access Port

The ADSP-2106x has a program memory (PM) bus, a data memory (DM) bus and an Input/Output (I/O) bus. The PM bus is used to access either instructions or data. During a single cycle the processor can access two data operands, one over the PM bus and one over the DM bus, an instruction (from the cache), and perform a DMA transfer. Special instructions include bit manipulation, division iteration, reciprocal of square-root seed, conditional subroutine call, single and block repeat with zero-overhead looping, average-of-two numbers, bit packing and unpacking fixed- to and from floating-point conversion, and conditional execution of most instructions. SHARC supports IEEE-754 single-precision floating-point, 32-bit fixed-point, and a 40-bit extended IEEE format for additional accuracy.

The ADSP-21000 family processors execute all instructions in a single cycle. They provide both fast cycle times and a complete set of arithmetic operations including `min`, `max`, `shift`, `rotate` in addition to addition, subtraction, multiplication, and combined multiplication/addition.

The DSP56301 24-bit digital signal processor of Freescale [21] has the following architectural features.

1) Highly parallel instruction set
2) Fully pipelined 24 × 24-bit parallel Multiplier-Accumulator (MAC)
3) 56-bit parallel barrel shifter (fast shift and normalisation, bit stream generation and parsing)
4) 24-bit or 16-bit arithmetic support under software control
5) Position independent code support
6) Addressing modes optimised for DSP-applications
7) On chip instruction cache controller
8) Nested hardware DO loops
9) Fast auto-return interrupts
10) On-chip concurrent six-channel DMA controller
11) On-chip emulation module
12) JTAG Test Access

The on-chip memories are: 1024-4096 × 24-bit program RAM (optional configurations) with 1024 × 24-bit instruction cache (if enabled), 2048/3072 × 24-bit X data RAM (optional configuration), 2048/3072 × 24-bit Y data RAM (optional configuration), 3K × 24-bit bootstrap ROM.

The TMS320C62x/C64x/C67x DSPs execute up to eight 32-bit instructions per cycle [58]. The C62x/C67x device's core CPU consists of 32 general-purpose registers of 32-bit word length and eight functional units. The C64x core CPU consists of 64 general-purpose 32-bit registers and eight units. These eight functional units contain:
1) Two multipliers
2) Six ALUs

The C6000 generation has a complete set of optimised development tools, including an efficient C compiler, an assembly optimiser for simplified assembly language programming and scheduling. Features of the C6000 devices include:

Advanced VLIW CPU with eight functional units, including two multipliers, and six arithmetic units. It executes up to eight instructions per cycle for up to ten times the performance of typical DSPs. It allows designers to develop highly effective RISC-like code for fast development time. The instruction packing gives code size equivalence for eight instructions executed serially or in parallel. Instruction packing reduces code size, program fetches and power consumption. They also allow conditional execution of all instructions which reduces costly branching and increases parallelism for higher sustained performance. Other features are: 8/16/32-bit data support, providing efficient memory support for a variety of applications. 40-bit arithmetic options add extra precision for vocoders and other computationally intensive applications.

The C67x has the following additional features:
1) Hardware support for single-precision (32-bit) and double-precision (64-bit) IEEE floating-point operations.
2) 32×32 bit integer multiply with 32- or 64-bit result.

The C64x additional features include:
1) Each multiplier can perform two 16×16-bit or four 8×8 bit multiplies every clock cycle.
2) Quad 8-bit and dual 16-bit instruction set extensions with data flow support.
3) Support for non-aligned 32-bit (word) and 64-bit (double word) memory accesses.
4) Bit count and rotate hardware extends support for bit-level algorithms.

Bibliography

[1] Analog Devices,
    http://www.analog.com/processors/processors/sharc/

[2] Antoniou A., *Digital Filters*, second edition, McGraw-Hill, New York, 1988

[3] Barnsley M., *Fractals Everywhere*, Academic Press, New York, 1988

[4] Barnsley M., Hurd L. P. and Anson L. F., *Fractal Image Compression*, AK Peters, 1993

[5] Barthel K. U., Schüttemeyer, J., Voyé T. and Noll P., "A New Image Coding Technique Unifying Fractal and Transform Coding", IEEE International Conference on Image Processing (ICIP), 13–16, 1994

[6] Bell T., Cleary J. and Witten I. H., *Text Compression*, Prentice-Hall, Englewood, 1990

[7] Bolton W. C. *Laplace and z-transform*, Longman, 1994

[8] Brey B. B., *Microprocessor/Hardware Interfacing and Applications*, Charles E. Merrill Publishing, Columbus, 1984

[9] Broomhead D. S., Huhe J. P., and Muldoon M. R., J. R. Stat. Soc. B **54**, 373, 1992

[10] Burrows M. and Wheeler D. J., "A Block-sorting Lossless Data Compression Algorithm", Digital Research Center Report 124, 1994

[11] Charniak E., *Statistical Language Learning*, MIT Press, Cambridge, Massachusetts, 1993

[12] Chassaing R., *Digital Signal Processing - Laboratory Experiments Using C and the TMS320C31 DSK*, J. Wiley, New York, 1999

[13] Chui C. K., *An introduction to wavelets*, Academic Press, San Diego, 1992

[14] Cohen A., Daubechies I. and Feauveau J.-C., "Biorthogonal bases of compactly supported wavelets", Comm. Pure and Appl. Math. **45**, 485–560, 1992

[15] Cormack A. M., J. Appl. Phys. **35**, 2908–2913, 1964

[16] Cybenko G., Mathematics of Control, Signals and Systems, **2**, 303–314, 1989

[17] Daubechies I., *Ten Lectures on Wavelets*, SIAM, Philadelphia, 1992

[18] Deller J. R., Hansen J. H. L. and Proakis J. G., *Discrete-Time Processing of Speech Signals*, IEEE Press, 1999

[19] Deslauriers G., Dubuc S. and Lemire D., "Une famille d'ondelettes biorthogonales sur l'intervalle obtenue par un schéma d'interpolation itérative", Annales des sciences mathématique du Québec, **23**, 37–48, 1999

[20] Elliot D. F. and Rao K. R., *Fast Fourier Transforms: Algorithms* Academic Press, New York, 1982

[21] Freescale semiconductors, http://www.freescale.com

[22] Funahashi K.-I., Neural Networks, **2**, 183–192, 1989

[23] Gailly Jean-Loup, *The Data Compression Book*, second edition, M. T. Books, New York 1995

[24] Grover D. and Deller J. R., *Digital Signal Processing and the Microcontroller*, Prentice Hall, New Jersey, 1999

[25] Hagan M. T., Demuth H. B. and Beale M., *Neural Network Design*, PWS Publishing, Boston, 1996

[26] Hardy Y. and Steeb W.-H. *Classical and Quantum Computing with C++ and Java Simulations*, Birkhauser, Basel 2001

[27] Hassoun M. H., *Fundamentals of Artifical Neural Networks*, MIT Press, 1995

[28] Haykin S., *Neural Networks - A comprehensive foundation*, Macmillan, London, 1994

[29] Helgason S., *The Radon Transform*, Birkhäuser Verlag, Basel, 1980

[30] Hornik K. M., Neural Networks, **2**, 359–366, 1989

[31] Huffman, D. A., "A method for the construction of minimum-redundancy codes", Proceedings of the IRE, **40**, 1098–1101, 1952

[32] Jacquin A., "Image Coding based on a Fractal Theory of Iterated Contractive Image Transforms", SPIE, **1360**, Visual Communications and Image Processing, 1990

[33] Kohonen T., *Self-Organizing Maps*, third edition Springer-Verlag, Berlin, 2001

[34] Kondoz A. M., *Digital Speech, Coding for low bit rate communication systems*, John Wiley, Chichester, 1990

[35] Kosko B., *Neural Networks and Fuzzy Systems*, Prentice Hall, 1991

[36] Kuc Roman, *Introduction to Digital Signal Processing*, McGraw-Hill, New York, 1990

[37] Linde Y., Buzo A. and Gary R. M., "An algorithm for vector quantizer design", IEEE Transactions on Communications **28**, 84–95, 1980

[38] Luo Fa-Long and Ungehauen R., *Applied Neural Networks for Signal Processing*, Cambridge University Press, Cambridge, 1997

[39] Mallat S., *A wavelet tour of signal processing*, Academic Press, London, 1999

[40] Madisetti V. K., *VLSI Digital Signal Processors*, IEEE Press, Butterworth Heinemann, Boston, 1995

[41] Nelson Mark, "Arithmetic Coding + Statistical Modeling = Data Compression", Doctor Dobb's Journal, February, 1991

[42] Nelson M. and Gailly J.-L., *The Data Compression Book*, M & T Books, New York, second edition, 1995

[43] Pitas Ionnis, *Digital Image Processing Algorithms and Applications*, Wiley-Interscience, New York, 2000

[44] Parks T. W. and Burrus C. S., *Digital Filter Design*, John Wiley, New York, 1987

[45] Parsons T., *Voice and Speech Processing*, McGraw-Hill, New York, 1987

[46] Quatieri T. E., *Discrete-Time Speech Signal Processing*, Prentice Hall, New York, 2001

[47] Rabiner L., "A tutorial on Hidden Markov Models and selected applications in speech recognition", *Proceedings of the IEEE*, **77**, 257–286, 1989

[48] Rabiner L. and Juang B.-H., *Fundamentals of Speech Recognition*, Prentice Hall, New York, 1993

[49] Radon L., Berichte Sächsische Akademie der Wissenschaften, Leipzig, Math.-Phys. Kl. **69**, 262–267, 1917

[50] Ramirez E. and Weiss M., *Microprocessing Fundamentals*, McGraw-Hill, Tokyo 1980

[51] Salomon D., *Data Compression: The Complete Reference*, second edition, Springer-Verlag, New York, 2000

[52] Sayood K., *Introduction to Data Compression*, second edition, Morgan Kaufmann, Burlington, 2000

[53] Shannon C., *The Mathematical Theory of Communication*, University of Illinois, 1949

[54] Steeb W.-H., Hardy Y. and Stoop R., "Discrete wavelets and filtering chaotic signals", Int. J. Mod. Phys. C **13**, 771–776, 2002

[55] Steeb W.-H., *The Nonlinear Workbook*, third edition, World Scientific, Singapore, 2005

[56] Tan Kiat Shi, Steeb W.-H. and Hardy Y., *SymbolicC++: An Introduction to Computer Algebra Using Object-Oriented Programming*, 2nd edition Springer-Verlag, London, 2000

[57] Terrell T. J., *Introduction to Digital Filters*, second edition, MacMillan, London, 1988

[58] Texas Instruments, http://www.ti.com

[59] Tocci R. J. and Laskowski L. P., *Microprocessors and Microcomputers, The 6800 Family*, Prentice-Hall, Englewood Cliffs, 1986

[60] Vich R., *Z transform Theory and Applications*, D. Reidel Pub. 1987

[61] Walker J. S., *Fast Fourier Transform*, CRC Press, 1996

[62] Welch T. A., "A Technique for High Performance Data Compression", IEEE Computer 17, 8-19, 1984

[63] Witten I. H., Moffat A. and Bell T. C., *Managing Gigabytes: Compressing and Indexing Documents and Images*, second edition, Morgan-Kaufmann, San Fransico, 1999

[64] Witten I. H., Neal R. and Cleary J. G., "Arithmetic coding for data compression", Communications of the Association for Computing Machinery, **30**, 520–540, 1987

[65] Ziv J. and Lempel A., "A Universal Algorithm for Sequential Data Compression", IEEE Transaction on Information Theory, IT-23, 337-343, 1977

Index

Printed in the United States
By Bookmasters